Introducing the Creative Industries

Introducing the Creative Industries

From Theory to Practice

Rosamund Davies and
Gauti Sigthorsson

Los Angeles | London | New Delhi
Singapore | Washington DC

Los Angeles | London | New Delhi
Singapore | Washington DC

SAGE Publications Ltd
1 Oliver's Yard
55 City Road
London EC1Y 1SP

SAGE Publications Inc.
2455 Teller Road
Thousand Oaks, California 91320

SAGE Publications India Pvt Ltd
B 1/I 1 Mohan Cooperative Industrial Area
Mathura Road
New Delhi 110 044

SAGE Publications Asia-Pacific Pte Ltd
3 Church Street
#10-04 Samsung Hub
Singapore 049483

Editor: Mila Steele
Editorial assistant: James Piper
Production editor: Imogen Roome
Copyeditor: Sarah Bury
Proofreader: Kate Harrison
Indexer: Caroline Eley
Marketing manager: Michael Ainsley
Cover design: Lisa Harper
Typeset by: C&M Digitals (P) Ltd, Chennai, India
Printed and bound by CPI Group (UK) Ltd,
Croydon, CR0 4YY

MIX
Paper from
responsible sources
FSC® C013604

Library of Congress Control Number: 2012949657

British Library Cataloguing in Publication data

A catalogue record for this book is available from
the British Library

ISBN 978-1-84920-572-6
ISBN 978-1-84920-573-3 (pbk)

Contents

Acknowledgements

We are grateful for the help, support and encouragement of those who helped us develop and write *Introducing the Creative Industries: From Theory to Practice*. Thanks to our colleagues in the Department of Communication and Creative Arts at the University of Greenwich, and of course to our students on Working in Media and Creative Industries.

Rosamund would like to thank Angie Daniell, Marcelle Bernstein, Brigid Davies and most of all Luke Clancy for their interest, help and support in the research and writing of this book. Thanks also to Marley Davies for putting up with me working at weekends and in the holidays for the last two years.

Gauti would like to thank for the opportunity to refine elements of this project through conference presentations: Futuresonic, In the City Music Conference, The Reykjavík Academy, University of Westminster, Erasmus University, the Cultural Studies Association, American Comparative Literature Association, Martin Barker at Aberystwyth University, and David Hesmondhalgh and Helen Kennedy at the University of Leeds. Thanks to Jón Ólafsson and Njörður Sigurjónsson for conversations and writer's retreats at Bifröst University. For inspiration, suggestions and help along the way: Steve Kennedy, Alev Adil, David Jeneman, Andrew Knighton, Margrét Sigrún Sigurðardóttir, Bjargey Ólafsdóttir, Andrew Carmichael, Jobeda Ali, Kostas Maronitis, Joy White, Neil Percival, and David Berry. For their many contributions, thanks to Paul Bay, Börkur Sigthorsson, and Vera Júlíusdóttir. *In memoriam* and with much gratitude to Anna Kristjana Torfadóttir (1949–2012).

Finally, we would like to thank our numerous interviewees, many of whom wish to remain anonymous – without their generosity this book would not exist.

Introduction:
How to Use This Book

The creative industries is a metaphor, which implies that creative production has been industrialized, set up in factory-like structures and managed along the same principles as the manufacture of any other mass-market goods. This is a simplification, but a useful one because it calls attention to the fact that, like any other industry, the creative industries are driven by the work of people. Therefore, while we rely on an extensive range of published sources, we have gone out and interviewed a wide range of creative practitioners, whose stories and insights inform most chapters of this book.

We do not confine ourselves to a specific area of the creative industries, for example audiovisual production, music, games, or publishing. Instead, we look at the creative industries by asking what the different specialisms share. There are great differences between the people we interview, in terms of expertise, skill sets, working conditions and economic circumstances. However, they share certain key concerns that provide us with the overarching themes of this book.

First, we look at the relationship between creativity and commerce. Legions of people make their creativity their profession – generating creative products or services – and they have been doing that for centuries. Artists, artisans, craftspeople, writers, performers, entertainers, musicians – they have been around for some time, and they are likely to continue to do so, but how (and whether) they make a living off their words, images and sounds is an entirely different question.

Second, we consider the cultures and routines of work in the creative industries. We look at what creative workers do, how they do it, and under what circumstances. Again, we are interested in shared cultures, routines and practices across specialist sectors, for example how freelancing makes networking necessary whether you work in advertising, fine arts or media production.

Third, we introduce the business structures that creative workers inhabit – commissioning, client-briefs, financing and entrepreneurship. While they may seem rather abstract, business structures influence the everyday lives of creative practitioners. For example, the ways in which content is commissioned (e.g., for radio, TV or a magazine) makes its mark on income, work habits and the social relationships among creative workers. How they find new business and perform their work imposes certain strictures and opens up possibilities.

The aim of this book is to expand our readers' horizons by showing how the various specialisms within the creative industries depend on one another for ideas, skills and talent. Different sectors share many of the same characteristics, and the skills and talents that apply to one apply in another. Someone starting out in the creative industries might begin in one area and migrate to another because an opportunity presented itself. The creative industries change very rapidly, new trends, products, technologies and markets emerge, while others fade out of fashion or become economically unviable. If there is one thing we would like to accomplish with this book, it is to help our readers spot the opportunities when they come along and take advantage of them.

1

What are the Creative Industries?

DEFINING THE CREATIVE INDUSTRIES

The creative industries don't exist – at least not as a unified category. In this book we treat the "creative industries" as an umbrella term that covers a variety of activities, products and services. Whether we consider fine arts, music, film/TV production, games design, events and festivals, or advertising and marketing (just to name a few examples), they are all connected by three defining features (UNCTAD 2010: 4): first, they all require some input of *human creativity*; second, they are *vehicles for symbolic messages*, that is, they are carriers of *meaning*; and third, they contain, at least potentially, some *intellectual property* that belongs to an individual or a group.

To put it in less technical terms, the creative industries are about experiences. A tremendous range of economic activity arises from the creation of *pleasure* and *meaning*. These experiences, when they take the forms of goods and services, provide work for a host of people ranging from computer programmers and engineers to writers,

Intellectual property rights (IPR): Intellectual property is "any form of original creation that can be bought or sold - from music to machinery" (UK Intellectual Property Office, 22/5/2012). There are a few different types of intellectual property: copyright, patents, trademarks and designs:

Copyright: The legal right to produce or sell copies of an item of intellectual property (book, image, record, film, etc.) for a given period of time, usually between 50 and 70 years after the originator's death. Copyright was invented for books, to identify the party legally authorized to print copies to be distributed and sold. This was also a convenient way for the authorities to keep track of the responsible parties in case they wanted to censor a publication.

Today copyright covers a wide range of original creations, including lyrics, scores, magazine and book layouts, software and databases. Copyright is an automatic right, which means that you do not have to apply for the rights to it and, until you have signed a contract assigning it to a third party, you retain the copyright to your creative work. Crucially, however, copyright applies only to the expression of an idea (in written, visual, audio form, etc.) but not to the idea itself. By law, ideas cannot be copyrighted. Since ideas are a central currency of the creative industries, this can be something of a conundrum for creative workers. Pitching ideas is the way that creatives establish contacts, secure meetings and win commissions, so sharing ideas freely is very often a better business tactic than hoarding them away out of reach. On the other hand, ideas do get poached and there is not necessarily anything you can do about it. As a creative practitioner, this is a call that you will repeatedly have to make and decide on a case-to-case basis.

Digital technologies and online distribution have complicated the enforcing of copyright laws considerably. Business models which relied on the sale of physical copies of music, films and books, have found themselves compromised by the willingness of consumers to copy and share copyrighted materials digitally. In turn, trade associations and corporations have attempted to stop consumers from engaging in copyright "piracy" by suing individuals and pursuing them for damages for lost sales. More constructively, the so-called crisis of copyright has spurred a great deal of innovation in recent years, particularly in the distribution of music and films online. Recommended reading: Lawrence Lessig, *Free Culture: How Big Media Uses Technology and the Law to Lock Down Culture and Control Creativity* (2005); Matthew Rimmer, *Digital Copyright and the Consumer Revolution* (2007); David Berry, *Copy, Rip, Burn: The Politics of Copyleft and Open Source* (2008); Matt Mason, *The Pirate's Dilemma* (2008); Vincent Miller, *Understanding Digital Culture* (2011).

artists and musicians. There are also many kinds of services, from public relations (or PR) to interaction design to retailing, where pleasure, meaning and experience are absolutely central to the business. Video games, for example, are deeply invested in providing pleasurable, meaningful experiences, but so are large, profitable businesses like Nike, Starbucks, or a certain fruit-themed computer company based in Cupertino, California. In other words, while some aspects of the creative industries might be regarded as frivolous, or at least not "serious" business, they contribute to and support a host of other economic activities, and entire industries.

The local and the global

One reason why the concept of the creative industries is so eclectic is the international diversity of what people consider "creative" in the first place. In some countries the local creative industries are primarily about heritage, tourism and managing access to sites of natural beauty or animal habitats – after all, not all countries produce film, music or video games on an industrial scale. In this broader sense, the creative industries are not just important for rich countries, but also the developing world, with some countries developing export opportunities around cultural heritage, festivals and tourism, for example around the Carnival in Trinidad and the Caribbean (Green and Scher 2007), while others in film and audiovisual media (Barrowclough and Kozul-Wright 2006; Keane 2007; UNESCO 2009: 11–16). In Africa, the creative industries can be seen to include gorilla-viewing tours in Rwanda, the "Nollywood" film scene in Lagos, Nigeria (Lobato 2010), and urban tourism in South Africa (Rogerson 2006). In short, there are many emerging, local versions of creative industries around the world.

Many creative products and services are distributed globally or attract an international audience; yet, the traditions, ideas, languages, skills and talent that they draw on are all in some way *local*. Where things come from is tremendously important in the creative industries – literature, music and dance, for example, have roots in local languages and traditions. Even when the distribution of a product is global, industries such as film and television have strong local characteristics, whether those might be the American twang of Hollywood, or the dance and song of Bollywood (Kavoori and Punathambekar 2008).

The creative industries also go hand in hand with the economies of cities and regions. One might even say that countries, cities and individual areas are themselves symbolic products – after all, places stand for a great many things (Evans 2003). For example, the creative industries are closely connected with tourism, because a thriving cultural scene makes for an interesting destination. Therefore, cities go to great lengths to cultivate their international image – to *brand* themselves as destinations for cultural tourism. This applies both to wider urban areas, such as the city of Bilbao which has been rebranded through the presence of the Guggenheim Bilbao, and to neighbourhoods

Patents: Taking out a patent provides legal protection for a new invention, which has an industrial application. Patents can be renewed for up to 20 years, providing an inventor with time to develop his or her invention, prepare them for commercial application and reap the initial commercial benefits, before others can enter the market. They are not automatic, they need to be registered officially and it costs money to do so. According to the UK Intellectual Property Office (www.ipo.gov.uk), the earliest known English patent was granted in 1449 to a certain John of Utynam. The patent gave him a 20-year monopoly on a Flemish method for making stained glass, which was not known in England and which was used to make the windows of Eton College (IPO 2012 11/8/12).

Trademarks: Signs used by organizations to distinguish their identity from other organizations. When such a sign is trademarked, other organizations are legally prevented from using them without permission. Trademarks, such as the Nike "tick", often form an integral part of the brand. They are very often visual logos, but they can also be textual or verbal slogans, sounds (such as the Intel processor sound), or even smells. Trademarks need to be registered and it costs money to do so.

Designs: Designs (both two dimensional (2d) and three dimensional (3d)) can also be registered, to provide the originator with legal protection against unauthorized imitation or reproduction. A wide range of designs might be registered. Examples might include a pattern for wallpaper, a craft or industrial ceramic item, a packaging design, etc.

or areas within cities, for example the "neo-bohemias" of urban areas keen to make themselves into "creative cities" (Evans 2005; Lloyd 2010). Imagine London's

Creativity and creatives (artistic and cultural): The concept of creativity is not a precise one. Sometimes it refers to a process, and sometimes the product or outcome of that process; sometimes it refers to the talents of the people involved. In practice, creativity has a lot to do with the context in which it resides - it is far more than simply the "input" of the creative industries (with innovation as its "output") (Pratt and Jeffcutt 2009). As James Donald, puts it, creativity can be seen as the "skill to make useful, enjoyable, or beautiful things, or a flair for making interesting things happen" (Donald 2004: 236). Creativity, in this sense, is not so much a skill or form of knowledge in itself; rather, it's a by-product of various specific (and trainable) skills, such as writing, drawing, or playing an instrument. "Creatives," in turn, are skilled people who contribute some form of expressive or original value to a production process (Hackley and Kover 2007). Across the creative industries, creatives are the people who invent, create and express in whatever medium is involved, from novelists and musicians to architects and graphic designers. When a creative has done his or her job, something exists that didn't exist before. In *Management and Creativity* (2007), Chris Bilton challenges the romantic notion that creativity is a form of useful madness (spontaneity, fantasy and inspiration) and that it is a characteristic of exceptional individuals; on the contrary, he regards it as a rational, manageable process that brings together many different roles. Looking beyond individuals, Bilton argues that successful creative environments and institutions cultivate a diversity of creative talents and allow individuals to play multiple roles. In short, the "creative" is not an exclusive, specialist role, although many creative roles involve specialist skills and training.

Bilton draws on a larger debate on the collective, shared process of creativity. One influential

South Bank without the Royal Festival Hall, Hayward Gallery, British Film Institute, National Theatre and the Tate Modern – this patch of the city would not be particularly exciting without them.

Symbolic products and services

A broad, inclusive concept like "creative industries" gives us a way of talking about the many things that different specialist occupations have in common, and what the people working in each can learn from the others. At first, it might not seem like a sculptor creating a unique piece of art might have anything in common with a programmer writing code for a mobile phone application. However, if you think about it, both the sculpture and the piece of software are *symbolic* products – the people involved make something that has meaning. This is why some scholars define the creative industries as a combination of *individual creativity* and *the mass-production of symbolic cultural goods.* This idea comes from economists and cultural critics who have pointed out that there are certain industries that use characteristic forms of industrial production and organization to produce and disseminate symbols (Hirsch 2000; Banks 2007; Hesmondhalgh 2008: 553).

Symbolic products are created in a variety of media. Moreover, when they are mass-produced and distributed they are usually not stand-alone creations; instead, they form clusters or "chains" of related products and services. *Star Wars* is the classic example of a creative product that became a brand through a successful film franchise which, through licensing, became merely one aspect of an entire universe of characters, stories, games, toys and lifestyle products (pyjamas, lunch boxes, special-edition hamburgers, etc.) (Curtin and Streeter 2001). The pioneer of branded entertainment, Walt Disney, called this systematic packaging of symbolic products *total merchandising*: one Disney product advertised another (so that the *Disneyland* TV show promoted the Disneyland theme park, populated by Mickey Mouse, Snow White, Cinderella and other characters and scenarios from Disney's films) (Anderson 2000). Following an identical pattern, the successful *Pirates of the Caribbean* film franchise was developed from a Disney theme park ride of the same title. Similarly, J.K. Rowling's Harry Potter has become a highly successful total merchandising brand: from a character in a book to films, computer games, action figures, clothes and a variety of other products – all of these symbolic products bring together creativity and industrial production knitted together around the character of the boy wizard, his friends and enemies (Kruhly 2011).

Working in creative disciplines, whether it's fine art, architecture, computer games or film, involves many different specialisms. At the same time, these specialisms are constantly being brought together, whether it's in teams working on a single project, or at the level of businesses and organizations. This is something that journalists have experienced in the recent past with the transition from print to digital publishing. While the fundamental skills of researching and writing stories remain the same, they have had to adapt to a new technological context (see Chapter 9). Newspapers and magazines

example of this thinking, in relation to the creative industries, is James Webb Young's *A Technique for Producing Ideas* (presented to students in 1939, published in 1965). Young broke creativity down into elements of a larger process of learning, thinking and experience – from gathering "raw materials" and processing them consciously and unconsciously, to the "a-ha moment" and the work of adapting an idea to artistic, commercial, technological and practical reality (Young 2003). In philosophy, anthropology, sociology and psychology, creativity has come to be regarded as a feature of human intellect and social life – the *resources* of creativity, such as language, skills, raw materials and techniques, are shared among everyone (for an accessible historical overview, see Johnson 2010). Talented individuals draw on this shared pool, a fact that does not detract from exceptional works of poetry, paintings, novels or music (Weisberg 1993; Sternberg 1998). In *The Gift* (2007, orig. 1983), Lewis Hyde suggests, from an anthropological perspective, that creativity can be understood in terms of reciprocal gifts that strengthen communal bonds, ties between the living and with past generations. At a more individual, psychological level, Mihaly Csikszentmihalyi has argued in his influential book *Flow: The Psychology of Optimal Experience* (1991) that creativity is one aspect of a broader range of pleasures associated with doing, making and being "in the moment" of activity. Therefore, the notion of creativity as an economic, professional activity, industrialized and systematized within the "creative industries" has been criticized as a rather reduced notion of human capacity, psychology and community (Osborne 2003; Banks and O'Connor 2009).

Platform: A technology or system that enables or allows other technologies or systems to work. Advanced technologies can be said to stand on many such platforms stacked on top of one another (e.g., power generators and the electrical infrastructure makes the telephone and data network possible, which in turns enables the internet, which I access through my smartphone, that runs the Android operating system, which in turn is the platform for the email app through which I check my mail on the bus). Computer operating systems are platforms that enable various kinds of software to run — whether it's the Windows operating system for a desktop, or iOS or Android on a smartphone. Platforms are only open to a certain extent, as anyone would find out if they tried running an Android app on an iPhone. More fundamentally, infrastructural platforms like electricity, the telephone network and the internet make a great diversity of technologies and activities possible. Therefore, platforms are not only technological, they are simultaneously cultural and social in the way they are adopted and in the behaviours they enable (Bowker and Star 2000). Changes in older platforms, or the introduction of new platforms have historically caused upheaval and radical changes in the creative industries - the introduction of sound in films transformed the making and experience of cinema, for example. More recently, digital media have changed how we relate to television, radio and other established mass-media, pushing media organizations to change their production systems and ways of working. Recommended reading: Henry Jenkins, *Convergence Culture* (2008); Mark Deuze, "Rethinking Convergence Culture in the Creative Industries" (2007b); Graham Meikle and Sherman Young, *Media Convergence* (2012).

Convergence or "media convergence": This is when previously separate kinds of media come together (or "converge") in a new medium. This applies particularly to digital media that bring

now publish across a range of **platforms** – their websites offer videos, audio podcasts, and versions of their publications customized for reading on mobile internet devices. Therefore, media **convergence**, online distribution and increased interactivity have fostered new products, practices and identities. A newspaper journalist has to be able not just to research and report on a story using text and photographs, but also to contribute to other formats like video, podcast, or blogs, and to interact with the audience through multiple channels, including social networking sites.

When we focus on the process – what we refer to later in this book as the **production chain** (Pratt 2004) – of creation, production, distribution and consumption, we do not tend to distinguish between "high culture" and "low" (or "popular") culture. In the study of economics, particularly the economics of culture, snobbery is of dubious analytical value. When viewed from this perspective, the branding of the boy wizard Harry Potter is not very different from the highbrow form of branding used by iconic art galleries like the Guggenheim in Bilbao and the Tate Modern in London. These internationally recognized galleries are involved in a sophisticated game of total merchandising, in part so that they are not forced to rely exclusively on public subsidies for their funding. The documentary film *Exit Through the Gift Shop* (2009), about the secretive graffiti artist Banksy, mocks the way in which art galleries routinely fashion themselves as branded destinations with their buildings, cafés and restaurants – not to mention the gift shops full of bags, t-shirts and mugs featuring their logos.

The idea that the creation and distribution of symbolic products can be regarded as a specific type of industry is not new. There is an older, widespread idea of **culture** and the *cultural* industries, which mostly applies to the production of cultural goods like fine art, literature, theatre, music, radio, film and television. As John Hartley points out, "the 'creative industries' idea combines – but then radically transforms – two older terms: the *creative* arts and the cultural *industries*. This change is important for it brings the arts (i.e. culture) into direct contact with large-scale industries such as media entertainment (i.e. the market)" (Hartley 2005: 6). This concept is very useful, but one reason why the broader concept of the *creative* industries has caught on is that it links the arts, media industries, and other forms of symbolic production and distribution by putting less of an emphasis on questions such as what counts as "art" or "culture" and focusing instead on related forms of production and labour.

STUDYING THE CREATIVE INDUSTRIES – THREE APPROACHES

In this book we rely mainly on three ways of looking at the creative industries: through economic data, creative industries markets, and creative labour:

Economic data can tell us something about the scale of the creative industries, such as estimates of how many jobs and businesses there are in the creative

together sound, image, text and video in new ways, adding participation, sharing, and other forms of interactivity to the mix. The media theorist Henry Jenkins (2008) has argued that a *convergence culture* is emerging, characterized by users' expectation that they "will be able to interact with, manipulate and share media socially".

Production chain: Very few creative products are the work of one single individual from start to finish. Each passes along a chain of individuals and organizations who contribute to it in some way. For example, in the audiovisual industries, a TV series passes from idea through development, pre-production, production, post-production and finally to distribution. At each of these stages there are specialists who contribute something to the eventual delivery of the project (for more detail, see our discussion of simple and complex cultural goods in Chapter 6). It's worth noting that Andy Pratt, whose work we cite throughout the book, uses this term in a particular way to describe "the situated nature of cultural production in terms of markets, technologies, organization and regulatory regimes (referred to collectively as governance)" (Pratt 2007: 43). For him, the Production Chain incorporates a far greater range of occupations, institutions, markets, and systems of governance than we indicate in our use of the term.

Culture: Like "technology", "economy", "society" and other large abstract terms, "culture" is used in many different senses depending on the context and the aims of the user. There are four basic ways of understanding the concept of culture and what the term describes. First, it can indicate that something has *value*. For example, it can refer to prized cultural artefacts (e.g., an artwork, an item of a people's "cultural heritage"), practices (e.g., the "cultivation of mind" through education, learning a musical instrument, or reading a book), qualities (e.g., by judging one kind of music as "trash" and another as "high culture") or even sensibilities (e.g., being "cultured"). Second, culture refers to the *practices* of a given set of people, identified by location, language, religion, ethnicity or other shared characteristics and habits - in this sense, culture is a "way of life" or "what people do" (Williams 1985: 87-93; Bennett et al. 2005: 67). Third, culture has been identified as a *resource* that serves a variety of social, economic and political ends (Yúdice 2003). Furthermore, if culture is a resource, then there are particular forms of cultural *labour* (Gill and Pratt 2008; Ross 2008) that are required for converting cultural resources into cultural commodities, for example the emotional labour involved in "handling" the participants in reality-TV programmes (Hesmondhalgh and Baker 2008; Harney 2010).

Policy and the creative industries: Policy is guidance; Individual policies are meant to serve as rules or guidelines for the decisions and actions of individuals within institutions – whether it's governments, organizations, businesses or even individuals. Policy is important because it steers decisions and actions along certain paths, not least with the aim of removing certain kinds of subjective bias or *ad hoc* decisions from the process. Businesses, for example, have company policies for dealing with customers (e.g., wearing a uniform, addressing them as "sir" or "madam"), human resources policies with rules for hiring staff, and privacy policies for handling customer data (e.g., when you sign up for a service online, you're asked to tick a box indicating that you've

industries, and how productive they are (DCMS 1998a, 2010, 2011).

The *markets* for creative products and services are characterized by uncertainty: art, entertainment, creative services – all the products and services of the creative industries are subject to fluctuating tastes, fashions, economic and technological changes, and the fickleness of the public (Caves 2000; Potts et al. 2008a).

Most importantly, we are interested in *creative labour*: by interviewing creative workers about their experience, conditions and their working life, we study what people who identify themselves as belonging to "creative" occupations actually do on a day-to-day basis, and the local contexts in which they do it (McKinlay and Smith 2009; Hesmondhalgh and Baker 2011).

Economic data, organizations and occupations

The creative industries are "those industries that have their origin in individual creativity, skill, and talent, and which have a potential for wealth and job creation through the generation and exploitation of intellectual property. (DCMS 1998a: 5)

The concept "creative industries" comes out of public **policy** – first in Australia, then in the UK, and later internationally. Since 1998, the UK government's Department for Culture, Media and Sport (DCMS) has identified 13 categories under the creative industries heading: advertising, architecture, art and antiques, crafts, design, designer fashion, film and video, computer games, music, performing arts, publishing, software and computer services, television and radio (DCMS 1998b). While this list is by no means complete, it enables government and policymakers to estimate how many people work in the creative industries, how many businesses there are in each area, the export value of creative services from the UK, and how much the creative industries contribute to the **gross value added (GVA)** of the UK economy as a whole.

This approach is primarily concerned with statistical questions such as how many people are employed in the creative industries, how many businesses there are, and what the value of their output might be. The answers, as with all statistics, depend on how one defines and measures the object of study. After all, you can't just go out and pile all the creative ideas, designs, inventions, films, music, radio, art works, plays, video games and publications in the country on to a giant scale and weigh them. Instead, the size, value and number of jobs involved in each sector can be *estimated* – for example, how much value the workers in each sector have added to the total value-added produced during one year for the UK economy as a whole. For example, the comparison in Figure 1.1 is based on official estimates of how much each of the creative industries contributed to the UK gross value added in 2009 (DCMS 2011):

Here we can see that in 2009 the four largest sectors of the UK creative industries (as measured by how many millions of pounds they contributed to GVA) were Publishing, followed by Advertising,

read and understood the company policy for what it can and cannot do with your personal data). Public policy guides the actions of the executive branch of the state, as directed by government and the law. "Creative industries policy" is one type of public policy, guiding how the state uses its resources, institutions and taxpayers' money to intervene in, shape or otherwise affect the creative industries as a sector. This can have large consequences, for example, if particular types of creative business were offered tax breaks in order to improve their competitive position in the international markets, allowing for cheaper exports and increased sales.

In the UK, the Creative Industries Task Force announced the arrival of a specific *creative industries policy* in 1998 (DCMS 1998a). The New Labour government took power in 1997 and the minister for the newly created Department for Culture, Media and Sport, Chris Smith, attempted to use the term "creative industries" (which had originally been coined in Australia) to secure increased funding for the arts. This strategy was criticized as a rebranding attempt – sprucing up Britain as "Cool Britannia" (Oakley 2004; Garnham 2005). This strategy shifted what used to be called arts funding into new categories alongside broadcasting, marketing, publishing and (most importantly) games and electronic publishing (Cunningham 2004). Previously, no-/low-profit performing arts had traditionally argued for public support on the basis of "market failure" – that they were essential cultural activities that could not survive commercially without state subsidy. In the new creative industries policy, the proudly non-commercial areas of artistic practice (visual arts, performing arts, dance, theatre, etc.) were lined up alongside established commercial media, design, architecture and the emerging sector of "new media" (Banks 2007: chapter 2; Flew 2012). Some scholars have argued that this shift in policy, dating back to 1998, has ironically led to less funding for the arts, and a reduced attention paid to them overall by policymakers, except as a potential source of creative inputs and talent for other, more immediately profitable areas of the creative industries (Banks and O'Connor 2009; Oakley 2009a). Others have suggested that the creative industries idea is even more appropriate to the networked economic and social spaces of the early twenty-first century than the original policymakers of the late 1990s might have imagined when they threw "the heavy duty copyright industries into the same basket as public service broadcasting, the arts and a lot of not-for-profit activity (public goods) and commercial but non-copyright-based sectors (architecture, design, increasingly software)" (Cunningham in Wright et al. 2009: 10). Recommended reading: Mark Banks, *The Politics of Cultural Work* (2007); Andy Pratt and Paul Jeffcutt (eds), *Creativity, Innovation and the Cultural Economy* (2009); Terry Flew, *The Creative Industries: Culture and Policy* (2012).

TV & Radio, and finally Music, Visual and Performing Arts. Using the same numbers, we can also compare the sectors by how many people each sector employs. Figure 1.2 shows how the creative workers of the United Kingdom stack up in the official figures for 2009 and 2010 (DCMS 2011).

Approximately 1.5 million people were employed in the UK creative industries in 2010. Music & Visual & Performing Arts has the most jobs, followed by Advertising, Publishing, and Design – all of which employ over 200,000 workers. Remember that these are estimates, and that the idea of "creative industries" is not fixed – the definition changes over time because the businesses, the jobs and the products themselves change so rapidly.

Creative activities take place in many different contexts, and in different sectors of the economy. Therefore, when we ask who works in the creative industries, we have to take into account the types of institution or organization involved in professional creative activities. The most common assumption about work in the most visible creative sectors, such as film, television, publishing and music, is that a few large employers sit at the top of each sector, with a large number of small firms and freelancers below them. The vast majority (84%) of companies are small (fewer than 10 people) and just 2% of companies are large (100 people and more), according to recent official estimates (Skillset and CCSkills 2011: 28). One key reason for this is that in all the media industries, but especially in film and TV, large organizations like the BBC, Channel 4 and ITV do not produce programming in-house, instead relying on a commissioning process to outsource production to smaller firms or individual freelancers. As Georgina Born argues, the 1990 Broadcasting Act, which imposed an independent production quota on the licence fee-funded broadcasters in the UK, had the effect of "casualising creativity" at the BBC and across the media industry:

> Where in 1979 almost all employment in television was accounted for by staff jobs in the BBC and ITV, by 1989 39 per cent of all employees were freelance, and by 1994 this figure had risen to 54 per cent. From a peak in the mid nineties, the percentage of freelance employment fell in the later nineties to around 45 per cent, and it has continued to hover at around this level. This shift is probably the single biggest change in the structure of British television in the last twenty years. (Born 2004: 180–181)

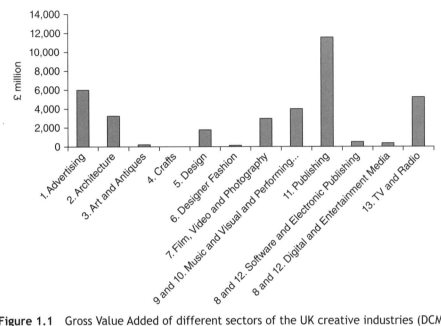

Figure 1.1   Gross Value Added of different sectors of the UK creative industries (DCMS 2011)

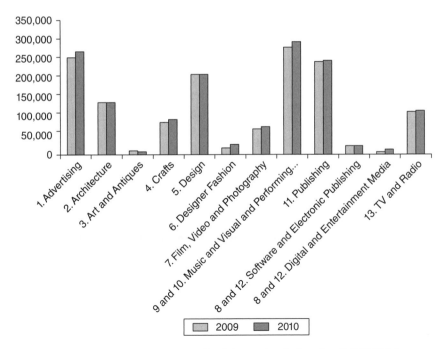

Figure 1.2   Estimated employment in the UK creative industries (DCMS 2011)

Content: The significance of the contemporary notion of content in the creative industries is that it makes a clear distinction between the medium and the content it contains. The increased use of the term, in preference to medium-specific terms such as "programmes", "books", etc., derives from the convergence of previously separate media formats, such as TV, radio and print, into digital formats that don't make that distinction in a straightforward manner. A news website will feature text, video and audio, whether the site belongs to a newspaper or a TV station, for example. In online media, content is seen as functionally separate from the platform on which it's distributed. There is, of course, no absolute separation between content and platform – audiovisual content, for example, has to be produced, edited and distributed in a medium that can convey moving images and sound with reasonable quality. However, it matters less and less whether this audiovisual "stream" comes to us through broadcast channels or online. When watching a live transmission from a sporting event, it matters more that we're watching something happening *right now*, than how we're watching it (that is, on TV or streamed online). Increasingly valuable to content producers are the intellectual property rights attached to content, which they can now exploit across a wide range of platforms, rather than in just one medium, such as print, or broadcast.

Focusing on the core functions of commissioning, financing and distribution, the large media organizations now outsource a substantial amount of their creative work to independent production companies specializing in developing **content** for TV, radio and film. Therefore, the bulk of all film and television in the UK is made by smaller firms or individuals, who come together (sometimes in very large teams) around specific projects, and then disperse once the jobs are completed.

This means that many creative workers are not employed full-time by a specific creative business or organization. Creatives also work as freelancers or independent **producers**; groups or teams work within specialist creative organizations; and people in creative occupations work within larger "non-creative" organizations (Pratt 2004; Cunningham and Higgs 2008: 15). The figures for the UK bear this out, since approximately 43% of the total creative workforce in the UK is employed outside the creative industries (Skillset and CCSkills 2011: 29). In other words, almost half of all the "creative" workers in the UK are working in companies that are not explicitly identified as belonging to the creative industries (Figure 1.3).

The "creative industries" label therefore applies to a diverse range of businesses and activities. For example, a graphic designer – let's call her Lucy – might at different times work as a freelancer or sole trader, as an employee at a creative agency, or as a member of the web team at a bank – whether she works as a freelancer, advertiser or banker, the designer takes the same set of skills into different institutions and contexts. This is why we focus in this book on the kinds of work people do *across* the creative industries, paying attention to how they use their talents, skills and time. We follow both people and products on this journey – sometimes focusing on individuals, sometimes on businesses, and sometimes on particular objects. Most symbolic (or cultural) products come into being through a production chain that contains many different stages, each of which can involve people contributing parts to the whole (Caves 2000; Bilton 2007).

Lucy provides us with a good illustration of the problem of defining the boundaries of the creative industries too narrowly. She may be counted as working in the creative industries while she works at an advertising agency, but she may fall into a different category when she moves over to the bank's web team, even if the two jobs are much the same. Lucy is hired to do similar work in her three different jobs, but for statistical purposes she is employed in three different industries. However, an "industry" is not a category that can be found in nature. Typically, industries are defined by the activity involved, the materials that are used, and the outputs they generate. The DCMS list of "creative" occupations is drawn from the Standard Industrial Classification (SIC), which is a classification system that aims to cover all occupations that UK taxpayers are likely to engage in. Every occupation is assigned a number in this classification system, which makes it possible for government to count how many people work in manufacturing, services, education, and so on. This classification system is appropriate when the majority of all economic activity can be defined by activity, input and output; however, it may not be as appropriate when the economic system has become more complex and service-oriented, as is the case in the creative industries.

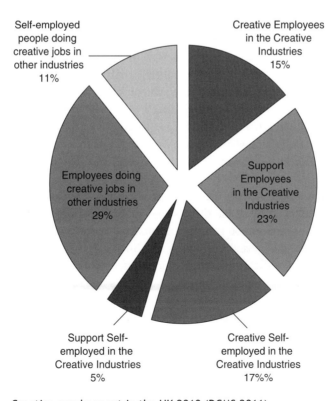

Figure 1.3 Creative employment in the UK 2010 (DCMS 2011)

Markets, novelty and uncertainty

One key feature of the creative industries is the *uncertainty* of the market for its products (Caves 2000). The creative industries produce novelty, but when something new is created, whether it's a song, TV programme or advertising campaign, there is no firm guarantee that there is actually a market for it out there. Therefore, risk is inherent to some degree in all areas of the creative industries.

To put this in more concrete terms, consider how works of art are priced, often through auction. One famous example of this is Damien Hirst's tiger shark suspended in a tank of formaldehyde. This work of art is titled *The Physical Impossibility of Death in the Mind of Someone Living*, or more prosaically "The $12 Million Stuffed Shark" (Thompson 2008). A full-size shark, preserved in this way, would for the average person be an expensive thing to source (not to mention transport and store). Expensive as that may be, it would still fall short of $12 million. The difference in valuation comes about because enough people agree that Hirst is an artist, that his shark is an important art work, that its contribution to modern art is unique, and therefore the shark has an artistic value that sets it apart from other preserved animals. Setting aside the question whether the shark has inherent artistic value, the *valuation* of it rests on social factors such as Hirst's recognition as an artist among people who are prepared to buy art works, and how unique or innovative they consider the work to be when they make offers on it at auction. The prices that bidders are prepared to pay for his shark depend on a market in which innovation is recognized socially and is also assigned monetary value socially – by art buyers and collectors who pick up cues from one another. These are social cues that answer key questions that a potential buyer might have: whether Hirst is regarded as an artist in the first place, whether someone's bought his work in the past, for how much, and what price the work might fetch upon resale. This happens through a complex social market we can call "the art world" – the social network of people operating in that market (Becker 1982; Currid 2007; Thornton 2008).

Novelty inspires uncertainty. In art as in most other areas, when something new appears most of us don't know about it, and those who do might not know what to do with it in the first place. So, any innovation gets filtered through a complex social system of choices made by individuals, groups and institutions. This market for choices about novelty and uncertainty can be said to define the creative industries, because "decisions both to produce and to consume are determined by the choice of others in a social network" (Potts et al. 2008a: 169). The creative industries are, in this view, the link between *novelty* and the *mainstream*, because they combine the choices made from the time when something is new and unknown to when it's become old news, widely known, or even an item of heritage.

This approach shifts the focus away from arts and heritage as "core" elements of the creative industries. Instead, the creative industries are seen as having three primary functions: *innovation*, the infrastructural *support for innovation*, and the *transformation* of novelty into the mainstream of lifestyle, culture and social activity. Therefore, some scholars have argued that the creative industries are best defined as *social network markets*, because these functions are all inherently social (Potts, Hartley, and Cunningham 2008b; O'Connor 2009a). This means that the creative industries rely more than others on word of mouth, taste, popularity and other social indicators, so that "individual choices are dominated by information feedback over social networks rather than innate preferences and price signals" (Potts et al. 2008a: 185). In short, we pay attention to others, when it comes to deciding whether a novelty is valuable or not, because by their choices they send out all kinds of signals that are useful for us in the form of trends, rumours, news and speculation.

Much of the work that people in the creative industries do is about processing such signals. Whether it's a freelancer looking for production work, a journalist seeking a commission or an advertising agency pitching to a potential client, they apply specific skills and tactics for gauging the demand for their services. As we will see later in more detail, there are business structures and work cultures that people learn to navigate as they become professionals. Networking, for

Keeping an Eye Out: Trendspotting, coolhunting, or simply being clued in — there are many terms for this basic necessity of working in media and creative industries. David, a senior planner at a large London advertising agency, says that a significant part of his role is to keep up with developments, trends and interesting ideas, and feeding this into the collaborative process of making advertising in a fast-changing market (David, 2010). Coolhunting as a specialism in marketing and advertising came of age in the 1990s with the emergence of trendwatching specialists like Faith Popcorn, author of the *Popcorn Report* (1992), and the research agency Look Look, profiled by Malcolm Gladwell in a 1997 *New Yorker* article, reprinted in *The Tipping Point* (Gladwell 2000). The initial focus of coolhunting on teenagers and trends emerging among youth consumers, as depicted in the documentary *The Merchants of Cool* (2001), has more recently given way to a broader approach by research agencies like Trendwatching.com and *Contagious* magazine, both of which focus on the business-to-consumer market (B2C) in general. Finally, trendspotting has become a popular practice among bloggers, as exemplified by the fashion blog *Facehunter* (Rodic 2010), the design blog *Cool Hunting*, and the art technology blog *We Make Money Not Art*.

example, is sometimes regarded as an almost mystical activity of conjuring "contacts" out of thin air. In fact, networking is a skill like any other, useful to creative workers in coping with the uncertainties of demand, the irregular income and work schedules of freelancing, and in searching for new opportunities (see Chapter 5). Portfolio working – on a project-by-project basis, often with a different team each time – makes it necessary for creative workers to be open to other kinds of expertise than their own, and to cultivate personal networks of people whose diverse talents can complement their own. This is particularly important when it comes to short-term projects for which a team is put together on a temporary basis to produce something against a deadline (see Chapter 3).

This gives rise to the radical proposition of social network markets: the creative industries are a set of relations between business, education, industry, the arts – they are defined by innovative *activities*, not by *where* those activities take place. Any sector of the economy can potentially be seen as contributing to the creative industries (Potts and Cunningham 2008). This gets around the problem we've seen above in the way creative occupations are classified as either "in" the creative industries or "outside" them (DCMS 2011). However, this approach has come under criticism for downgrading the distinctiveness of the creative industries: if they are defined by servicing other sectors rather than bringing something specific to the table, that leaves little room for the question whether economic value is all that matters in the study of the creative industries.

In short, the social network market may leave little room for cultural policy. The role of cultural policy is to decide how the power and the resources of the state, as a representative of the taxpayers, are to be used. Justin O'Connor argues that to separate the creative industries from cultural policy is to ignore the intrinsic value of creative goods. The creative industries draw on and operate within a cultural realm that is not simply about business, he suggests. Creative goods have an intrinsic value – they are about pleasure, meaning, identity and expression in ways that go far beyond mere exchange value. They are never merely functional and their benefits never solely pertain to business. "If [creative goods] are also part of active citizenship then they are to be judged on this basis – how far do they enhance this citizenship?" (O'Connor 2009a: 400).

Furthermore, if creativity is seen as a generic component of the "knowledge economy" at large, then what's so special about the "creative industries"? Mark Banks and Justin O'Connor suggest that we have arrived at a moment "after the creative industries", because "the creative industries appear increasingly to be viewed less as distinctive industry sectors requiring help to support and develop, and more as sources of innovation and creativity that input into other sectors and the economy at large" (Banks and O'Connor 2009: 366). While this emphasis on innovation has been important for creative industries policy (particularly around government support for innovation-led sectors such as computing and design), it has led to a diminished emphasis on the arts, which have gradually faded from creative industries policy, at least in the UK (Oakley 2009a). This has important repercussions for practitioners, not least those who work in the arts, education, and other areas that feed into and support businesses in the creative industries at large.

Creative labour, working in the creative industries

In part, understanding the contemporary creative industries involves talking to the practitioners. In researching this book, we have interviewed creative workers, asking them to tell us about their working lives, the context they work in, and not least to tell us about what it is they value personally about their professions, communities and occupations. These interviews are then put into the larger context of business models, financing and patterns of employment.

We draw on the work of a number of scholars who have studied the experience of creative workers: Angela McRobbie studied British designer fashion (McRobbie 1998) and the politics of creative entrepreneurship in late-1990s London (McRobbie 2002). Andrew Ross, particularly in *No-Collar* (2003), raised important questions about the working conditions, hours, pay and circumstances of freelancers and temporary workers in new media and other creative work. Using methods such as interviews and observation in studios, offices and other workplaces, McRobbie and Ross paid particular attention to the **precarity** of creative labour – the strains on the individuals (usually self-employed contractors, responsible for their own pensions, unemployment, taxes, and health insurance), the demands that "flexible" working hours place on the workers' time and home lives, the intense competition for jobs in the more glamorous sectors of the creative industries, and the constant threat of one's skills becoming outdated with new technologies coming along.

Looking at this topic from the point of view of organizations, Chris Bilton, in *Management and Creativity* (2007), draws on his experience as a film producer to argue that creativity is spread across organizations and teams – that it is, in fact, a product of systems and processes, specific to each sector. Similarly, Mark Deuze's *Media Work* (2007a) brings together an extensive selection of interviews with people working in various media industries ranging from Finland to the USA. Another very influential study of creative labour, which attempts to chart systems and processes from the point of view of the workers themselves is Rosalind Gill's *Technobohemians or the New Cybertariat?* (2007). This study brings together interviews with 50 "web workers" in Amsterdam, and casts a light on some of the contradictions experienced by the "web-workers" she interviews: on the one hand, they experience anxieties about their job security and income, the long hours, competition and the struggle to keep up with new technological developments; on the other hand, these people are very invested in their work, with a sense of self-worth and pleasure in doing good work.

This notion of "good work" sits at the heart of David Hesmondhalgh and Sarah Baker's extensive study *Creative Labour: Media Work in Three Cultural Industries* (2011). Drawing on the work of Ross, McRobbie and other critics of self-exploitation and precarity, they interview journalists, musicians and television workers in order to find out what

Precarity: When workers themselves take on business risks and responsibilities that otherwise would be assumed by the employer. The life of "precarious workers" is "characterised by risk, insecurity and contingency in which more and more of the costs of work are borne by the workers themselves" (Gill 2011: 250). Freelancers, for example, work on a project-by-project basis, without a predictable income, job security or the benefits that come with long-term employment. They are responsible for their own budgeting, taxes, pensions, insurance, as well as their own equipment, training and skills. Recommended reading: Andrew Ross, *No-collar* (2003); Rosalind Gill and Andy Pratt, "In the Social Factory? Immaterial Labour, Precariousness and Cultural Work" (2008); Terry Flew, *The Creative Industries: Culture and Policy* (2012).

counts as "good creative work" (and conversely, what makes for "bad" creative work) in their experience. In particular, they pay attention to the practitioners' accounts of making "good products", autonomy, and self-realization (both as individuals and members of a community of creative professionals). In other words, they pay attention to the pleasures of creative labour as well as the anxieties and risks that come with it. Similarly, Mark Banks has called attention to the "moral economy" inherent in creative work, that is, how social and political values may be just as important (and even more important for some) than economic values (Banks 2006). Money is not the prime motivation for the cultural entrepreneurs interviewed in Banks' study, even though their lives are subject to what Banks refers to elsewhere as the "instrumental leisure of the creative class" (Banks 2009) – the erosion of free time by the demands of work.

The concept of the "creative class" has been both influential and extensively critiqued. It derives from the work of Richard Florida, and refers to occupations in which people "add economic value through their creativity" – and to **knowledge workers** more generally. Creative workers sell a *creative capacity*, rather than sharply defined skills or products, a capacity which is "an intangible because it is literally in their heads" (Florida 2002a: 68). Because the creative capacity resides in the people themselves, Florida argues that it's economically necessary for corporations, cities and industrial clusters to think strategically about how they can attract and retain creative workers, not just by paying them good money, but by offering an environment in which they would like to live. It's not enough for an area to have jobs, Florida argues, it has to have the various things that the creative classes appreciate in their everyday life: good transportation, good communications infrastructure, broad choices of cultural opportunities and entertainment, an ethnically diverse population, high degree of social tolerance, and access to a social circle of likeminded people (Florida 2010c).

Therefore, it may be possible to gauge the robustness and the potential for growth in urban areas by looking at certain indicators of local cultural and social life (Hansen, Asheim, and Vang 2009). One such measure

Knowledge workers: Any worker relying on specialist training, skills or knowledge to provide services can be said to be a knowledge worker. Often, the term "knowledge economy" is used to describe an advanced economy in which the emphasis has shifted away from manufacturing and the processing of raw materials and commodities, to a high-tech economy characterized by the more high-skilled and high-margin manufacturing and processing, and above all to *services*. Communications, information technology and access to highly trained specialists able to apply new scientific knowledge to software, patentable technological innovations, health care, retail, tourism, financial services, and a myriad of other knowledge-based businesses and public services (Perrons 2007). The creative industries can be seen as a subset of the knowledge economy – and creative workers grouped with knowledge workers in general. This is why creative industries policy links the traditional arts and media production with "new" media such as electronic publishing and software, and with specialist services such as advertising and marketing, design and architecture (Cunningham 2002; Garnham 2005; Foord 2008).

is the Bohemian Index, which "charts the concentration of working artists, musicians, writers, designers, and entertainers across metropolitan areas" – mapping the concentration of the creative classes in particular areas (Florida 2010a). Florida argues that the presence of "bohemians" in an area creates an environment that attracts other types of talented individuals. In turn, innovative, technology-intensive industries will be attracted to the area because it will be easier to recruit high-quality employees, and new businesses will be created to take advantage of the same opportunities (Florida 2002b). The Bohemian Index (and similar indexes like "the diversity index" or "gay index") therefore has implications far beyond the circles of what he calls *artistic and cultural creatives* – a subcategory of the larger set of creative class occupations. By defining a class of professionals through the importance of "creativity" for their work, Florida's "creative classes" category has expanded over the years to include all occupations that involve a high degree of education, training, skill and intellectual engagement. In his later work they are not primarily identified with the creative industries in the narrower sense; instead the jobs of the creative classes involve the creation of new ideas, new content and new technologies in general. Therefore, the creative classes include workers in "science and technology, business and management, health care and law, and arts, culture, design, media, and entertainment" (Florida 2010b).

Some critics of Florida have argued that his work has spawned an industry of consultants paid handsomely to offer advice to struggling post-industrial cities on how to attract more creatives to their abandoned factories and warehouse districts (Nathan 2005). This form of consultancy has even acquired a specific name – "doing a Florida thing" (McGuigan 2009). However, Florida himself can't be blamed for what others do with his work at the local level, as Kate Oakley has pointed out in the case of Sheffield (Oakley 2009b). The most commonly cited shortcoming of the creative class hypothesis is that by prioritizing a certain category of people, Florida is putting the cart before the horse: without adequate infrastructure, economic opportunities, housing, transport, education, and so on, the creative class won't do much for a local economy (Nathan 2005; Pratt 2008). Therefore, policy initiatives have to look beyond the question of how to attract creative workers to an area or a city. Florida's "beatific notion of creative work" (Hesmondhalgh and Baker 2011: 6) is therefore seen by some as oversimplified and out of touch with the realities of labour in the creative industries. Furthermore, Florida's language of creativity and "bohemians" risks glamourizing casual, freelance employment practices and labour that is in actuality often badly paid, insecure, and positively hostile to the kind of work–life balance that people need in order to make a living, raise families, and sustain their careers (Gill and Pratt 2008; Banks 2009). In other words, the study of creative labour in practice tends to cast doubt on the utopian claims made for the autonomy and freedom of the "creative class", while at the same time providing interesting and detailed insights into the working life of creative professionals that are neither reducible to simplistic notions of the glamour of creative practice, nor the dire predictions of precarity, self-exploitation and impoverished overwork.

By focusing on the people who work in various creative occupations, scholars are able to pay close attention to the specifics of what it's like to work in the media and creative industries, and to the contexts that people work in. The creative industries share many features across national borders, but they turn out to be quite local in practice. Cities and urban areas turn out to be extremely important, not just as places to live and work, but as the living, breathing social fabric into which the stories of creative practitioners are woven (Pratt 2004; Evans 2009). Just to name a few examples of how cities emerge as key elements in this work, there is London's Hoxton and Shoreditch area (Pratt 2009); New York City (Neff, Wissinger, and Zukin 2005); writers, producers and film crews in Hollywood (Mayer, Banks, and Caldwell 2009); Manchester's media and music scene (Banks 2006; Robb 2009; Johns 2010); the "neo-bohemia" of Chicago (Lloyd 2010); the web-design studios of Amsterdam (Gill 2007); the flourishing arts, design and media scene in Berlin's Prenzlauer Berg and Kreuzberg (van Heur 2009; Heebels and van Aalst 2010); the filmmakers of Lagos (Nollywood) (Lobato 2010); the Hindi film industry of Mumbai (Bollywood) (Kavoori and Punathambekar 2008); and the emerging "creative clusters" of Singapore (Kong 2009), Beijing (Keane 2007, 2009) and Shanghai (O'Connor 2009b; Wu Wei and Hua 2009).

SUMMARY

This chapter has introduced the creative industries as a concept. It is an umbrella term that covers a range of different but related economic activities (products and services) for which *creativity* is important, particularly when it concerns *symbolic production*, and the generation of *intellectual property*. We also introduce our approaches to studying the creative industries, through the use of economic data, the study of market characteristics, and the stories of creative practitioners. We ask what are the *characteristics* of the creative industries, what do they *produce*, and what it's like to *work* within them.

RECOMMENDED READING

Bilton, Chris. 2007. *Management and Creativity: From Creative Industries to Creative Management*. Oxford: Blackwell. A study of the creative industries, with a focus on management and understanding the business fundamentals.

Hesmondhalgh, David and Sarah Baker. 2011. *Creative Labour: Media Work in Three Cultural Industries*. London: Routledge. Using interviews and participant observation, the authors study managers and workers in television, music recording and magazine publishing. This is an important and thoroughly researched study of the conditions and issues surrounding creative work.

Johnson, Steven. 2010. *Where Good Ideas Come From: The Seven Patterns of Innovation.* London: Penguin. An accessible historical study of creativity and innovation in science, industry and the arts.

Kong, Lily and Justin O'Connor, eds. 2009. *Creative Economies, Creative Cities, Asian European Perspectives.* New York: Springer. Good overview of the international trade in cultural goods, and the ways in which creative industries work in the Asian context, compared to Europe.

McKinlay, Alan and Chris Smith, eds. 2009. *Creative Labour: Working in the Creative Industries. Critical Perspectives on Work and Employment.* Basingstoke: Palgrave Macmillan. Essays on various aspects of working in the creative industries, ranging from networking and skills to labour union politics.

McRobbie, Angela. 1998. *British Fashion Design: Rag Trade or Image Industry?* London: Routledge. A groundbreaking study of the London fashion industry.

Pratt, Andy C. and Paul Jeffcutt, eds. 2009. *Creativity, Innovation and the Cultural Economy.* London: Routledge. A collection of essays on the different sectors of the creative industries, with two chapters each for advertising, music, film and TV, new media, design and museums/visual arts/performance. All the essays touch on the question of *where* the relevant activities occur, and the institutions and networks within which creative professionals work.

Thornton, Sarah. 2008. *Seven Days in the Art World.* London: W.W. Norton. An entertaining and informative set of observations ranging from an art school seminar to a Christie's auction.

2

Creativity and Commerce

The relationship between economics and culture, between commerce and creativity, is very important when studying the production of commercial symbolic cultural goods and services. It may be tempting to romanticize artistic creativity, inspiration and talent as "art for art's sake" which cannot be reconciled with "selling out" – succumbing to the base materiality of utility, commerce and profit. This relatively recent separation of art from commerce, according to Raymond Williams, relies on the idea that an artistic inclination and talent will exclude the artist from any involvement in administrative or commercial matters. One is either an "Aesthetic Man" or an "Economic Man", with the former committed to a freewheeling bohemian life of non-conformist refusal of the values of work, prudence, family and profession that characterize the latter (Williams 1961, 1965).

Aesthetic Man and Economic Man are stereotypes that some artists and musicians have used to great effect to build a public persona for themselves – Bob Dylan, for instance, writes in his autobiography *Chronicles* (itself an exercise in self-stylization) that he studied the American folk tradition intensely and put that heritage to use in creating his own musical persona as the itinerant folk musician, poet and rambler, modelled on predecessors like Woody Guthrie and Ramblin' Jack Elliott (Dylan 2003). Developing in the opposite direction, bridging the roles of Aesthetic and Economic Man, another musician of more recent vintage has written about overcoming his own bohemian financial illiteracy: the bassist Duff McKagan of Guns n' Roses went to university after a stint in rehab in 1994, taking charge of his own business affairs (McKagan 2011). "Becoming a suit, without the suit," he eventually founded a money management firm for musicians alongside recording and touring with his new band (Kimes 2011).

Disdain for commerce wouldn't get us very far in the study of how people actually make their living from creative labour. The main focus of this book is contemporary, and we assume that our readers are curious about the experiences of practitioners making a living in a variety of professions across the creative industries. In telling those stories, we draw on a number of historical concepts that require a bit of elaboration. While it would be impossible to boil down the entire history of commercial creative production into a single chapter (or even a book), this chapter aims to illustrate how the intimate relationship between commerce and cultural creativity has worked in ways that have been around for many centuries.

Figure 2.1 "Not for Sale" Graffiti, Redchurch St, London, August 2012 Photo credit: Gauti Sigthorsson

Who pays? Who makes? Who buys?

The fundamental business relationships and funding models that apply in the contemporary creative industries have a long history. We consider three such models in this chapter. First, we look at *patronage* and commissioning, using the example of Michelangelo and other artists of the Italian Renaissance. Then we look at the marketplace for Shakespeare's plays and how a paying audience takes the place of the patron. Finally, we consider the *industrial production* of creative goods, first as

Industrial Revolution: There is more than one "beginning" ascribed to the Industrial Revolution, but in Britain it has often been dated from the mid-1700s, when coal-fired steam engines were harnessed to mechanize the manufacturing of textiles. One of the most influential features of industrialization was the standardization of parts and components of machinery, along with the standardization of the functions of labourers and managers within the manufacturing process (Beniger 1986). This was the great difference between the diverse, small-scale, crafts-based manufacturing that preceded the Industrial Revolution, and the standardized, large-scale, hierarchical manufacturing that industrialization made possible (Hobsbawm 1999). Industrialization would not be confined to manufacturing for long — all aspects of life became industrialized, from the jobs and professions that were created, the mass-migration from the country to the cities, in which "the working classes" took shape out of the dispersed labourers of agricultural society (Williams 1965), to the mass-produced goods and standardized technologies that emerged in the course of the nineteenth century and in the twentieth century (see also **Fordism**). For example, the modern newspaper was made possible through mechanized printing, speedy distribution, and communications technologies such as the telegraph that made it possible for information to travel at the speed of electricity through a wire, rather than at the same speed at which a human

exemplified by the invention of print, and later by the **Industrial Revolution** of the eighteenth and nineteenth centuries. These are key developments behind the emergence of mass-production, mass-distribution and the kind of mass-mediated popular culture that we are familiar with today.

PATRONAGE: WEALTH, POWER AND RELIGION IN ITALIAN RENAISSANCE PAINTING

The fourteenth, fifteenth and sixteenth centuries saw a period of cultural development in Europe that is now referred to as the **Renaissance**. The Renaissance is often seen as having marked the end of the **Middle Ages** in Europe and the beginning of the modern era in European history. In fourteenth-century Italy, **classical** Greek and Roman art and culture were rediscovered and promoted by artists and intellectuals. This was a scholarly, religious, artistic and scientific movement that spread across Europe in the next three centuries, and coincided with a remarkable period of technological, political and economic change.[1] It was also a Golden Age of **patronage** in the arts, when the rich

---

[1]Much of this new knowledge came to Europe from Asia. One centre of scholarship was Constantinople (now Istanbul in Turkey), the capital of Byzantium, which was the last surviving part of the Roman Empire. When Christian Constantinople was captured by the Ottoman Turks in 1453 and became part of the Muslim Ottoman Empire, there was a substantial exodus of Greek scholars to Europe, bringing contemporary Arabic and classical learning with them. Prior to this, Islamic scholarship had also spread into Europe in the Middle Ages from centres of scholarship on the Islamic Iberian peninsula (modern-day Spain and Portugal), including translations of the classical philosopher Aristotle, previously unavailable in Europe.

merchants and aristocrats of Florence, Venice and other Italian city-states began commissioning artworks of great quality and ambition to ensure that their names and likenesses would endure long after their own day.

Painting in Renaissance Culture

Prior to the Renaissance, images and decoration had been important in Catholic Christianity, which was the dominant religion in Europe during the Middle Ages and at the beginning of the Renaissance. There were two main reasons for this. First, much money and effort was expended on making churches majestic and beautiful, in order to reflect the glory of the divine and so to inspire awe in the congregation. At a more practical level, paintings were used to communicate the key messages of the religion to the largely illiterate congregation, who could not read the Bible. During the Middle Ages, painters would use valuable pigments, such as gold, to reflect the importance of the subject of the painting and the church itself (Baxandall 1988). The use of precious metals and minerals not only gave the painting sensual appeal through bright colours and lustrous surfaces. It also made the painting a materially valuable object, which represented the importance of the contribution and therefore spiritual worth of the Church authorities or the private donor who had commissioned and paid for the painting. Consequently, the commissioning body or individual would stipulate to the

could (Mattelart 1996). The railway, impossible without standardized, mass-manufactured components that conform precisely to standards (tracks, engines, carriages, etc.), effectively "industrialized time and space" in the nineteenth century, making long-distance transportation possible at greater speeds than ever before (Schivelbusch 1986). Standardization, in turn, has had a profound, widespread social, cultural and technological influence in the areas of transportation, energy and communication (Bowker and Star 2000). In turn, the industrialization of creativity can be traced through the history of industrialization in many different ways: design and architecture are profoundly influenced by standardization, manufacturing technologies and infrastructure (electricity, water, sewage, communications). Mass-communications and mass-media, from the newspapers of the nineteenth century to the games studios of the twenty-first, are all "industrial" operations in their reliance on standards, specialized workers, technical skills and systems of production and distribution.

Patron and **patronage:** Derived from the Latin word for "father", a patron is a defender or protector, someone who lends support and influence. "Patrons of the arts", for example, are institutions or individuals who fund artistic practice of some kind, protect an artist or a group of artists, collect and preserve artwork for posterity. Patronage in the classical sense, like the Medicis' patronage of Michelangelo, later came to mean something closer to a 'customer' — someone who regularly purchases the product in question. In the digital era, however, the old sense of "patronage" has been revived to describe, not only **public funding** and corporate and individual sponsorship of the arts, but a wider range of practices, for example, how musicians make up for the lost sales of physical copies of CDs by licensing their music for use in advertisements or turn to their fan base for direct donations — effectively relying on a crowd-sourced form of patronage for their income. See Chapter 10 for a fuller discussion of some of these forms of patronage. Recommended reading: Jerry Brotton, *The Renaissance: A Very Short Introduction* (2006); Paul Allen, *Artist Management for the Music Business* (2011).

Value: "What is a cynic?" asked Oscar Wilde. "A man who knows the price of everything and the value of nothing." In valuing something we ask "what is it worth?" and in so doing we compare it with other things of a similar nature. The notion of value is therefore inseparable from social *evaluation* or *estimation*, through which value is established. This is how we come to value one thing more or less than another, constructing *hierarchies of value* from "low" to "high", and differentiating "good" from "better and "best". Because we can evaluate the same thing in many different ways, the term "value" often comes with a qualifier in front of it, such as "*economic* value", "*aesthetic* value", or "*moral* value" (Edgar and Sedgwick 2008: 375). This means that *valuation* is essentially a social activity, either in a marketplace or among a particular social group which can recognize and establish the value of something, for example the work of a new designer or an artist (Currid 2007). When comparing economic, aesthetic and moral value, the first (economic value) might seem the simplest to figure out, but in economics there is a difference between *exchange value* (measured in money — what someone is prepared to pay for it) and *use value* (of how much use a thing is to someone) (Bennett et al. 2005: 366). In other words, we may be able to measure some types of value with money, but it's a crude measurement

painter how much gold or other precious materials should be included in the painting. So, when considering how these paintings might have functioned as symbolic cultural products, we should bear in mind that the spiritual **value** of medieval and early Renaissance Italian painting was closely tied to its material value. This practice can still be found in contemporary art, most famously in the case of Damien Hirst's "For the Love of God" (2007) – a platinum cast of a human skull, encrusted with diamonds, but with the teeth from the original skull inserted in their anatomically designated places.

Medieval painting did not have realism as its primary aim. The aim was rather to symbolize certain key aspects of the religion and to provide devotional images.

However, during the Renaissance, Italian painters began to attempt to paint scenes that recreated the natural world more closely. They began to use a system called one-point or linear perspective – a mathematical formula that facilitated a representation of space as three-dimensional. This system was a valuable tool in architectural design, allowing architects to represent on paper, and thus design, structures that had previously been too complex. As the Renaissance progressed, it became an equally vital **technology** for painting. Italian painters became increasingly preoccupied with using it to arrange figures in convincing three-dimensional space. Piero della Francesca was one painter whose paintings demonstrate a central pre-occupation with perspective. At the same time, painters, such as Michelangelo, were also inspired by classical sculpture in their representation of the human figure.

Figure 2.2   Piero della Francesca (1415/20-1492): Flagellation, c. 1455.Urbino, Ducal Palace. Tavola. cm 59 x 81,5.- © 2013. Photo Scala, Florence – courtesy of the Ministero Beni e Att. Culturali

Although these Renaissance painters were still producing religious paintings, it is noticeable that their focus had shifted onto the representation of the human figure, architecture and the natural world and away from the primacy of religious symbolism.

The Renaissance painter

As painters became more skilled in this form of realistic, figurative representation, their client's focus also shifted (Baxandall 1988). The value of a painting came more closely to be allied with the skill of the painter, rather than the use of valuable materials. Church authorities and private patrons began to value the painter over his materials and would seek to engage a particular artist for a commission, rather than stipulate particular precious materials. As a consequence, artists began to sign their work and whereas prior to the Renaissance painters were regarded as artisans and had no higher status than other craftspeople (all craft activity had fairly low social status), late Renaissance painters, such as Michelangelo (1475–1564) and Raphael (1483–1520), were celebrated as geniuses.

Italian Renaissance painting thus marks an increased importance in the individual human subject, both in the paintings themselves and in the social status of the painter.

when it comes to questions of people's motivations, behaviour and the choices they make, often based on considerations that have little to do with money and a lot to do with other, less concrete forms of value. For example, *novelty*, *innovation* and *creativity* are important criteria for the evaluation of potentially lucrative ideas, designs and objects (Potts et al. 2008a). Therefore, they can have tremendous value without being immediately measurable in cash terms.

Technology: The ancient meaning of technology as 'systematic treatment' of something, whether artistic or industrial, is still implicit in contemporary use. In the simplest sense, technology is the reduction of processes (material, physical, social) to physical systems or systematic procedures. This is why technology is both *physical*, in the sense of devices, machines or tools, and also *social*. Techniques, habits of thought and divisions of labour are themselves technologies. In factory production, for example, the division of labour is a technology for organizing the work of many into an "output" of some kind. Technologies, in short, are as much social as they are mechanical. Recommended reading: Tony Bennet et al., "Technology" in *New Keywords* (2005: 342–344); Craig Hanks, *Technology and Values: Essential Readings* (2010).

The artist as genius: The enduring notion of the artist as a special person endowed with unusual gifts dates from the Renaissance. Giorgio Vasari, in his collection of artists' biographies, titled *Lives of the Artists* (or rather, *Lives of the Most Eminent Painters, Sculptors and Architects*), first published in 1550, inaugurated a new form of art-historical writing in which the history of art is told through biographies of the artists themselves. In regarding artists as exceptional human beings, Vasari established a tradition that continued to develop from the Renaissance onwards, as several scholars have pointed out (Batschmann 1997). It was a fundamental idea in the Romantic movement of the early nineteenth century, which we discuss later in this chapter, and continues to underpin contemporary discourse about art and artists.

Production and financing structures

The high status of the painter in subsequent centuries has meant that the history of Renaissance painting has often focused on the achievement of individual artists. However, it's important to note that the majority of Italian paintings were produced as a part of a workshop system of production. Established painters had their own workshops, in which they trained apprentices and employed a team of painters to assist them in the execution of commissions. Thus, although the artworks of course bore the stamp or signature of the master of the workshop, Italian Renaissance paintings were most often produced as part of a production line, rather than as the sole work of a single individual. The artist's name and signature, therefore, served in the same way as a brand in contemporary commerce, a guarantee of quality and authenticity provided by the master of the workshop.

The workshop system involved significant overhead costs for the artists who ran them and painters were reliant to a large extent on patrons commissioning work. They tended not to produce paintings speculatively, but sought clients who would commission a particular work and pay for its production. The Catholic Church had, until the Renaissance, been the chief patron. As the most powerful political entity in Europe, the Church drew enormous wealth from the kings and aristocrats whose claims to their thrones and bloodlines were validated by the doctrine of divine right. Wealthy patrons would commission paintings for the Church as a way of demonstrating their piety. This tradition was taken up by the merchants that grew rich from the shipping trade in the Mediterranean that bestowed enormous wealth on the city-states of Italy. These were cities which functioned as independent states and, as they grew richer, private commissions also began to flourish.

Paintings were increasingly commissioned not only for churches and chapels, but for public buildings and private homes. In the city-state of Florence, which was perhaps the centre for art and sculpture in the whole of Renaissance Italy, the richest and most powerful family and the chief patrons of the arts were the Medici. The Medici family used patronage of painters, sculptors, poets and philosophers as a way of establishing power and influence. Just as painting served to communicate the power and majesty of the Church, it also served to communicate the power and majesty of the Medicis, securing and maintaining their status as the richest and most culturally discerning family in Renaissance Florence (Brotton 2006).

Aesthetics, religion, power and status were therefore closely linked in the commissioning and production process of Italian Renaissance painting. As an artefact, a painting's worth was derived from a complex aggregation of spiritual, commercial, social and political values, which had multiple and different significances for different people involved in its production, distribution and exhibition. While twenty-first century patronage is usually far removed from religion and spirituality, the association between aesthetics, power and status is still present in the corporate sponsorships of events or individual artists, funding partnerships, co-branding (for example, when a brand becomes part of the name of a book awards or film awards), or other substantial public affiliations between corporate patrons and the arts (see Williams (1981) for a fuller discussion of different types of patronage).

THE MARKETPLACE: ENGLISH THEATRE IN THE TIME OF SHAKESPEARE

In 1564, the year that the Italian Renaissance painter Michelangelo Buonarroti died, the British playwright William Shakespeare was born. He went on to act and write plays as part of a theatre company, the Lord Chamberlain's Men, in London at the end of the sixteenth century. Since our interest here is in the cultural economy of theatre in Shakespeare's time, we will set aside discussion of his writings and his role in the canon of English literature. Instead, we will look at what political and cultural factors might have contributed to his success, and consider the business model of the company of actors he belonged to.

Patronage vs the marketplace

At the end of the sixteenth century, England, like Italy, had seen an influx of people to the cities. London was a busy capital city with many residents and many more traders and visitors passing through. By law, theatre companies needed an official patron

Market and marketplace: A market or market-place is, in the simple sense, a place where people come together for the purchase and sale of goods, usually in public. The more abstract, modern sense of 'market' retains this ancient meaning. Wherever exchange happens, a market takes place. In a marketplace the value of something is established through comparison and trade: goods, services, skills, information - tangible and intangible things are traded in markets, both large and small. As a creative producer, taking your product to market has quite different implications from receiving a commission from a patron to fund your creative work:

1 The key financial difference is that you have to invest upfront in the product and then hope to recoup your investment and a profit later. It may be that, rather than risking all your own money, you find an investor to invest their money in the project. An investor is looking for a financial return on their investment, rather than the benefits of power and influence that we associate with patronage of the arts. Their calculation is that the finished product can be exchanged in the marketplace for more than the costs of producing it, thus obtaining a profit.

2 A key aesthetic consideration is that you are not producing something to satisfy the requirements of a particular individual or organization. You are producing something for an unknown consumer. You will therefore need to have a pretty good idea of the tastes of your target audience, whether they are Tudor theatregoers; Victorian novel readers; cinema audiences; wearers of t-shirts with slogans on them; or craft enthusiasts, buying hand-turned wooden bowls.

Recommended reading: Peter Antonioni, *Economics for Dummies* (2010).

in order to perform. But in practice the Lord Chamberlain's Men operated a very different **business model** from that of the Italian Renaissance painters (Williams 1981: 38–44). Shakespeare and his fellow actors, who all had **shares** in the company, relied not on commissions by wealthy patrons, but on paying audiences to make their living. The theatre audiences of Tudor London were not made up solely of the royals and aristocrats who patronized painting, music and poetry. They were a mixed bunch of anyone from noblemen to trade apprentices (Berry 1985; Shurgot 1998; Gurr 2006). In writing his plays, Shakespeare had to think about what might appeal to a mixed public from very different classes and backgrounds, courting as wide a popularity as possible at a time when the theatre was emerging as a professional and commercial venture in the late sixteenth century.

The Lord Chamberlain's Men's business model relied on many people each paying a small amount of money to see a performance. This meant that the theatre as a creative form had a much lower social status than the painting, since the majority of its patrons were commoners, ordinary people not part of the royalty or aristocracy. Actors too had a very lowly social status. A key disadvantage of appealing to the commoners in the marketplace like this was also that the theatre company assumed the financial risk for the production of the work. If the audience didn't attend performances, the company might lose money or even go bankrupt. On the other hand, the theatre company retained ownership of the plays, which was important to their business model: "Companies performed six days a week in the public playhouses, putting on a different play each day. A new play would be added every two weeks or so, with more popular plays repeated and others abandoned" (McEvoy 2000: 120). Having a repertoire was essential, since companies could perform plays again and again, reviving older plays and adding new ones to attract audiences. This also made theatre companies and playwrights very protective of their "**intellectual property**" (long before this concept was invented in the legal and commercial sense), resisting printed publication of the text of the plays to prevent competing theatres from getting their hands on it and mounting performances.

In contrast, under the system of patronage, once a Renaissance painter had completed his painting, he would hand it over to the patron who had commissioned it and start a new work from scratch.

> **Public funding:** In many countries, government funding is available to support cultural activities, including creative practice, in a range of sectors. This includes subsidies and grants for the performing and visual arts as well as for film and digital media. Usually intermediary organizations are set up with government funding to manage allocation of and application for funds, such as the National Endowment for the Arts in the United States, the Australia Council for the Arts, or the UK Arts Councils. Typically, such organizations provide funding both for specific projects and for organizational development. See Chapter 10 for a fuller discussion of public funding policies.

The two funding methods outlined so far, the first based on elite patrons' commissions and the second relying on the marketplace, are each related to the particular socio-historical context of production and the particular features of the medium to which they belong. Painting has retained its status, and along with the other "fine arts" is often funded through patronage by individuals or public or private bodies. Theatre, meanwhile, has clawed its way out of the muck of the sixteenth-century marketplace to a higher cultural status than it could ever hope for in Shakespeare's time. At the same time, as cinema, radio and television drama have replaced theatre drama as the staple of popular culture, many theatres now find it difficult to survive purely on performance receipts. Contemporary theatre therefore often operates a mixed model of financing, relying simultaneously on patronage, in the form of **public funding,** and the **marketplace,** in the form of ticket sales (Caves 2000).

Mainstream cinema and popular music, however, are two examples of contemporary creative production that are funded through the marketplace, one which has been vastly expanded through modern recording and distribution technologies. It is, moreover, a marketplace characterized by corporate structures and industrial production and so is also very different from Tudor-era theatre, as we will go on to investigate.

REPRODUCTION AND MASS-PRODUCTION: THE PRINT REVOLUTION

Very often a new venture, which will ultimately rely on consumer sales, requires a large amount of money or **capital** invested upfront to pay for the expense of starting up

Capital and **capitalism:** Capital is wealth that generates more wealth, primarily through ownership of or investment in businesses that produce profits (for example, through stocks, **shares** or money invested directly as "venture capital"). Capital*ism*, by extension, is a social system that favours the ownership of capital. This can take different forms, ranging from various forms of market-led capitalism in which property is regarded as the fundamental right of individuals, to state capitalism, which places all property under the collective ownership of the state, subject to central planning and management. There are, in other words, multiple capitalisms, and within them the creative industries take on local forms, for example, the ways in which the idea of creative industries has been adopted in the context of Chinese state-capitalism (Keane 2007). Recommended reading: Tony Bennett et al., "Capitalism" in *New Keywords* (2005: 22-26); Nigel Thrift, *Knowing Capitalism* (2005): Peter Antonioni, *Economics for Dummies* (2010).

the business before it makes any sales. The development of the European publishing industry, which arose as a result of the invention of a printing press in Germany, in the middle of the fifteenth century, provides an early example of this kind of capital investment in new business. The innovation introduced by German goldsmith and printer, Johannes Gutenberg, was the use of movable type, a technology that was already known in China, but not in Europe. This meant that any page of text could be reproduced using individual letters arranged together for each page, whereas the method of block printing that was used prior to Gutenberg's innovation necessitated producing a unique printing block for each page to be printed.

Gutenberg the innovator

Gutenberg has been compared to the contemporary technology entrepreneurs of Silicon Valley by Jeff Jarvis, in the ebook *Gutenberg the Geek* (2012), and by the technology journalist John Naughton, who argues in *What You Really Need to Know About the Internet: From Gutenberg to Zuckerberg* (2012), that "the Internet is special because it's a powerful enabler of disruptive innovation [...] a global machine for springing surprises – good, bad and indifferent – on us" (Naughton 2012: chapter 3). Jarvis points out that Gutenberg, like contemporary technology entrepreneurs and innovators, engaged in research and development, or **R&D**, keeping the type foundry, typesetting and printing in separate workshops to reduce the risk that the employees might abscond with the invention and set up their own printing shops before he could recoup his considerable investment – which he never did, in fact. "He was the inventor of history's greatest platform. Atop it, countless people have built political revolutions, scientific revolutions, art, cultures, businesses, education, and so much more" (Jarvis 2012).

The impact of the printing press

Printing changed established institutions in a profound manner, providing one of the prime motors of the Renaissance, the Reformation and the rise of modern science (Eisenstein 2012). Prior to the printing press, when books in Europe had either been written or block printed by hand, very few copies of any book would ever be produced. Few people who did not belong either to the priestly or aristocratic classes ever so much as saw a book, and fewer still possessed them. Books were mainly found in the libraries of monasteries, noblemen and kings and were, according to Briggs and Burke (2002), mainly of a religious nature and usually written in Latin. However, Williams suggests that while a doctrinal distinction between religious books as desirable and other books as undesirable was widely ascribed to, in practice those who were both literate and had access to books did read many other kinds of non-religious material (Williams 1965: 178–179).

Certainly, when the printing press gave rise to the large-scale production of text, different cultural movements seized on the possibilities of this new invention and a wider range of books and other documents were produced. Indeed, printed books became popular with surprising speed. By 1500, at least 20 million books had already been printed, and by 1600 that figure had grown to 200 million, which led Francis Bacon to believe that in the 150 years of print "the appearance and state of the world" had been changed (Febvre and Martin 1976: 248–249). Not least, the mass-availability of print led to a demand for books to be printed in languages other than Latin, namely the vernaculars or national languages spoken across Europe but little used for written communication. Latin, the language of the Church and scholarship, had a limited reach. Febvre and Martin estimate that the market for books in Latin would have been saturated by the late 1600, with the demand for books in the various common tongues growing ever stronger.

Printing enabled the Vatican to sell so-called papal indulgences on a large scale across Europe. These were letters, signed by the Pope, releasing the buyer from any penance or acts of contrition they might be due to make up for sins they'd already confessed to and been absolved of by a priest. Likewise, printing allowed the reformist Protestant religious movement, which originated in Germany, to communicate its protest against the selling of these mass-produced indulgences to all and sundry. Protestants enthusiastically embraced the printing press as a way of widely communicating its message of religious dissent through pamphlets, posters and other printed matter in the sixteenth century. In fact, Martin Luther's 90 theses, which were nailed to the church door in Wittenberg, became so influential because they were immediately translated into German and published as pamphlets. Luther was the first best-selling author in history, "the first writer who could 'sell' his *new* books on the basis of his name" (Anderson 1991: 38).

In the seventeenth century, across Europe, the use of both government-sponsored and unofficial pamphlets to communicate important news and elicit the political support of a wider public for various causes became a common phenomenon. Business too seized on the potential of the printing press. Rich merchants, with money to invest, saw this new technology as a profit-making opportunity and often joined together to set up printing presses as business ventures. This level of capital investment and speculation was a novel feature that marked the beginnings of the economic system of **capitalism** (Briggs and Burke 2002). The rise of printed news is connected to the growing fortunes of the merchant class and the demand for information about markets, transportation and commerce. The first newspapers in Europe emerged at the end of the seventeenth century, providing international trade and investment news to a commercial readership. By the middle of the eighteenth century, newspapers and periodicals were well established in Europe, catering to the political, economic and cultural interests of the expanding middle classes (Williams 1965: 197).

The print revolution and the writer

The wide circulation of printed matter, and a growing audience that could read it, provided an alternative source of income for writers. Poets and essayists who had previously relied on royal or aristocratic patronage to support their writing, might now conceivably turn to the marketplace and earn a living from the sale of their work in written form, and celebrated authors were able to sell their manuscripts to publishers who bought them as reliable investments based on their authors' reputations (Anderson 1991: 40). A new type of writer, the journalist, had emerged and the first **copyright** law was passed in England in 1709. This law granted authors, or their assignees, the exclusive right to print their work for 14 years after its creation (in the twenty-first century, under European law, this right now extends to 70 years after the death of the author).

Writers emerged as a distinct class of professionals who made a living from writing books, pamphlets, journalism and other works distributed through the medium of print. They were part of the expansion of the middle class in Britain in the eighteenth century, which also provided their readership. As part of this expansion, painters and sculptors too began to carve out a separate professional identity by disassociating themselves from **trade guilds**, which were seen as artisanal or working-class organizations, and to set up instead clubs or societies, resulting in the establishment, among others, of the Royal Academy of Arts (Vaughan 1999: 100). Like writers, artists also had to balance the prestige of noble patronage against the potentially more lucrative funding stream of middle-class consumers. A good example of this is William Hogarth, who made his name and his living from selling widely-reproduced engravings to the middle classes, but as a result struggled to obtain painting commissions from noble patrons, who tended to dismiss him as a commercial artist, and therefore an inferior one.

INDUSTRIAL PRODUCTION

Growing wealth from international trade and from its colonies at the end of the eighteenth century, contributed to a development in Britain which was to spread to much of the rest of the world, with far-reaching consequences for creative production – the **Industrial Revolution**. According to Porter (1990), the combination of increased manufacturing and increased birth rate were two closely linked drivers of this transformation. New agricultural equipment was manufactured which, together with land reform,[2] facilitated large-scale agricultural production that could feed an expanding workforce. The development of the waterway system, which could facilitate the large-scale and cost-effective transport of raw materials, was another. Britain began to produce and export iron and steel in large quantities. Furthermore, the invention of new technologies and imports of raw cotton from India permitted the mechanization and cheap production of textiles. The cloth was then mostly exported back abroad to Britain's colonies, becoming Britain's number one export.

British mass-production and export of textiles made attractive and affordable clothes available to many who would not have been able to afford them before. It also put an end to cotton processing and manufacturing in India and meant that in Britain previously independent artisans, who had practised weaving on a small scale as a craft, could not compete with the new cotton mills on either price or quantity. They often found themselves either without employment or obliged to work as employees in large factories in dangerous conditions for long hours with low pay. Factories operated a **division of labour** which meant that they could employ unskilled (and therefore very cheap) workers, often women and children. Porter (1990) has argued, however, that while the Industrial Revolution created appalling working conditions or unemployment for some, it provided new high-skilled and reasonably paid opportunities for others in activities "such as puddling iron, fitting machine parts, pottery painting, and many sectors of Black Country metal manufactures" (Porter 1990: 316).

Division of labour: Simply, the division of labour involves separating large, complex tasks into smaller, simpler ones and dividing them among workers to be completed and assembled. In industry, this is one of the great inventions of the Industrial Revolution – multiplying output by modularizing the making of an object or machine into small, specialist tasks that can be distributed among dozens, even hundreds of people, from the manufacture of small components to the assembly of the finished product. The division of labour necessitates administration – a system of managers and workers who direct and monitor the work of others. As James R. Beniger suggests in *The Control Revolution* (1986), the control that modern bureaucracy and administration enabled can be seen as one of the drivers of the Industrial Revolution – bureaucracy made the division of labour possible, which in turn allowed factories to operate at a large scale.

---

[2]In particular, the practice of enclosures, whereby landowners enclosed fields and pasture that had previously been open to common use by villagers. This facilitated more efficient land use and higher productivity, using modern agricultural technologies, but left many rural poor with worse or no access to arable land and pasture.

The industrial revolution and the designer

Another new creative role that was produced through the division and mechanization of labour was that of the designer (Forty 1995: 34, 47). In artisan production, the activities of design and production are integrated and the translation of the idea into a physical form may be a fairly intuitive, informal process. However, in mass-production the relation between the two stages is entirely distinct. The designer produces a **prototype** and/or a set of instructions that can be followed by others in order to produce a standard product. The division of labour thus had the effect of elevating the role of design, in which painters and sculptors were often employed, and devaluing the role of production, which became divided into a set of lower skilled tasks.

From worker to consumer

The scale and depth of the changes produced by industrialization were nothing less than revolutionary. Both great benefit and terrible suffering have been ascribed to it. Industrialization depopulated rural areas while it over-populated the cities in a short period of time, resulting in the creation of vast urban slums. A large urban working class of men, women and children emerged around the factories, working in unhealthy and dangerous conditions for very long hours and very little pay. Karl Marx, who lived in Britain as a Russian exile in the mid nineteenth century, based his analysis and critique of capitalism as an economic system on his observation of British industrialism and its exploitation of the working classes. With Friedrich Engels, who owned and ran a Manchester textile mill, he wrote *The Communist Manifesto* (1849), an influential call to the workers of the world to unite against the oppression of the owners of the means of production. Marx and Engels were not alone in their condemnation of the inhumanity of industrial practices. Throughout the nineteenth century, social reformers in Britain campaigned against child labour and some of the other worst abuses, and by the end of the century some of these horrors had been alleviated. These reform movements continued into the twentieth century, with developments such as the legalization of unions. At the same time, the Industrial Revolution also resulted in a huge leap in the circulation of commodities to an expanded consumer base. Catering first largely to the middle classes, mass-production made products available to people who could not have afforded them otherwise, extending this possibility first to the middle and then, by the end of the nineteenth century, to the working classes.

Romanticism: The divorce of "Aesthetic Man" and "Economic Man"

The Industrial Revolution, from the eighteenth century onwards, had particular implications for creative production. It exacerbated the tension between the idea of creative expression as a spiritual and aesthetic pursuit and the practice of creative skills and products exchanged for money. With craft activity in areas such as textiles and ceramics increasingly industrialized, the manufacturing of products came to be seen more and more as separate from art. In industrial Britain, this view was given weight by the Romantic movement, which reacted against the Industrial Revolution as ugly and destructive. British Romanticism was part of a wider European movement in the early nineteenth century, which emerged as a reaction to the social and political upheaval of the time. The French Revolution (1789–1799) had failed to establish a Republic in France, while the Industrial Revolution was turning Britain into "the workshop of the world". Both seemed to signal the failure of the **Enlightenment** to achieve social change for the better. Romanticism challenged Enlightenment values of objectivity and logic, whether in writing, painting or music (Brown 2001). Instead it championed art as individual expression, inhabiting it as a form of rebellion against oppressive social and political structures and exalting it as a kind of magical or divine activity. British Romantics, such as the poet William Wordsworth, eulogized nature and saw art forms such as painting and poetry as a way of preserving spiritual and emotional values in opposition to the capitalist material values that seemed to reign supreme.

The Romantics' alignment of art with nature and individual freedom rather than industrial, social and political structures and their vision of the artist as rebel and outsider was an innovation that gained lasting cultural influence. However, in many ways the Romantics conformed to existing cultural norms. Their emphasis on art as a spiritual and 'special' activity privileged traditional and established forms of creative production such as poetry, painting, sculpture and classical music. These forms continued to be accorded high cultural status, and were seen as requiring sophisticated aesthetic understanding from their audience, who were themselves made 'special' by their ability to appreciate them. They retain this special status in contemporary culture.

Meanwhile, the newer creative forms that were linked to industrial processes, such as industrial design, illustration or journalism, did not have the same high cultural status awarded to the traditional arts. As Raymond Williams points out, the choice between art and commerce for the creative worker became ever sharper over the course of the nineteenth century as mass-production expanded certain areas of creative production, such as design and publishing (Williams 1961). A would-be writer might be faced with the perceived choice between being a high-minded but penniless poet or an unprincipled hack on a newspaper.

Art as moral improvement

This perpetuation of a perceived conflict between creativity and commerce, and the division between high culture and low culture that accompanied it, had further consequences. By the second half of the nineteenth century, the Industrial Revolution had seen the urban middle classes become the dominant social class and, having claimed high culture for their own, they set about bringing it to the lower classes, who had previously been left to their own devices. This was part of a wider movement of social reform, which tried to counteract the worst abuses of the new industrial manufacturing conditions, including child labour. As well as campaigning for an improvement in conditions, at the heart of the social reform movement was a belief in self-improvement. The prevailing idea was that morally upright behaviour and hard work would ultimately be rewarded. Movements of social reform therefore often concerned themselves as much with the moral as the physical well-being of the poor. While this could at times seem like a patronizing and interfering approach, it was also the driving force behind the passing of laws to provide free education to all and public access to museums and art galleries, as high culture was seen as a civilizing force for good for all.

The emergence of the "general public"

Middle-class zeal for reform of the working classes can also be attributed to the fact that the Industrial Revolution had greatly swelled and concentrated their numbers, creating huge urban populations in major cities in a way that was unknown in the eighteenth century. After an outbreak of attempted revolutions in Europe in the 1840s, the influence of "the masses" of the new industrial cities on politics and society became a nineteenth-century preoccupation. In the eighteenth century, the majority of the lower classes were illiterate, they could not vote (as they did not own property), and were largely excluded from public life. By the beginning of the twentieth century, voting rights had been extended to all adult males in several countries in Europe, including Britain, and, with the establishment of compulsory and free education, literacy rates were much higher. Consequently, while in the eighteenth century the "public" for a politician or a creative producer was a relatively small and homogeneous group of people, by the twentieth century, the concept of the "general public" had emerged and both artists and lawmakers had to take their views into account. As "the masses" finally attained the status of enfranchised citizens, with voting rights, they also became "consumers" in the contemporary sense – buyers of goods and services in a mass-market – to whose tastes a whole industry of cultural production would soon seek to cater.

INDUSTRIALIZED MEDIA PRODUCTION: THE STUDIO SYSTEM

Technological invention continued in the field of creative production in the twentieth century. The technique of recording light on paper, discovered in the nineteenth century, facilitated the emergence of photography and filmmaking as new forms of creative production, which, in the twentieth century, were quickly incorporated into the industrial mass-production model and so into the status of mass, or popular, culture.

Photography and film lent themselves to becoming a commodity rather than a work of art because they could be mass-produced, like other **commodities**, such as cloth or ceramics. Photography became an increasingly essential component of newspaper and magazine publishing, as epitomized in the *Picture Post* (1938–1957) in the UK and *Life* magazine (1936–1972) in the USA. These magazines pioneered photojournalism, targeting it at a mass audience, the general public.

Meanwhile national film industries expanded rapidly, above all in the USA, and, by the 1930s, film was perhaps the most popular global creative product of all. The Hollywood studios, for example, obtained up to 50% of their revenues from export abroad. The Hollywood studio system of the 1930s and 1940s is an important example of the way that the principles of mass-production, already in operation in areas such as textiles or ceramics and in newspaper publishing, came to be applied to the new creative forms afforded by visual and audio recording technologies.

The Hollywood studios operated a production line, just like the manufacturing industries. When a particular film idea was selected to go into production, it would be written up into a script, which functioned like a design blueprint for the director and crew to follow. The director would shoot the film according to the Hollywood continuity system, which involved shooting a standard range of shot sizes and angles, from wide shot to close up. This would allow the **editor** to assemble the finished scene, according to the script, without the need for the director to be there. Indeed, when the film was in the edit, the director would already be shooting another film. Thus the Hollywood studio system enforced a strict division of labour. Each crew member, from the director to the costume assistant, had a specialized role on the production line, which operated according to standardization. Not only was the continuity system adhered to as a way of shooting the films, but also each of the main studios used the same stars and stuck to particular genres as part of their house style (Bordwell, Staiger, and Thompson 1985).

The organization of the Hollywood studio system is often referred to as a type of **Fordism**, because of its similarities to the organization of the Ford Motors factories, owned by Henry Ford. Ford successfully spearheaded the low-cost mass-production of automobiles in the early twentieth century, opening up a mass-market for motor cars, which until then had been unaffordable luxuries for the average consumer. The Ford factories and the Hollywood studios were both also characterized by vertical integration between production and distribution, that is to say they controlled distribution as well as production of their products. With the Hollywood studios this meant that they either owned film theatres or had a deal with theatre owners that guaranteed the distribution of their films. Distribution was clearly an essential key to the success of all the mass-media.

Film production is a hugely expensive process. As with the production of newspapers and magazines and other recording media, it relies on recuperating the high initial cost of originating the product through low-cost reproduction and distribution of multiple copies. Mass-production necessitates mass-consumption.

Fordism and **post-Fordism:** The car manu-facturer Henry Ford is credited with having invented a new form of industrial production using standardization to mass-produce a prod-uct for a price which the general public could afford. He didn't invent the assembly line, but he adapted it most successfully to produce the landmark Model-T Ford — the first mass-market automobile, introduced in 1908. Therefore, Fordism usually refers to three related elements of industrial production: *standardization* of the product and production process (e.g., through standard components), use of *specialist tools* to decompose complex tasks into simple ones, and the *elimination of skilled labour* (as far as possible). Fordism is also associated with the tendency of corporations to do as much as pos-sible in-house, integrating the whole production process along a single assembly line.

Post-Fordism, by contrast, refers to the tendency of corporations to strip down their operations (and therefore their fixed costs) to the core functions of the particular business, outsourcing anything that can be done more cheaply elsewhere. In this way, businesses use the principles of Fordism (standardization, routine, elimination of skilled labour) to make certain functions portable, so that they can be outsourced, often to a different country where labour costs are low enough to offset the costs of transportation of the eventual products. Furthermore, post-Fordism is associated with more attention to services, customization and ever-more nuanced niche-marketing to par-ticular groups of consumers — all of which is enabled by information technology, commu-nications and more sophisticated methods of gathering intelligence about the habits and tastes of consumers themselves (Smythe 2006; Flew 2012: 117-120). Recommended reading: David Harvey, *The Condition of Postmodernity* (1992); Ash Amin, ed., *Post-Fordism: A Reader* (1994).

Standardization and specialization facili-tated both cost-effective production and the acquirement of a high level of skills in film employees. It also meant that the audience knew exactly what they were get-ting when they went to see a film. However, not all creative workers blossomed in this environment. The famous director Orson Welles was a notorious critic of the studio system, where, after two high-profile and expensive commercial disappointments, he could not find employment, while the actress Judy Garland, as an adult, blamed her drug addiction on her studio, MGM, where she said she and other child stars had been given amphetamines to help them cope with the rigours of the production line schedule, followed by sleeping pills to help them sleep.

Along with sound cinema, the music industry also flourished as an area of mass-production. Music has been part of people's lives for centuries, but as with the moving image, sound recording and playback tech-niques first developed at the end of the nineteenth century made it possible in the twentieth century to sell music recordings to the general public. And so the music indus-try was born. The sale of gramophones and records took off in the 1920s, with early record labels producing recordings of famous singers and musicians. The development of radio initially had a negative impact on record sales, but, as Frith (1988) points out, ultimately aligned the businesses of music and radio so that, by the end of the 1930s, record companies were no longer seeking to record popular live acts, but rather to cre-ate 'recording stars' who would be popular on radio and jukeboxes and promote their records. Meanwhile radio companies gained hours of cheap programming from the alliance. The 1930s saw the major record labels, such as EMI, RCA and DECCA, expanding into music publishing and concert promotion, building 'stables' of artists and creating their own star system, like the Hollywood studios. These companies oversaw all aspects of the production chain, from deciding what songs to record, to distribution and promotion of recordings.

The industrial nature of the record companies was not accidental. The music mogul Berry Gordy, founder of Motown Records in Detroit, writes in his autobiography how he consciously modelled the company after the Lincoln-Mercury assembly line he had worked on as a young man. "At the plant the cars started out just as a frame, pulled along on conveyor belts until they emerged at the end of the line – brand spanking new cars rolling off the line. I wanted the same concept for my company, only with artists and songs and records" (Gordy 1994: 140). There were, in short, many similarities and cross-overs (of strategies, markets and talent) between the manufacturing, film and music industries. Like the film industry, the music industry developed an international reach based on the principles of industrial production.

SUMMARY

This chapter has provided a brief historical overview of four key concepts for the study of the contemporary creative industries: *patronage*, the *marketplace*, *mass-production* and *industrialization*. These will appear in different variations throughout the chapters of the book, often in radically different guises. For example, internet-based social media have enabled a new form of patronage – crowdsourcing – which has allowed small producers to combine small donations from individuals to fund creative projects through websites like Kickstarter. It's a long way from the Medicis to Kickstarter, but the idea of patronage applies in both cases. In the chapters that follow, we will return to key aspects of the business of creative production, such as finance, production and distribution structures, similar to the historical precedents we have explored here. We will look at the role of the creative producer in the workplace and examine the different ways in which creative producers generate economic value through products and services. We will also study the impact of new technologies. In the course of our enquiry we will discover both similarities and ruptures between the past and the present, both of which should help us to understand the particular features and implications of the creative industries of today.

RECOMMENDED READING

Baxandall, M. 1988. *Painting and Experience in Fifteenth-century Italy: A Primer in the Social History of Pictorial Style* (2nd edition). Oxford: Oxford University Press. A detailed account of the working practices and institutions of the Italian Renaissance artist.

Bordwell, David, Janet Staiger and Kristin Thompson. 1985. *The Classical Hollywood Cinema: Film Style and Mode of Production to 1960*. London: Routledge. Introduces the working practices and institutional organization of the Hollywood film industry.

Briggs, A. and P. Burke. 2002. *A Social History of the Media: From Gutenberg to the Internet*. Cambridge: Polity Press. The chapters on the printing press and the ensuing "print revolution" are very useful for contemporary readers.

Brotton, Jerry. 2006. *The Renaissance: A Very Short Introduction*. Oxford: Oxford University Press. An accessible, general introduction to the Renaissance.

Caves, Richard E. 2000. *Creative Industries: Contracts between Art and Commerce*. Cambridge, MA: Harvard University Press. A wide-ranging introduction to the creative industries as a business, mainly from a US-based perspective.

Forty, A. 1995. *Objects of Desire: Design and Society since 1750*. London: Thames & Hudson. Key case studies in the history of design.

Porter, R. 1990. *English Society in the Eighteenth Century*. London: Penguin. Very useful for understanding the expansion of the middle classes in the eighteenth century and the Industrial Revolution.

Williams, Raymond. 1965[1961]. *The Long Revolution*. Harmondsworth: Penguin. A classic book of British cultural history, especially of the reading public, publishing and the press.

Williams, Raymond. 1981. *Culture*. Glasgow: Fontana. Chapter 2 is a historical account of the "relations between producers and institutions", which examines the implications of patronage and markets.

PART 1

Working in the Creative Industries

There are three chapters in Part 1, each one of which explores aspects of what it is like to work in the creative industries, from a particular perspective.

Chapter 3 focuses on the kinds of organizations and employment structures that you will find in the creative industries and examines the practices which characterize them. You will meet a cross-section of people who work in these organizations and employment structures and find out more about what their work consists of and their daily work routines.

Chapter 4 will explore business principles and operations in further detail. You will learn more about the legal frameworks within which organizations operate, about aspects such as intellectual property and contracts, and about a range of business models that operate within the creative industries.

Chapter 5 considers in more detail different work routines and cultures associated with employment, freelancing and portfolio working. You will find out more about the social element of working in the creative industries, such as the necessity of networking, and also about potential obstacles faced by new entrants and how they can be approached.

3

Institutions, Ownership and Entrepreneurship

As we have seen, the creative industries are made up of different sectors. Although the creative output of each sector may be different, institutional organizations and employment structures across all sectors have much in common. The institutional landscape of the contemporary creative industries is made up of three types of organizational structure: **freelance** workers, small-to-medium-sized enterprises (**SMEs**) and large, often multinational, **corporations**.

Freelancers are temporary workers hired on a short-term contract, for their specific skills, knowledge or experience (Osnowitz 2010: 4). They may receive hourly, weekly or monthly wages or a flat fee for each **project**. Freelancers have clients, rather than employers; usually businesses or organizations, more rarely individuals. The relationships with the clients are usually short-term, and contracts are agreed either directly between the freelancer and the client, or through an **agency** (e.g., talent agency).

SMEs very often contract freelancers, rather than employing full-time staff because, in a **project-based** industry, it allows them more staffing flexibility. Large corporations, on the other hand, will tend to employ a large number of staff on permanent contracts. However,

Freelancer: The word itself derives from a medieval term for itinerant mercenaries, soldiers who would hire their lance to any nobleman who could afford them, hence a "free lance". In the modern, non-violent sense, freelancers are workers who either hire out their services to a company for a set amount of time (usually the length of a project such as a film, a play, the recording of an album, etc.), or supply them with a particular product, such as a book, an article, a line of clothing or jewellery. Skillset, the official training body for the UK film and broadcasting sector, defines freelance employment as any contract of less than one year's duration, and **employee** status as any contract of more than one year's duration (Skillset 2009).

Sometimes a freelancer may supply their services or products direct to the public, instead of contracting with a company. They might, for example, depending on their particular sector, publish their music or writing online, set up a market stall, play in clubs or pubs, etc. Examples of typical job roles which are often freelance are: actor, writer, filmmaker, musician, photographer, or designer.

In the creative industries overall, a substantial proportion of workers work on a freelance basis. As recent figures for the UK show, the balance between employees and freelancers in different specialisms varies greatly. For example, Skillset has published research on the employment profile of workers in film, TV, radio and animation:

> Overall, 25% of those working or available for work in the Creative Media Industries are 'freelance' and the remaining operate on an 'employee' basis. Amongst employees in the Creative Media Industries, four fifths are employed on a full time basis and one fifth part time. [Many] sectors of the Creative Media Industries are characterised by high levels of freelancing, especially those areas most closely involved in the production process, for example Film Production (89%), Independent Production for Radio (61%), Photo Imaging (67%), Corporate Production (54%), Animation (46%) and Independent Production for TV (44%). In other sectors such as Advertising the figure is closer to 20% or below. (Skillset 2011: 26)

The transition to freelancing from full-time employment can often be difficult. For example, Georgina Born points out in her study of the BBC that uncertainty in employment is a major cause of stress for freelancers. "Women face freelance status more than men, and find it more stressful. Because of uncertainty, workers are impelled to diversify their sources of income; a significant proportion consider leaving the television profession, particularly experienced workers" (Born 2004: 211). However, some find that the variety and flexibility of freelancing outweighs the risks. Paul, a freelance communications consultant, says that it would

they also contract work out to SMEs and freelancers, particularly in the area of content creation, as we will go on to examine.

These different structures affect the experience of work in the creative industries perhaps as much as the particular sector in which it takes place. A freelancer, the managing director of an SME and an **employee** in a large corporation in the publishing sector will each have a similar work experience, in certain ways, to their counterparts in the games industry, for example.

THE ORGANIZATION OF PRODUCTION

What determines whether a creative worker goes freelance, sets up their own company, or works as an employee in a large corporation? There are many answers to this question and they relate to both industry trends and personal choice. Government regulation, market conditions, de-industrialization and trends in theories of business management have all had their role to play.

As we have seen in the preceding chapters, there was a tendency in the first half of the twentieth century for the entertainment industries and mass-media to consolidate into large, **vertically integrated** companies which took care of all aspects of production – from ideas development to distribution – **in house**. Typical examples of this are the Hollywood studios in the USA in the first half of the twentieth century, or the BBC in the UK in the second half. In this production context, the majority of creative workers were full-time employees.

There are still many large organizations in the creative industries, but, by the end of the twentieth century, various political, economic and social factors had worked some changes. One example is the transformation of the Hollywood studios, once the epitome of Fordism in the creative industries. In the 1950s, television significantly lessened Hollywood's market share of audiovisual entertainment and the Hollywood studios had to slim down their operations to survive. Rather than keep a permanent 'stable' of actors and armies of technicians on the payroll, as they had done in the 1930s and 1940s, they moved to a 'packaging' model, in which they continued to commission and distribute films but began to outsource the actual production to independent production companies.

Post-Fordism

Outsourcing became an influential business model in the second half of the twentieth century, across all business sectors, part of what is often referred to as **post-Fordism**, which saw the model of the integrated factory, in which a product is put together on an assembly line, broken up into multiple manufacturing processes which could be divided up between manufacturers, sometimes in separate countries. The influence of **neoliberalism** on government policy was another important factor in changing organizational structures, mainly through the privatization of state-owned institutions and businesses and the relaxation of state-control through **deregulation**. In many countries across the world, attitudes towards broadcasting changed and many regulations were lifted, as were other restrictions on

be difficult to return to full-time employment after years of successful freelancing, even though some of his clients want to hang on to him: "Companies sometimes don't realise that some of us are unemployable – we don't want to be employed" (Paul, 2011). Freelancers may, in the course of their career, move on to setting up their own company, delivering creative products either direct to the public or to larger organizations. A freelance producer might set up a production company, a shoemaker might set up a shoe shop, a writer might set up a magazine. However, many freelancers, including actors, writers, musicians, film and TV technicians, will remain as freelancers throughout their working life.

Project: The contemporary sense of the term "project" dates back to the Cold War. Previously, a "project" would be understood as a draft, proposal or a proposed idea. But with the armaments race of the 1950s and the complex technological developments necessary to achieve aims such as developing weapons systems or putting humans on the Moon, a new understanding of the concept of a project emerged:

> Development processes that earlier were conceived as separate activities were now conceptualized as an integrated entity, called a "program", "system" or "project". The overwhelming scale of these projects in terms of financial and scientific resources as well as their ambitious timing created formidable problems of co-ordination and control. (Grabher 2002a: 207)

In this context, the role of the "project manager" — a professional coordinator of a team (or teams) of people working to achieve a common outcome — became indispensable. Various jobs in the creative industries involve this kind of coordination, particularly when teams have to be coordinated to produce a complex output (Caves 2000; Ekinsmyth 2002). As cross-platform production becomes more prevalent (Skillset 2011: 17), the role of the project manager has now migrated from technology and software to the production of films, TV shows, radio and computer games. Recommended reading: Stanley Portny, *Project Management for Dummies* (2010); Peter Morris et al., eds., *The Oxford Handbook of Project Management* (2011).

SME: SME is an acronym for Small-to-Medium-sized Enterprise. It refers to an organization (usually a partnership or a limited company; see Chapter 2) employing fewer than 250 people. Often SMEs in the creative industries are very small. A company, such as a talent agency, a television production company or a design agency, may consist of a partnership of just two people (in which case they are often referred to as a microbusiness). When an SME has a project in production, it will expand the work team with the addition of freelancers.

Project-based work: This is work that is not part of an uninterrupted daily, weekly or annual routine, such as running a shop, but focused on the delivery of individual products or of services, tailored to specific clients. In a large organization, such as a broadcaster, there will be many jobs (from programme commissioner to marketing officer, to transmission staff) which are staffed by permanent employees and are part of the routine work of the organization. By contrast, the jobs that are most closely involved with the actual production of the film or TV programme tend to be staffed on a freelance basis. Project-based working is prevalent in a variety of production and post-production roles beyond film and broadcast media. Across the

international trade and finance. This meant that it became much easier for broadcasting companies to expand and to operate for commercial gain, usually by merging into larger companies, often with an international reach.

As Hesmondhalgh (2007) and others have pointed out, this political and economic climate of the second half of the twentieth century and the combination of changes in regulation and vertical disintegration meant an increase in both the presence of large **conglomerates** and the number of SMEs and freelancers active in the creative industries. The 1990s in the UK, for example, saw a concentration of ownership of the television companies making up the Independent Television Network (ITV) after the lifting of ownership restrictions in the Broadcasting Act 1990. However, the UK government of the 1980s and 1990s saw the country's competitiveness as dependent on the development of a more **entrepreneurial** society, with a place for small business as well as large conglomerates. Consequently, the same act also required both the BBC and ITV to commission 25% of their programming from independent companies (Born 2004). This was after the establishment of Channel 4 in 1982, as a publisher broadcaster, had already opened up broadcasting in the UK to independent production companies (Brown 2007).

The stark contrast between large and small companies in the creative industries – with a handful of major companies dominating the sector and a large number of small enterprises, self-employed creative and two- to three-person businesses making up the rest – is often referred to as the "hourglass structure". There is a "missing middle" to the creative industries in this respect (Pratt 2008: 46). In the United States, for example, the four largest firms in the sectors of broadcast television, advertising, publishing and recorded music industries account for over 80% of **market share** (Flew 2012: 117).

Whales and Plankton: The ecology of the creative industries

The contemporary creative industries constitute, then, a very particular **ecology** characterized on the one hand by a high number of freelancers and **microbusinesses**, which are largely involved in content creation, and the dominant presence of extremely large, often multinational, corporations on the other. These large organizations tend to control commissioning, publishing and distribution (Hesmondhalgh 2007; Pratt 2008; Flew 2012).

Evans (2004) memorably defined this particularity of "a handful of high profile global players, stars and multinational companies, dependent upon vast shoals of project-based micro-enterprises" as an ecology of "whales and plankton" (Evans 2004: 9). This picks up on an important feature of the creative industries, namely the gatekeepers or *filters* that so much creative production has to pass through. Gatekeepers such as publishers, studios, and broadcasters, connect the artists/creators to consumers/audiences (Hirsch 2000). Just as whales filter plankton out of seawater, cultural gatekeepers filter the outputs

creative industries, freelancers and small businesses form "networks of project-based enterprise" (Bilton 2011: 38), with large businesses such as advertising agencies and media agencies built around projects (Grabher 2002b). Recommended reading: Chris Bilton and Mark Deuze, eds., *Managing Media Work* (2011).

How would you answer? Here is a sample of some of the questions we asked creative workers about their work and employment structures. See if you can think how freelancers, directors of SMEs and employees of a large corporation might each answer these questions. Then, once you have read the interviews, return to these questions and see if you would answer differently.

- Do you work "normal office hours"?
- Do you belong to a union/professional guild? Why? What does being a member involve?
- What are the highs and lows of your job?
- Do you consider the scope of your work national or international?

Vertical integration: This is when a company keeps all or most of the production chain in-house, from development through production to distribution. When a process is vertically integrated, "successive stages in production and distribution are placed under the control of a single enterprise" (Bannock, Baxter, and Davis 2003: 399), which enables control of the overall process. In volatile sectors like the creative industries, the downside of vertical integration is that while it ensures the lion's share of the revenue from each product, it also concentrates risk, so that an expensive flop can bankrupt a large, vertically integrated enterprise. The Hollywood studio system was, famously, vertically integrated on the model of **Fordist** manufacturing in the years 1918 to 1948. The whole filmmaking process took place within the same organization — from idea-generation and writing through production and exhibition at studio-owned theatres. This integration began to come apart in 1948, when the studios were forced to separate production and distribution from exhibition. They sold off their theatres, and a gradual process of dis-integration began, in which production, distribution and exhibition were separated (Bordwell, Staiger, and Thompson 1985: 399-400). Recommended reading: Jennifer Holt and Alisa Perren, eds., *Media Industries: History, Theory and Method* (2009).

Neoliberalism: A school of thought in economics and politics which seeks to minimize the role of the state in all areas of society, and leave as much as possible to the functioning of the "free market". The signature policies of neoliberals are privatization of state-run services and businesses, deregulation (i.e., the loosening of regulatory frameworks that may constrain the operations of businesses), a thoroughgoing individualism which, in some cases, rejects the notion of "society" as merely a collection of individuals pursuing their private goals. Therefore, neoliberalism is strongly antithetical to all forms of collective mobilization and bargaining — trade unions, in particular. The neoliberal deregulation of banking and finance in the USA and UK in the 1980s and 1990s is sometimes credited with having sown the seeds of the credit bubble which resulted in the credit crunch of 2007 and the crash of 2008. Recommended reading: Manfred B. Steger, *Neoliberalism: A Very Short Introduction* (2010); Nick Couldry, *Why Voice Matters: Culture and Politics after Neoliberalism* (2010); Gérard Duménil, *The Crisis of Neoliberalism* (2011).

of writers, artists and musicians for mass-audiences, selecting some for fame and some for obscurity.

Furthermore, while the whales would starve without the plankton, the relationships between the whales and the plankton are constantly shifting. Whales often swallow up plankton and incorporate them, as has been evident in video games in the twenty-first century, which has seen extensive consolidation. Companies such as Electronic Arts and Ubisoft have bought up smaller development studios. At the same time, however, the studios that make up such multinational developers and publishers tend not to be completely subsumed into the identity of their parent organization. They "have distinctive personalities, and in many cases are proud of their 'small-studio' mentality" such as the various studios under the umbrella of Electronic Arts (Edge 2012). Similarly, Google has acquired a number of new media startups in recent years, most famously YouTube, the entertainment giant CBS bought Last.fm, and Facebook bought Instagram, just to name a few prominent examples. These new media developments conform to trends in the longer-established media sectors, such as film, TV and music.

The pros and cons of flexible labour

The **casualization** of work and outsourcing, which typify the networked, post-Fordist model, offer several advantages to large companies in the creative industries. It reduces their overheads and offers them increased flexibility and competitiveness in the makeup of project teams.

Many SMEs and freelancers in the creative industries also prize the relative autonomy and flexibility allowed to them by this organization of production. Clive, a film and television screenwriter, works from home and enjoys not having to go into an office every day.

> "I don't have to worry too much about when I go to bed and therefore when I get up... it's a cliché but you are your own boss... I'd find it pretty difficult to do a 9–5 job." (Clive, 2011)

Likewise, Chris, the **director** of a small commercials production company, says that the main reason for setting up his own company was because he felt it would give him more freedom to choose the kind of jobs he took on and how he organized his time. After working for several years as a freelance **director** on the books of a large commercial production company, he says:

> "We knew the game... knew the people, we wanted to make the calls ourselves on what jobs we did and how." (Chris, 2011)

Chris and his partners also wanted to gain more time and resources to develop other projects besides commercials. Chris is currently working on two feature film projects, with two different writers and has another TV series idea he is working on, as well as running a short film scheme for the New Zealand Film Commission. Having their own production company and premises gives Chris and his partners the contacts and material resources to facilitate these kinds of projects more easily.

Regulation and **deregulation** of broadcast media: All states *regulate* media at the national level, to some extent. In most European states, broadcast media are subject to regulations regarding content (e.g., the 9 o'clock "watershed" rule for adult themes and violence on broadcast television in the UK), without resorting to direct censorship. States have a direct hand in the licensing of broadcast media, since radio and television use portions of the radio spectrum — "the public airwaves" — allocated to them by a government agency, the Office of Communications (Ofcom). In exchange for use of this public resource, broadcasters (both commercial and public service) must abide by certain regulations in order to retain their broadcasting licences. By contrast, *deregulation* of broadcasting in the 1980s and 1990s involved, first, the loosening of the state's hold on broadcasting in the UK and opening up television and radio to private operators funded through advertising. Furthermore, deregulation in Britain, Europe and the USA involved loosening the regulations on media ownership, enabling large conglomerates to own many media outlets (this is sometimes called *cross-ownership*), and the opening of the media markets to new entrants. Recommended reading: Graeme Burton, *Media and Society: Critical Perspectives* (2010); Paul Hodkinson, *Media, Culture and Society* (2011); Georgina Born, *Uncertain Vision* (2004); David Hesmondhalgh, *The Cultural Industries* (2007); Maggie Brown, *A Licence to be Different: The Story of Channel 4* (2007); Peter Lunt and Sonia Livingstone, *Media Regulation: Governance and the Interests of Citizens and Consumers* (2012).

Entrepreneur: Someone who starts a business, building it from an idea to a commercial product or service. Being *"entrepreneurial"* means having the skills and motivation to turn an idea into a working business, either as a stand-alone operation or located within a larger company or organization. Entrepreneurship is also strongly associated with creativity, problem-solving and having an eye for spotting gaps in the market: "Creativity suffuses business. It's the entrepreneurial spark that finds a solution to a problem, meets a need or fills a gap in the lives of people. By creating value for people, capital flows" (Dubber, in Wright et al. 2009: 16). Recommended reading: Kathleen Allen, *Complete MBA for Dummies* (2008); William Bygrave, *Entrepreneurship* (2011).

Ecology: A common metaphor for various networks of mutual support and dependency. In biology, an "ecology" or "ecosystem" is the connected whole of all organisms within a specific context. This context can be large or small — an ecology can be viewed at a micro-level (e.g., a single pond) or a macro-level (the Earth). The term is used in computing, media and communications to indicate a connected network of hardware, software, and practices relating to them. For example, a mobile phone operating system might be said to have an ecology of software providers creating applications for it, creatives generating content, and users paying for it through purchases or advertising. In analyses of the creative industries, the various "gatekeepers" (Caves 2000) can be described in ecological terms, for example the mutual dependency of artists, galleries and buyers in New York (Currid 2007). Gernot Grabher has used this ecology metaphor in his studies of the UK advertising sector, looking at clustering in the "advertising village" of Soho (Grabher 2001)

Flexibility of labour structures can therefore offer benefits to both the "plankton" and the "whales". If a competitive pitching environment means that the best person or company is taken on to do a job, rather than permanent members of staff who are on the payroll and need to be kept occupied, this should in theory both improve quality of the end product and also offer greater access to new entrants. Furthermore, since media companies rely on the creativity of workers, they are often prepared to pay high rates to key personnel. Film stars, earning millions of dollars for a movie, are the most obvious example, but successful directors, directors of photography and other key talent can also command high rates.

However, in a media ecology in which a few large multinational companies tend to control the distribution of products (along with PR, marketing and other business activities), the majority of freelancers and small companies, who are supplying products and services to the larger ones, find themselves in a buyer's market and in fierce competition with each other. As a result they may often find themselves forced to submit to lowering rates and prices or agreeing to very long working hours (Randle and Culkin 2009). This means that a segmentation is in place within the creative workforce, especially in high-volume industries like film and TV, where non-unionized and low-paid workers will be employed on low-budget productions and "unionized A-list craft and talent" are utilized on high-budget productions (Christopherson 2009: 82).

The role of trade unions

Trade unions have an important role to play in supporting and protecting the rights of creative workers (Christopherson and van Jaarsveld 2005; Saundry, Stuart, and Antcliff 2007). The practice of individual workers joining together to exercise collective strength in fact has a long history. In the middle ages, individual artisans belonged to **trade guilds**. Industrialization saw these guilds lose their power, but in the twentieth century trade unions emerged, out of fierce political struggle, to represent the rights of workers. The power exercised by trade unions has varied widely in different countries at different times, their political status varying from being illegal organizations to constituting a central pillar of political influence.

When they are powerful, trade unions may operate as gatekeepers as well as support structures. In the UK, for example, Equity, the actors' union, and BECTU, the entertainment workers' union, effectively operated a **closed shop** (Saundry, Stuart, and Antcliff 2007; Daniels and McIlroy 2008: 33) until the end of the 1980s, when the UK government forced them to end the practice. Margaret Thatcher, UK prime minister from 1979 to 1990, worked systematically to reduce the power of trade unions, across all economic sectors, seeing their political and economic power as a stumbling block for the UK's international competitiveness, and certainly this reform of the unions helped to open up the creative industries to new entrants and independents. 1988 was a watershed year for British commercial broadcasting, when commercial television employers unilaterally ended national **collective bargaining** (McKinlay 2009). This shifted more work to the independent production sector which

and working practices in advertising, describing them as a "project ecology" (Grabher 2002a). His approach has also been used to study the film and TV industry in Manchester (Johns 2010). Recommended reading: Matthew Fuller, *Media Ecologies* (2005); Gernot Grabher and Oliver Ibert, "Project Ecologies" in *The Oxford Handbook of Project Management* (2011).

Agents and **Agencies**: Agents and agencies act as intermediaries between those who require a service and those who can deliver it. *Agents* usually work on an individual basis. For example, screenwriters, directors and other film/TV creatives have agents who will represent them, get their proposals and screenplays seen by commissioners, represent them in negotiations with producers, and assist in other ways. The same applies to literary agents, music agents, and other specialist agents. Established film and TV professionals, such as directors of photography and editors, will often use diary services — booking agencies who manage their workflow and liaise with production companies in scheduling new work. Agents and agencies have an important role to play in project-based work across the creative industries, sourcing and recruiting talent for a great variety of roles, skills and talents. Specialist *agencies* usually focus on a particular service, or a range of services, that most clients would not normally have in-house. Communications agencies, for example, provide their clients with an integrated communications strategy to promote their company's brands and products. They will engage organizations and individuals to fulfil different elements of the strategy, for example by creating a brief and inviting creative agencies to pitch for a particular advertising campaign (for more on creative, media and communications agencies, see Chapter 10). Talent agencies, to give a different example, represent individuals such as writers, directors, actors or creatives of some kind, both by promoting their clients to relevant organizations (e.g., a literary agency would send an author's novel to publishers) and by providing a point of contact for organizations looking for a particular service (such as that of an actor to play a role in a television series).

picked up the work outsourced by the broadcasters through the commissioning process.

Conversely, however, the period after 1988 also saw an influx of workers who were prepared to work for lower pay and longer hours than union rules allowed (Saundry and Nolan 1998). This situation has continued.

Despite the diminution of the powers of trade unions in the UK media industries, screenwriter, Clive, and Judy, a games writer, both stress how important it is to them to be members of the Writers' Guild of Great Britain, which has been instrumental in negotiating national standards for rates of pay with broadcasters and video games developers, for example.

Negotiating contracts is also the role of the **agent**, whose job it is to make sure that they get the best deal possible for their client, as we will discuss further in the next chapter. Clive says that he relies on his agent to negotiate on his behalf:

> "They represent lots more famous people than me, which gives them strength and authority, which I wouldn't have by myself. Which I think probably means, in some cases definitely means, that I get paid more." (Clive, 2011)

However, Clive also says it is equally important to him to be a member of a trade union:

> "I think they're very good for writers without other representation and I think it's important for writers who do have representation, i.e., writers with more other muscle, to be members of it, because it gives it more weight. If it was only representing writers without agents then it wouldn't be." (Clive, 2011)

As Clive points out, whereas powerful agents and well-known creative talent can negotiate extremely high rates on an individual basis, it is important that standard rates are set across the industry, which all creative workers can benefit from, and this is the role of the trade unions. Certainly Judy, who doesn't have an agent, says she relies on the Writers' Guild for support and advice.

In the UK, however, joining a trade union is now more a matter of choice than necessity, if you want to work in the creative industries. By contrast, in the United States creative workers' trade unions, such as the Writers' Guild of America, still operate something much closer to a closed shop. This, together with the fact that large teams of writers are employed full-time on many US television shows, meant that the Writers' Guild of America strike of 2007–2008, which lasted for three months, had a severe impact on television programming (Stahl 2009: 60; M. J. Banks 2010).

Getting past the gatekeepers

The "plankton" – the individuals and small businesses whose creativity sustains the corporate "whales" – can therefore wield some organizational clout. Nevertheless, the inherent inequalities of size, access to capital, distribution networks and marketing budgets can be seen across the creative industries. In sectors such as craft and fashion, small producers, like their media counterparts, need to pass through gatekeepers, such as retailers, and also struggle to get distribution and fair prices for their products.

However, in the fashion and design sectors there are some other options for content creators, besides selling to the retail giants. There are also small boutique shops, which sell clothes, jewellery and other products directly to the public. Producers can therefore work with retailers on a smaller, more local scale. They may also set up their own market stall or shop. In audiovisual media, on the other hand, this small-scale distribution has historically not been an option. Television and cinema distribution has been much more tightly controlled by large corporations, forcing producers of content to go through their channels if they want to find an audience (Garnham 1990). However, the changing dynamics of distribution and retail, enabled by digital technologies, are affecting these models significantly, as we will explore in Chapter 10.

Having explored the broader characteristics of the organization of production, we turn now to a more detailed investigation of what it is like to work within the employment structures we have outlined. Let's begin with the workplace itself.

WORKPLACES

Depending on the sector you work in and your job, workplaces in the creative industries can differ hugely. Artists may work in studios, product designers in labs. Audiovisual technicians may work in recording studios, as will actors and musicians, who will also perform on stage. Meanwhile, film and television production crews may find themselves working on location anywhere from the middle of a field to a tiny terraced house. In between jobs, however, the permanent work base of many freelancers is at home. Depending on their job, for example, if they are a designer or a writer, they may also carry out a large part of their work at home. Some freelancers may choose to rent or convert a part of their home into a separate office. Others may operate a less formal division between their workplace and their home. Clive says that, although he has a spare room, where he could set up an office, he prefers to work in his living room:

> "because it means I've got everything that I generally need... I can play music, I can stop and watch the television, I can nip into the kitchen and make a cup of tea. All that stuff is ready to hand so I really like working there." (Clive, 2011)

Workspaces: Here are some photographs of different workspaces/desks. Which do you think might belong to which of the three?

Figure S.1   Workspaces a,b,c

Startup companies may also begin at home. Chris, the commercials director, says that when he and his partners set up their company, to keep down their costs, they operated out of the garage of one of the partners. Once they had become a little more established, they rented office space in the centre of town. This situates them close to the offices of agencies, post-production houses and other organizations they are likely to do business with, making meetings easy to arrange, even at short notice.

Being based in London, the capital of the UK, most of the meetings Clive has are also easy for him to get to, with producers and production companies based in the same town. However, he says that he does not think it would affect his career greatly if he did not live in London, particularly as new communication technologies make it fairly easy for him to have a long-distance face-to-face discussion with project collaborators, such as a production company in Denmark that he has been working with recently. Although new technologies certainly facilitate such project collaboration, at the start of a project, project initiators will nevertheless tend to want to meet potential collaborators in the flesh. For new entrants, even more than for established talent, being 'on the ground' and engaging in such face-to-face contact is vital, as we will go on to discuss in relation to networking in Chapter 5.

Chris says that he and his partners made a conscious decision to have an open-plan office, where all the work, including discussions and meetings, takes place, because he thinks it "gives people a better sense of what is going on" (Chris, 2011), although there is a separate room for more private meetings if necessary. This kind of informal approach is typical of work culture in the creative industries, where workspaces are often improvised and changed according to the requirements of ongoing projects.

The workspace of radio drama producer, Kevin, is very similar, although he works within a much larger, much more structured organization, as we will go on to see. Kevin works in a radio department that encompasses arts, features and documentary programmes, as well as drama. Like Chris, his office is open plan. It features signs suspended from the ceiling, which designate the different areas of programme output. He and other production staff do not have one designated desk, but will move around the office, to sit at different desk clusters, arranged under these signs, according to what programme they are working on. This arrangement reflects the fact that the producers and researchers in the department are expected to work across the range of programmes produced by the department, even though, like Kevin, they may specialize in one area. The spatial organization of the office thus reflects and facilitates this mixture of specialist and generalist activity that each employee is expected to engage in. As Kevin says, the layout makes it "easy to jump from drama to working on an arts journalism programme to making your own feature ..." (Kevin, 2011). This **hot-desking** arrangement also means that all staff have networked IT profiles that can 'migrate from any PC to any PC' (Kevin, 2011).

WORK STRUCTURES

A small company such as Chris's will typically have few permanent employees and a larger pool of freelance workers to draw on. Besides the three partners who set up Chris's company, the company has only two other permanent members of staff: an office manager and a director's assistant, who provides administrative support. As projects come in, this small team will expand to encompass many other freelance workers, such as producers, director, designers and other production staff, who will use the office as a base for the length of the project they are involved in. A huge variety of people will therefore come and go in the course of the year.

Kevin's workplace, the Irish national broadcasting company RTE, has a more stable structure. RTE has a large campus in the suburbs of the capital city of Dublin, which houses many permanent departments, including those responsible for programming areas, such as news, current affairs, entertainment, music, etc., and those that are responsible for centralized activities, such as programme planning and facilities, sales and marketing, publicity, as well as services such as printing and duplication. The drama team consists of three staff producers.

As in Chris's company, however, their number will be swelled at various stages of production by people such as the writer, director, cast and other technical personnel. The writer, director and cast will be engaged on a freelance basis, whereas technical personnel, such as a sound engineer, will be in-house RTE-staff assigned to the production by the programme planning and facilities department.

There is a clear and established hierarchy within Kevin's team, in which one of the three producers has a more senior role as a series producer and takes the lead in deciding what projects they will do. He reports in his turn to the drama **editor**, who also oversees arts, features, documentaries and independent productions. Ideas that are generated by the production team will need to make their way up this chain of command to the editor for approval, before they can go ahead. Ideas will also come down the other way and the editor is also responsible for overseeing and managing the workflow, assigning staff to particular projects as needed. The editor is herself answerable to senior management within the organization.

For freelancers and SMES, working along a production chain, this higher authority, which says yea or nay to projects and the course of their development, often comes from outside their own organization. In advertising, as Chris recounts, it is the client who must have the final say. When a commercial is being shot, both the creatives from the advertising agency and a representative from the client company will be present on set. If they do not like what the director is doing, they will say so, which can make some jobs quite uncomfortable for the director if there is a lack of trust or the client is very exacting. But, as Chris says, the work is ultimately being done for the client and so the director has to learn to relinquish control.

Similarly, Clive finds himself required to satisfy the wishes of several different parties involved in the production chain. On a television project he will usually get notes from the script editor, the producer, the director and finally from the executive producer for the broadcaster. As Clive says, it can sometimes feel as if, "being a professional writer, your life consists of being criticized" (Clive, 2011). Usually, however, he says people do respect his creative input as a writer and make suggestions, or point out problems, rather than dictate exactly what he should write. In the end, though, it is the production company and/or the broadcaster who are the final decision makers, and, if they don't like what a writer has written, they will fire him or her and get another writer. This is one of the reasons why a writer's contract breaks the writing process into different stages: if the company is unhappy with the writer, then they may decide to terminate the contract at the end of one of those stages and engage someone else for the next stage. A writer may be brought in to carry out revisions on the first draft written by another writer, for instance.

Freelancers are more easily hired and fired than staff employees and so, while they may, like Clive, often enjoy a feeling of being 'their own boss' because they have quite a large amount of freedom and flexibility in the organization of their time, at other times they may also experience strong feelings of anxiety and powerlessness because of their lack of job security or, more sharply put, "the fragility of creative careers" (Hesmondhalgh and Baker 2011: 145). Consequently, they may find themselves spending more and more of their time on their work.

Creative work, particularly when conducted at home or in a self-directed manner outside the confines of a structured workplace or office, is often difficult to separate from other aspects of one's life – family, friends, leisure. As Mark Banks (2009: 668) has called it, this "instrumental leisure of the creative class" makes all of one's time potentially subject to the demands of work.

This state of affairs is not confined to the creative industries. As Melissa Gregg points out, in her book *Work's Intimacy*, short-term or casual contract workers often face anxieties over their status in the "flexible, multi-tasking, web-based workplaces typical of information jobs today," in which short-term, casual and sometimes unpaid apprentice-workers labour (Gregg 2011: 56–63). We will return to these questions in Chapter 5.

WORK PATTERNS

"With each new project, there's a phase where I spend a lot of time getting distracted... Then something clicks and I can find it hard to stop... maybe writing from 10am to 9pm." (Clive, 2011)

"There's no typical day. It depends on whether you are in production, in pre-production or post-production. But in fact I could be all of these stages at once on different projects... When I'm busy I'm up at 7 and finish at 8, then read stuff in the evening. When you shoot, everything else stops." (Chris, 2011)

"The days are quite different. In production you're in the drama studio making drama that has to be turned around in five days, or you're doing all the support tasks at your office desk to get that into production. You read scripts, find sound, engage a sound designer, have lots of discussions with colleagues about finding the right actor...." (Kevin, 2011)

These three comments show how the majority of work in the creative industries is project-based and give an idea of how the rhythms of a project regulate the

Development: A term used particularly in the audiovisual industries (i.e film, television, games) to describe the stage at which ideas are brainstormed and worked up. Typical activities include: meetings and discussions, preliminary sketches, written outlines, plans, scripts, prototypes, research, fund raising. Development may be part of an in-house project, such as a video game or a radio programme. It may be a more informal and quite possibly unpaid process in which one or two individuals try to get a project off the ground. The vagueness and uncertainty of development as a project status, covering everything from early ideas to a fully financed script, prototype, or startup venture, has led to the oft repeated refrain 'I've got several projects in development' being understood as a euphemism for 'I haven't got any work at the moment'.

Pre-production: Another standard term in the audiovisual industry, this is the stage in which all the steps are taken to put things in place for production. The crucial difference between development and pre-production is that pre-production starts when a project has been **greenlit**. So pre-production starts when full finance is in place for the project and it forms part of a defined project schedule, which includes **production and post-production**. Unlike development, it does not and cannot go on indefinitely. Typical activities include: engaging of personnel, casting, rehearsal, booking of equipment and space, meetings and discussions, sketches, plans and other documents. One of the key differences between development and pre-production is that pre-production can only start once finance is secured and will always be part of a set schedule for completion of the project.

Production and post-production: These are standard terms in the audiovisual industries, with "production" also a standard term in use across many sectors of the creative industries. Production describes the process of audio, film or video recording; live performance; manufacturing, printing or publishing. "Post-production" describes the stages, through which a product goes, after production, to make it ready for distribution. These include: audio, video or film editing; track laying and mixing; image grading (adjusting the colour, saturation and other qualities of the film or video image). People working closest to *production* are most likely to be freelancers, because production work tends to be project-based and temporary – it involves "ephemeral undertakings" (Menger 1999).

work patterns of the people who work on them. Despite the differences between the employment structures of freelancers, SMEs and large companies, there are, therefore, also many similarities between the work patterns of people working in creative production, whatever their employment structure. The research and development (**R&D**) and **pre-production** stage of a project is often the longest and necessitates the most diverse range of activities and time scales. The **production** stage of a project engenders the most intensive work patterns and involves a very particular, tightly focused set of activities, completed in a relatively short time scale. Overall, people may put in quite long hours at this stage of the process. **Post-production**, an important stage in the creation of audiovisual products, is a time of reflection and revision and is usually longer in duration than the production stage. We will go on to examine in more detail the implications of project-based work and work rhythms in the creative industries in Chapter 5 and will look in more detail at the different stages in the production cycle of creative projects in Chapter 7.

FINDING WORK

There are differences between specialist areas within the creative industries. One of these differences is how people in different employment structures get to work on projects in the first place.

Clive, a freelance screenwriter, gets work largely through his **agent**. The latter sends out Clive's work to film and television drama **production companies,** or he will be approached by companies looking for a writer for a project. Clive has also built up relationships with a few production companies through working on projects, and will often work with them again on new projects. At the time of writing, Clive has four projects on the go. Two of them are scripts which he has been paid to write, for which the producers are now raising production finance. On a third project, the producer is awaiting development money, which will then be used to pay Clive to write the script. The fourth project is an idea for a drama series which Clive and a producer are **pitching** to television.

Chris, who directs his own commercials company, also relies on contacts with other organizations to find work. His company will be invited by advertising **agencies** to **pitch** for briefs, along with three or four other companies. These briefs are put together by a writer and art director who work for the advertising agency and they then put the brief out to directors, usually through a commercials company like Chris's. As well as running the company, Chris also directs commercials, as does one of the other partners in the company. Four other commercials directors work for Chris's company on a freelance basis. There is one in-house producer, who is also a partner in the company, and other producers also work for the company on a freelance basis.

Pitch/pitching: A prepared introduction of a creative product or service, aimed at persuading a potential buyer, investor or client. More generally, of course, a sales pitch refers to any attempt to persuade someone to buy or invest in something. The term comes from baseball — the accurate delivery of a ball from a pitcher into a catcher's mitt, past the hitter. Pitches take many forms, from the short "elevator pitch" (which takes its name from Hollywood screenwriters taking advantage of happenstance meetings with producers to pitch entire screenplays in a matter of seconds) to formal pitch meetings at which a project, product or service is presented. Each specialism has its own conventions and practices around pitching: journalists pitch stories to commissioning editors, writers pitch screenplays to film producers and directors, producers pitch ideas for programmes to TV commissioners (see Chapter 9 for more detail), while marketing and advertising agencies pitch campaigns to clients (see Chapter 10) (West 1993; Hackley and Kover 2007; Grabher 2002b).

It is clear, then, that both Clive and Chris are part of a **production chain** which links organizations and individuals together in the process of developing and producing projects. Freelancers, who carry out individual roles on the project, are at one end of this chain and financers, who pay for the project, are at the other. There may be several other companies of various sizes, including agencies and production companies, forming other links in the chain. The detail of how this works varies from sector to sector. In advertising, commercials are financed by client companies. They will typically work with a communications agency or creative agency which will put out a brief to production companies who make commercials. These companies will then engage directors and other crew members to make the commercial.

In television, a writer like Clive will be engaged either directly by a broadcaster, or by a production company, who will make the programme for a broadcaster, which will finance most or all of the costs. Film and television production companies often prefer to engage screenwriters through agents. However Judy, who works as a video games writer, does not have an agent and says that she finds all her work through direct contact with games developers. Usually, like Chris, this means she will be required to take part in a pitching process. What this involves, she says, will vary according to project and company:

> "From writing a couple of cut scenes, writing some AI dialogue [i.e., dialogue for the non-player characters, controlled by artificial intelligence], doing a whole reworking of the main story arc... it depends on what the company requests." (Judy, 2010)

Freelancers and production companies are thus constantly seeking to establish and become part of new project delivery chains in order to develop and produce new projects. They participate in a shifting landscape of connections and collaborations, which comes together for each new project and then disbands again. They will be paid on a project basis – either getting a fee for the whole job or a day rate. Judy, working on video games, says she prefers to get a day rate because she never knows how long a project will take. Clive's fee for television drama scripts is calculated on the length of the final programme, with the payment set at a certain amount of money for each programme-minute. However, he will receive different payments at different stages of the process (we will look in more depth at contracts in Chapter 4). Chris's company will take a production fee, as well as his fee as director, as part of the budget for the commercial.

Kevin, on the other hand, who is not a freelancer, but employed as a staff producer at a public radio station, is not paid per project, but on an annual salary basis. Projects are generated from inside the company and he has set slots to fill for regular programme strands. The same is true for writers, producers and other employees working in-house in other large corporations, including television broadcasters, newspapers, large film and TV production studios, and games publishers.

CAREER TRAJECTORIES AND PORTFOLIOS

People working in the creative industries, although they will tend to have specialist skills, may well work on a diverse range of projects in their career as well as having varied career trajectories. Drama producer, Kevin, for example, was in a band, which, although it got a record deal, didn't make very much money, prompting him to work in arts administration for a while, before retraining in radio production. He then got a job as a production coordinator on a classical radio station, before becoming a producer at RTE Radio 1, where he worked generally in arts, features and documentary, before specializing in drama. By comparison, Judy started off as a journalist, writing about video games and, through the contacts that she gained doing this, she eventually found work as a games writer.

Portfolio careers

Much project-based employment is quite irregular, with intensely busy periods followed by not much going on. The risk of unemployment has to be factored into the plans of every freelancer – not least making sure that the money earned on one project can be made to last until the next one comes along. In television production, for example, freelancers will seek to diversify their income sources as a way of coping with uncertainty about income and regularity of work (Dex et al. 2000). **Portfolio working** is characterized by "obtaining and doing a variety of pieces of work for a number of different clients or employers" (Clinton, Totterdell, and Wood 2006: 179; see also Handy 1995), and portfolio workers are sometimes said to have **portfolio careers**.

This sense of "having a portfolio" is implicit in terms such as "CV-building" or when graduates are encouraged to take on unpaid work to "build the portfolio" by gaining experience, skills, training and contacts instead of being paid wages. The value of experience and skills is "employability" – the various professional attributes that ensure longevity in the job market (Osnowitz 2010: 147). In an interview with the journalist Elizabeth Day, actress Louise Brealey, who starred as Molly Hooper in the BBC series *Sherlock*, describes her portfolio career, "juggling acting jobs with journalism," at one time serving as deputy **editor** of *Wonderland* magazine: "'At one point, I was rehearsing at the Royal Court and editing a piece about *Twin Peaks*' 20th anniversary in my tea breaks.' More recently, she has been working as a documentary researcher and has just produced a children's comedy drama for the BBC, *The Charles Dickens Show*" (Day 2012). It's not surprising that portfolio workers often describe their careers as "juggling" (Platman 2004: 591; Osnowitz 2010: 147) – being self-employed, they have to keep many balls in the air at the same time.

The range of things that a person may do, particularly as a freelancer, will define the portfolio they build over time. Rachel, for example, works as a journalist, is writing a novel and also teaches part-time. Emily, a film producer and an executive coach, splits her time between the more predictable, scheduled work of coaching and the less predictable work of developing and financing film productions.

Sometimes portfolio careers and changing career trajectories are part of a deliberate long-term strategy to achieve specific aims for the person involved. Certainly this

> **Portfolio working** and **portfolio careers:** A portfolio is a book-shaped folder for carrying loose sheaves of paper. It has become a metaphor for any organized gathering of selected materials, from stocks to artworks to professional skills — we all have portfolios of one type or another. In this sense, a *portfolio worker* is employed (as a freelancer or part-timer) for more than one individual or organization. For example, a journalist might work at a newspaper two days a week and teach journalism at a university during the remaining three days. When this becomes a long-term arrangement, a worker can be said to have a *portfolio career*. Research has shown that many artists hold multiple jobs, often subsidising their artistic practice through work in a different sector (Throsby and Zednik 2011). Recommended reading: Mark Deuze, *Media Work* (2007a); Alan McKinlay and Chris Smith, eds., *Creative Labour: Working in the Creative Industries* (2009); David Hesmondhalgh and Sarah Baker, *Creative Labour: Media Work in Three Cultural Industries* (2011).

is a key element of the career advice given to young hopefuls looking to gain a foothold in the TV and film industries (Richmond 2012). Someone might, for example, juggle bar work or temping with work as a runner on film projects because ultimately they want to be a film director or producer.

People's interests and skills may also change and develop over time without necessarily being part of a planned strategy, and may open up new opportunities which develop their careers further. Judy's move from journalism to games and Kevin's move into drama are both examples of careers which changed and developed organically over time, through a mixture of chance and design.

Creative careers have an element of "self-realization" to them, as Hesmondhalgh and Baker point out (2011). In their interviews with creative workers, there emerges a strong association between what people do and their sense of themselves, their talents and passions – their love of what they do is closely connected to their sense of self, personal development, and even dignity. "Self-realization in relation to labour involves a sustained sense of good work, so that work may contribute to a sense that a person might have – and other people might also share – that they are developing, flourishing, achieving excellence in forms of work activity that are valuable" (Hesmondhalgh and Baker 2011: 140). They quote a writer who had transitioned from being an actor, and had recently become a father. Despite his new responsibilities and the inherent precariousness of a writer's income, he says: "I feel as though it's more worthy somehow, that I can go to a room and spend all day writing and I feel it's a more appropriate way to make a living rather than getting on a train and going down to Soho and going to a room for two minutes and pretending to be a chicken or whatever for a commercial and then getting on the train and coming home again" (Hesmondhalgh and Baker 2011: 145). Contrary to how portfolio careers have been identified with freedom and autonomy, and cast as glamorous and exciting ways to make a living, Hesmondhalgh and Baker argue that creative careers are inherently fragile. However, they are careful to note that a substantial number of their interviewees care deeply about their creative work and their identities as writers, musicians, and the like – deeply enough to accept the risks that come with their lines of work.

Entrepreneurship

Entrepreneurship is sometimes regarded as a form of creative expression in the creative industries. Many creatives will often instigate their own projects or set up businesses on their own. Chris's commercials company invests its own time and resources into drama projects because this is an area that they would like to move into. New entrants into the creative industries may do bar and restaurant work in order to support their nascent careers as actors, musicians, dancers, writers, etc. They might equally be doing so because they hope to set up their own bar or restaurant or club and want to get experience in the area.

Another entrepreneurial career trajectory is to have an original idea, realize a gap in the market that it could fill and make money out of it. In the creative industries, such ventures often closely align business opportunities with personal tastes. Robin, company director of Vegetarian Shoes, wanted to make vegetarian (i.e., non-leather) shoes because he was himself vegetarian. He soon found that there was a sizeable demand for such shoes, from other vegetarians. First, he made the shoes himself, but then outsourced the shoe production to a factory, allowing him to grow his business and increase his sales. Similarly, the founders of Last.fm were interested in sharing music recommendations and built a **dot-com** company around this concept.

> **Dot-coms, Dot-com bubble:** A company that does business primarily online. During the dot-com bubble (or "dot-com boom") businesses sprang up around the act of attaching the ".com" suffix to a generic term and creating a company out of it (e.g., Pets.com). Recommended reading: Michael Lewis' *Next: The Future Just Happened* (2002) provides an early post-mortem on the dot-com era; Lori Gottlieb's insider account *Inside the Cult of Kibu* (2002) is a very funny example of this genre of books; Rory Cellan-Jones' *Dot.bomb: The Rise and Fall of Dot.com Britain* (2001) documents the dot-com boom in the UK; for a critical overview of literature on the dot-com boom and bust, see Geert Lovink, *My First Recession* (2003); finally, for a humorous, autobiographical take on the aftermath of the dot-com era and the early Web 2.0 years, see Paul Carr's *Bringing Nothing to the Party* (2008).

The canny upstart who recognizes and exploits a gap in the market is the classic model of the **entrepreneur** (Neff, Wissinger, and Zukin 2005). The typical next step is then to sell the company to a larger concern, making a lot of money out of the deal, and move on to a new business venture. However, while Last.fm, like many new media startups, was sold to a larger company (CBS), Vegetarian Shoes did not take this route. It remained a small business, albeit with a large mail order reach. Such differences will always be partly a question of market forces: new media is an emerging area with vast possibilities for growth. It has already been the subject of one speculation bubble (the so-called **dot-com bubble**) and continues to feature hugely inflated **market valuations** for startups. The shoe industry is a much more mature and stabilized sector, with much less interest from speculators. As discussed by Leadbeater and Oakley (1999), however, not all entrepreneurs in the creative industries have making large profits as their primary aim – often the value of what they do in the context of a community, their recognition by their peers, and the quality of the work they do will outstrip financial considerations. We will explore this further in Chapter 4.

NATIONAL AND INTERNATIONAL PERSPECTIVES

In this chapter we have read about the experiences of creative workers in different national contexts. We can take their experiences of work patterns and structures as broadly representative of those of freelancers, SMEs and employees of media corporations in the UK and other countries. However, there are always specific national, political and other factors that affect these experiences.

The national and the local

Because so much work in the creative industries takes place in project networks – bringing together the talent and efforts of a diverse group of people and organizations – most creative workers rely on their local contacts. There are some key reasons for this: First, individuals' industry *contacts* and work opportunities are often concentrated in a particular city or area, which is why networking is such an important skill for creative professionals (Blair 2009). Second, credentials and training are often very important for recent graduates seeking to get into certain sectors where *local knowledge* and understanding of how things work are essential – for example, in film/TV production and performing arts (Guile 2010). Third, particular sectors of the creative industries have a tendency to *cluster* geographically around institutions, markets, financing opportunities and local talent pools (Flew 2012: 146) – we will discuss this further in the next chapter.

State regulation and legal frameworks play a large role as well. For example, economic and political conditions (such as taxation and access to capital) are likely to be more favourable to the establishment and survival of SMEs in some countries than in others. In some, the media are largely under state control and subject to censorship; elsewhere they are largely under private ownership. However, all media are *regulated* to some extent at the state level (Freedman 2008; Chalaby 2010). In the UK, the Office of Communications (Ofcom), for example, exists in order to "further the interests of citizens and of consumers" (Lunt and Livingstone 2012: viii).

Such macro-level social, political and economic factors will of course have an impact on the micro-level (i.e., the experience of the individual worker). For example, an independent producer in the UK-market would have to pitch very differently to a commissioner at a broadcaster with a public service remit than to one with no such duties.

The international dimension

Creative professionals do not, however, operate in an exclusively national market. Let us consider three examples.

Clive, a freelance UK screenwriter, recently wrote two episodes for a drama **co-production** between Irish national broadcaster RTE and UK national network ITV. Furthermore, almost all the film projects he has worked on have had an international component, involving producers and organizations from a range of countries, including Denmark, the United Arab Emirates and the USA. International co-production is even more of a feature of film production than it is of broadcasting (as we shall explore further in Chapter 10).

Video games content director, Luc, is employed by a large international video games company. It is French owned and its head office is in France. But France is not the sole, or indeed the primary market for the video games the company publishes. Its primary markets are the USA and Asia. It has studios all over the world and its employees need to be international in their outlook. Luc previously worked for the company in Shanghai. He is French, but speaks fluent English and spends a lot of time travelling internationally and liaising between his company's head office, its games studios and other enterprises worldwide.

Meanwhile, based in New Zealand, Chris's production company also has representation in Australia and is developing a film project with another production company in Canada. Chris directs work for clients in Australia and Asia as well as New Zealand, and he gets work through international advertising agencies that have branches all over the world. American companies sometimes shoot commercials in New Zealand, as crew rates are lower, so Chris also sometimes works on commercials for a US audience.

We might conclude from these three examples that, in the contemporary creative industries, freelancers, SMEs and employees in large corporations may all feel the international reach of what they do.

Even national public service broadcasters, such as RTE and the BBC, which have a primary responsibility to their national audience, the licence-fee payers, also enter into international co-productions and distribute their programmes internationally (see Chapter 9 for more details). Drama producer Kevin also recounts how he attends the European Radio Awards each year, a trade event, which provides an opportunity for professional support and development and networking at an international level. Such international events are features of all sectors of the creative industries.

The relationship between the local and the global is complex. A strong local product may also be what makes a strong global product. A strong domestic market for broadcasters is important for their participation in the international market for media content – especially TV, radio and film. Hollywood has, of course, exported American culture to the world for nearly 100 years and the British Broadcasting Company (BBC) has also become a global brand, running the **BBC World Service** (Wood 2000) and selling its programming internationally through its commercial arm, **BBC Worldwide**.

We might conclude, then, that the audience for creative products is global. Wherever they are made, creative products are marketed and sold across the world. However, despite being a growing area of international trade, at the same time, all creative industries are, in a sense, also locally based. As Terry Flew points out, "there is much work to be done on better understanding which products and services developed by the creative industries best 'travel' between nations and cultures, and which do not" (Flew 2012: 132). To understand in more depth the micro- and macro-organization of employment in the creative industries in particular countries, it will always be necessary to carry out further specific research into the particular country or market-territory in question.

SUMMARY

We began this chapter looking at *institutions and ownership*: the contemporary creative industries are characterized by a high number of freelancers and microbusinesses (largely involved in production), on the one hand, and the dominant presence of extremely large, often international, corporations on the other (who tend to control commissioning, publishing and distribution). These different types of company are connected through production chains, in which each has a particular role to play in the project, from conception through to distribution. Work in the creative industries tends to be project-based and creative workers often work flexible, irregular and long hours, according to the demands and rhythms of the project. Typically this will mean a research and development period, which involves a diverse range of activities and time scales, and a production stage, which is much more intense and tightly focused in its activities and completed in a relatively short time scale. Since they are only engaged for the length of a project, freelancers will always need to keep looking for new projects to work on once the current project(s) is/are finished.

Workplaces can be very varied for people working in the creative industries. They may work at home, in large or small offices, shops, workshops and studios, markets, film/TV/radio location shoots. The same person may work in several different types of workplace, depending on the stage of the project. Office space is often organized to facilitate informal and flexible working patterns and teams, including open-plan offices and hot-desking.

Careers are unpredictable, and there is no set path into the creative industries. People enter into the creative industries through diverse, sometimes unexpected routes, and portfolio working is common. Positions are often publicized and filled via word of mouth and personal contacts, so networking is an important skill to acquire and practise. The scale of the work is often *international*. Many creative industries organizations have an explicit focus on the international rather than the domestic market, while for others the domestic market may be primary, with the international market as secondary. However, most creative workers will, in some way, feel the international reach of what they do.

RECOMMENDED READING

Deuze, Mark. 2007. *Media Work: Digital Media and Society*. Cambridge: Polity Press. Interviews with creative workers, international in scope and highly informative, particularly on work in and around the media industries.

Hesmondhalgh, David and Sarah Baker. 2011. *Creative Labour: Media Work in Three Cultural Industries*. London: Routledge. Extensive study, based on interviews and participant observation in three industries: television, music recording and magazine publishing.

Hjorth, Larissa. 2011. *Games and Gaming: An Introduction to New Media*. Oxford: Berg Publishers. A concise introduction to games and gaming as both an area of study and an industry.

Lewandowski, Natalie. 2010. "Understanding Creative Roles in Entertainment: The Music Supervisor as Case Study." *Continuum: Journal of Media & Cultural Studies* 24 (6): 865. Accessible, informative study of the role of music supervisor in practice.

Martin, Chase Bowen and Mark Deuze. 2009. "The Independent Production of Culture: A Digital Games Case Study." *Games and Culture* 4 (3): 276–295. A case study of the production process in a studio.

Miller, Vincent. 2011. *Understanding Digital Culture*. London: Sage. Accessible overview of key issues in digital media and their cultural implications.

4

The Business of Creativity

This chapter explores business principles and operations in the creative industries. We compare lifestyle businesses and growth businesses, learn more about the legal frameworks within which organizations operate, about aspects such as intellectual property, contracts, finance, and about a range of business models that operate within the creative industries. We will also consider key factors that might affect the success of a business.

SOLE TRADERS AND MICROBUSINESSES

In the previous chapter we were introduced to the idea that the contemporary creative industries are characterized by an ecology of a few very large companies and many small-to-medium companies (SMEs). We learnt, moreover, that many small companies are often very small indeed, since a large number of creative workers are freelancers, whose legal status of **self-employment** defines them as a particular type of small business, called a **sole trader**. Even creative businesses which consist of more than one person tend to be smaller than average. They are often in fact **microbusinesses**.

Setting up business as a freelancer

As we saw in the last chapter, freelancers value their independence. Screenwriter, Clive, commented on how, being a freelancer, he feels more like 'his own boss' and, indeed, since he is the sole proprietor of his business, this is literally the case. With this independence also comes responsibility for things that, if he was an employee, his employer would take care of, since sole traders are responsible for paying their own tax and national insurance, which are deducted automatically at source from the wages and salaries of employees. Clive needs to make sure that he doesn't spend all his **gross** income, but keeps back enough to pay his yearly tax bill.

Covering tax and national insurance are not the only budgetary aspects a sole trader needs to manage. In order for a business to succeed, at the most basic level, it needs to bring in more money than it spends in order to deliver its product or service. As a creative producer, you need to turn a **profit** if you are to make enough money to earn a living. But what does it actually cost to produce a creative product? This needs to be calculated quite carefully and it is something that new creative producers often underestimate. If you are working as a freelance journalist, selling an article to a newspaper or a magazine, for example, what resources and costs are involved? First, there is your labour as the key resource. But how many days work go into the article? There's the time you spend writing the article, for sure. But what about the time you spent researching the story? And what about the time you spent pitching ideas and otherwise finding somebody to publish your story in the first place? Then there's the time spent on invoicing the magazine or newspaper in order to get paid. Your labour adds up to more than the time you spend writing the final piece. Furthermore, you've also spent money on telephone and internet services, on stationery and travel perhaps. As discussed above, you will also have to remember that you cannot keep the **gross** amount of your fee, a percentage of it will have to go to the government in national insurance and tax. These are all costs that your fee for the articles you write needs to cover and exceed if you are to make a living out of journalism. Ideally, having calculated these costs, you would then determine your price for your service. However, you are unlikely to have much control over what the newspaper will pay you for your story, particular as a new entrant to the creative industries. So you will have to turn your budgetary control on yourself and make sure that you don't allow the time and resources you invest in producing your articles to rise above a sustainable level. So far so good on paper, but in practice this is tricky, as radio presenter and producer, Luke, explains:

> "Being a very small company it's quite identity based, in that you are so closely identified with what you do that shoving out stuff that you make quite cheaply isn't really an option for you...." (Luke, 2012)

As a creative microbusiness, you are always chasing your next job and one of the ways that you do this is through pleasing existing clients with the quality of your work and impressing future ones with your show reel. Trying to juggle this with keeping your costs down is a hard act to pull off.

Luke produces a daily arts and culture slot on the radio and says that one of the ways he manages costs and resources is by getting interviews that can generate more than one show:

> "One of the strategies that I definitely do is that I try and get people who have three shows in them... to find people who aren't necessarily Maria Carey or Rhianna but who have a lot of audience with them, which is good for us in a kind of global way, people listen to podcasts all over the place. So people who have a global audience

and a back catalogue of books or ideas that they've been through and therefore you can set up a couple of hours with them and get three days out of it and that can be a great thing. That's as close as we come to an **economy of scale**." (Luke, 2012)

Operating in a highly competitive environment, with very slim margins, creative micro-businesses have to be both careful and creative about how they allocate their resources to their activities if they are to succeed. However, all startup businesses do need to anticipate and plan for a significant period of making a loss, before they start to turn a profit. This is one of the motivations for portfolio working, examined in the last chapter. Indeed, even established businesses factor in **loss leaders** as part of their strategy and practice.

As a sole trader, like any other business, you can also offset your business costs against **revenue**, so that your profit, and therefore also your tax bill, is reduced. Allowable costs may include things like a percentage of your electricity and telephone bill if you work from home. It will include travel, consumables such as stationery and also capital expenses such as equipment. Luke admits that he often forgets to record small items – buying something on i-tunes to use for a story, for example – because, even though they are legitimate expenses that would bring his tax down, it takes time and organization to record such payments in the company **books** with the necessary receipt. However, the fact that good quality equipment, which will add value to his creative output, can be offset against profit is something that he finds invaluable to his business:

"I can remember people who were photographers when I was younger and they always had fantastic gear and I wondered how they managed to do that and actually there's no reason not to have the best gear, because it will sound the best and to have the most convenient kind of set up. I feel often encouraged to do that." (Luke, 2012)

However, Luke relies on his accountant to tell him what he can and can't claim. The rules about what expenditure you can and can't offset against income are very strict and quite detailed. This is one of the reasons why most self-employed people pay an accountant to advise them and prepare their tax return.

Setting up business as a partnership or limited company

As Leadbeater and Oakley (1999) point out in their study of the creative industries at the end of the twentieth century, the next step for some freelancers may then be to venture more fully into business management by going from being a sole trader to setting up a **partnership** or **limited company**. Chris, the commercials director we met in the previous chapter, is an example of this. Having worked for many years as a freelance director in advertising, he set up a partnership with another director and a producer.

However, new companies are also often set up by people who move from employment in larger companies into starting up their own ventures. The deregulation of the broadcasting industry in the 1980s and 1990s, for example, prompted the establishment of independent production companies by previously in-house broadcasting staff. In the UK, the arrival of Channel 4 and the new regional and independent production quotas, encouraged many producers to leave in-house positions in the BBC and ITV and set up production companies supplying their former employers, as well as other broadcasters, with content.

The move from employee to entrepreneur may equally be motivated by individual circumstances. Carole found herself setting up her own company as a literary agent almost by accident, after she lost her job working for a publisher.

> "I was going to interviews with publishers and thinking 'I don't want to work for you.' And then authors were calling me and saying 'look if you're going to become an agent...' ... Then I realised actually I already had an embryo client list. So I sort of fell into being an agent. I was married. I had a house. I had a spare room where I could run the agency from. So, back then in 1977, it didn't seem much of a risk.... And so I kind of just fell into being a literary agent." (Carole, 2011)

The history of startup companies often seems to be one of luck and chance as much as design and strategy. Robin, unlike Carole, set out deliberately to start his own shoemaking business. He had identified what he thought was a gap in the market (vegetarian shoes, for people who didn't want to wear leather), and had also identified a breathable, microfibre material that he planned to use to make the shoes. He then worked for a year to save money, doing as much overtime as possible, living with his parents and doing everything he could to keep his costs down. It was then that chance intervened:

> "It was the very last lift of a long trip on a holiday I'd rewarded myself before I started the business, because I knew that I wouldn't have any holiday for a few years... and the very last lift that I didn't have my thumb stuck out for, because it was getting dark and I was walking away. He stopped and we got talking and I shared with him my secret, because up until then I'd been saving money for this fantastic idea that I hadn't told anybody about. I was worried that someone would nick my idea or... you know I was very naive, I had no business background, no history of business so I didn't know it was going to work, but I had a lot of energy and determination... so I told this fellow and he told me about this material that he had found and I tracked it down and the next week, when I started business, I started with this material that I hadn't been planning a year ago to use, but it turned out to be what we use now even, really good stuff." (Robin, 2011)

The 'lifestyle business' vs the 'growth business'

If you want to be a writer, a director, a musician, a film or television technician, a designer and so on, most openings will be on a freelance basis. Thus many creative workers become microbusinesses because they are interested in a particular creative activity rather than because they are inspired to set up and grow a successful business. Partnerships and limited companies may be similarly motivated. Advertising director Chris, for example, says he and his partners set up their partnership to establish a space in which their individual development could flourish and they could find personal fulfilment, which they felt freelancing for others didn't offer them. This affects their goals for the company, as they value having time to develop drama and other projects that they find creatively fulfilling over higher revenues that might come from focusing purely on expanding their advertising activities. Robin too explains that, although when he first set up the business he invested all his time and energy into it, now that it is well established he is keen to maintain his work/life balance:

> "You've got to work hard at the beginning of your life and you can take it easier at the end... I've gone from running everywhere and working maybe six or seven days a week to the quality of life, you know. The bills are paid... Someone once said 'How much do you want?' and the answer is always 'just a little bit more'... actually... I've got enough. I don't need any more." (Robin, 2011)

He says he now tries to work four rather than five days a week and most of the staff at the shop are also not 100% full-time:

> "You get to go away and ride your motorbike. That makes a lot of sense you know. Not everyone here works full-time and they don't earn so much because of it. Because you're working less days. But some people (some do some don't), some prefer to have the time... Some people think that's a bit weird... it's not perhaps part of the more conservative way of doing life. It's more alternative." (Robin, 2011)

This kind of business is often termed a lifestyle business in that its owners' aim is primarily to support a particular lifestyle. This term is sometimes seen as having negative connotations, suggesting a lack of professionalism. But in fact many lifestyle businesses are perfectly viable concerns (Harper 2003: 205; Bygrave 2011: chapter 14).

However, unless creative businesses embrace entrepreneurship to some degree and practice good business management, problems can result. Although, as we have seen, luck and chance may play their part in business success, they are not usually enough. Even with a company consisting of one person, a range of factors need to be weighed and managed. Robin explains how he managed **cash flow** for his first order of shoes, which he designed and had made up by a factory and sold by mail order:

> "I think the minimum order was 100 pairs and I didn't have enough money to buy 100 pairs of shoes. I had enough money to buy the material and I had enough money to supply the factory with, because they did the making and the other components and they charge you. I had enough money to place an advert... So I aimed to get my advert out a month before the shoes arrive then hopefully collect some orders and then when the shoes arrive pay for the shoes with the money that I've collected from the orders. Magic... And then, when the shoes finally arrived, this was how naive I was, I assumed that as soon as you get something, you have to pay

for them. I had **30 days credit** anyway... But I did get enough orders and paid for the shoes and put another order in and it was OK." (Robin, 2011)

As a company expands, the number of elements that need to be planned for and managed multiply and become more complex. One of the problems that can beset creative companies is the competing requirements of project management and business management. Creative industries tend to be project-based, meaning, as we saw in our freelance journalist example above, that financing is usually gained on a project-by-project basis: an article, a book, a script, a commercial, a design is commissioned. The price that the customer pays for the product then has to cover all the associated **direct and indirect costs** involved. While this might be fairly straightforward to manage when dealing with one product at a time, as with Robin's first pair of shoes, as a business expands, more skill is required to manage budgeting and cash flow, so that both the business and its projects can flourish. Multiple projects/products must be juggled simultaneously, while trying to make sure they cover the costs of the increased infrastructure and **overheads** of the business itself, as well as of each individual project.

Carole's literary agency eventually developed from a one-person business operating out of her house into a partnership (with screenwriting agent Julian Friedmann), the Blake Friedmann agency, occupying the top floor of an office block and employing 10 people. Carole says she has to divide her time between looking after the authors that she represents and 'looking after the business of the business' (Carole, 2011), the bulk of which, for Carole, is "**HR** stuff: looking after staff" (Carole, 2011). Carole is proud of the agency's record of retaining staff long term and says: "You don't fall into having long-serving staff by ignoring them, or by treating them just as job descriptions" (Carole, 2011). Since Blake Friedmann is an agency, offering a representation service to writers, its most valuable assets are its **human resources** – the people who work to represent the interests of the writers – so it is no surprise that Carole prioritizes this aspect of the business.

In a similar vein, Matt Webb, CEO of design consultancy Berg, who writes regularly about his job on the 'weeknotes' strand of the company blog, stresses that how he manages attention, that is, his own time and that of his co-workers, is as crucial as how he manages cash flow and assesses risk:

> "I monitor three budgets: attention, cash, risk. All are flows to be directed. Attention: how many minutes do we have as a studio, and how many can be spent in experimental or undirected ways? Cash: how can cash-flow be managed to build up working capital to invest, versus spend freely to buy more attention to spend? Risk: how tolerant are the attention and cash budgets to delay or failure?" (Webb 2010)

Both Carole and Matt continue to practise their creative specialism – as an agent and as a designer, respectively. But both are also committed to their role as a creative manager. Creative businesses are more likely to expand successfully and remain sustainable when creativity is invested in the business as well as the projects, and this may result in different priorities for the company's founder, with their focus moving on to the business rather than its projects, as film producer Hamish Barbour explains:

> "We used to concentrate on making all the films and documentaries ourselves. But then we realised we could be creative with the company rather than with the product. Rather than pursue an ambition to be a big director I decided to focus on building the company." (in Leadbeater and Oakley 1999: 27)

Burns (2011: 19) proposes that true entrepreneurs (as opposed to managers) are those who found 'growth firms', that is companies which expand and grow beyond simply supporting the lifestyle of their founders. In particular, he foregrounds the economic value to national economies of **high growth firms** – growth firms which expand rapidly. Although they tend to make up only a small percentage of all small firms, these latter generate the most wealth and jobs, accounting for the bulk of the 50% of GDP generated from small firms in the USA, for example (Burns 2011: 7).

Burns does, however, comment that sometimes the aims of an enterprise may change; a lifestyle firm may become a growth business. It may indeed be hard at the outset to classify a business as one or the other. High growth internet companies, such as Google or Facebook, grew out of their founders' personal interests and talents. Children's author, J.K. Rowling, started out as a lifestyle firm (a freelance author), but her Harry Potter series became a global phenomenon, creating wealth and jobs internationally as well as nationally (Economist 2009; Kruhly 2011).

However, although the beginnings of all large companies may be traced back to small startups, comparatively few startups actually do become growth companies. In fact, many creative startups fail in their first three years. A recent report commissioned by the Work Foundation found the three-year survival rate of creative startups in the UK to be somewhere between 73% and 54%, depending on the sector (Reidd et al. 2010).

Few of those creative startups which do survive go on to metamorphize from "plankton" to "whales". Nor do many turn into some middle-sized beast to occupy the mid-ground between them. Instead, the most standard route for successful small companies to follow is to get bought out by big ones. In publishing, for example, Penguin Books, a paperback publisher set up in 1935, remains a household name as an **imprint**, but was actually bought up by Pearson in 1970. Consolidation in publishing has been very much the trend, since the 1970s, creating a kind of Russian doll effect, with companies being bought up by other companies which are bought up by other companies in their turn. Even the huge publishing group Random House, with many divisions and imprints under its umbrella, is itself owned by an even bigger company, German media conglomerate Bertelsmann, as Carole explains:

> "You know people think Random House is American, it isn't, it's German... a bunch of American publishers are owned by Germany or France or Spain... Hodder, Headline, Orion, Weidenfeld, Gollancz, they're French. They're owned by Hachette... Scratch the surface and you find somebody else." (Carole, 2011)

As Flew (2012) points out, high **fixed costs** and high **risk/return ratios** tend to promote this industry concentration, making it hard for small companies to compete with large ones, and much more profitable and much less risky for them to sell out to them. Therefore, the same 'Russian dolls' structure is in operation in other sectors of the creative industries, such as games, TV and film production, advertising and marketing.

However, many small companies in the creative industries do remain small, like Robin's Vegetarian Shoes and the Blake Friedmann agency. Both these businesses are established, successful companies with a track record of 30 years or more. Yet, although they have expanded substantially from zero to eight or 10 employees, they are still small businesses and both Carole and Robin say that they don't intend to grow further.

This attitude can be frustrating for economic development agencies (Evans 2009) since economic policies tend to be predicated on growth as a measure of economic success. In their 2010 report on the creative industries, Reidd et al. emphasize the potential of the creative industries as 'an engine of growth'. However, while this may be true of certain sectors, it is questionable whether this can be extrapolated out to cover all of them. Using statistics from the creative industries in Barcelona, Berlin and London, Evans (2009) states that growth performance and potential can only really be linked to certain commercial sectors of the creative industries (which also feature concentration of ownership), such as publishing, media production and software. He questions the wisdom of applying the logic of growth indiscriminately across all sectors.

Even where growth sectors are specifically targeted for support by governmental economic policy, in an attempt to help SMEs to develop and populate the 'missing middle' (Flew 2012) between microbusinesses and multinational corporations, such efforts may not meet with success. According to Evans, many creative industries policy initiatives have focused almost exclusively on supporting startups and SMEs, with the result that "those with the highest take-up of support (i.e., training, business advice) exhibit the poorest growth and improvement" (Evans 2009: 1029).

Factors such as the norm of project-based activity and a lifestyle approach to business certainly might seem to mitigate against such growth. However, Lloyd has made a more nuanced case for the compatibility of artists' values with those of contemporary business, claiming that "the do-it-yourself ethos of **bohemia** fits in well with the entrepreneurial imperatives of neoliberal capitalism" (Lloyd 2010: 245). Lloyd points out that sectors such as media, design and advertising draw heavily on the creative talent of art school graduates, who are trying to balance creative aspirations with making a living. Microbusiness and SME structures offer these creative producers a less institutionalized and more flexible working environment than large multinationals, giving them the sense that they have maintained their creative freedom.

Lloyd then goes on to argue that the networked production chains of the creative industries often mean that the smaller companies are working for larger agencies,

Bohemia: The artistic fringes of society, eschewing conventional manners and morality. "Bohemia" and the "bohemians" who belong to it have been described in various ways since 1850, but no simple definition of bohemia has ever stuck, as Elizabeth Wilson suggests in *Bohemians: The Glamorous Outcasts* (2000). The bohemian has historically taken that position on the margin, the artist-as-rebel, both an identity for individuals to occupy or aspire to, as well as a stereotype for popular consumption: "As soon as the bohemian appeared on the urban stage there were eager consumers of stories of glamorous and sordid individuals, men and women of genius and eccentricity, who lived exciting lives and challenged the conventions. The vicissitudes of the bohemian way of life, its excesses, its triumphs, its failures and its aura of grim seriousness, incongruously expressed in performance and pose, have always been good copy" (Wilson 2000: 3). These connotations of bohemia persist into the present, with different people, groups and places assuming the role of cool marginality. "Bohemia" is not just about the bohemians themselves, but *where* they might be found. As Richard Lloyd argues in *Neo-Bohemia* the various urban refuges of society's weirdos have been turned into the lifestyle bohemia of hipsters, coffee shops, cool bars and funky retail — bohemia as a form of urban regeneration through art and commerce in post-industrial cities (Lloyd 2006). This is the sanitized bohemia of Richard Florida's "Bohemian Index" (Florida 2010a), at a safe remove from any actual squalor, decadence or danger.

whose clients are in fact multinational conglomerates. He cites an example of one SME, where both directors and employees identify as belonging to a creative culture, which they see as the antithesis of "the stultification and injustice of corporate capitalism" while at the same time they are "working twelve-hour days making recruitment ads for Nike" (Lloyd 2010: 246). Thus, according to Lloyd, the **precarity** of the artist's lifestyle and the precarity of post-Fordist capitalism are a good match. In a corporate world, in which flexibility is expected of all workers, artists are particularly able to rise to the challenge and indeed value it as freedom. Lloyd's argument is that, even though they themselves may not grow, the productivity of microbusinesses and SMEs is nevertheless harnessed by large companies and contributes to their growth. Even less commercial areas, such as poetry or painting, are also fertile areas for creative labour in the commercial sector, since "the paltry returns for most artistic efforts are precisely what enable the incorporation of local artists into these other labor contexts" (Lloyd 2010: 248). According to Lloyd, corporate capitalism is thus able to profit from the precarity, long hours and low pay to which creative practitioners are habituated, while the creative practitioners themselves remain comparatively poor. Growth sector creative businesses may therefore benefit from being located near to centres of artistic activity, particularly in urban areas, on whose pool of labour they can draw (Power 2003; Heebels and van Aalst 2010; Scott 2010).

The chains and networks of production that Lloyd describes are complex and dependent on many factors. Policy debates continue as to whether it is more productive to try to work with distinctive features of the creative industries such as those cited above or to try to overcome them. We will return to further discussion of this later in the chapter.

FINANCING A CREATIVE BUSINESS

Starting up

As we have seen, both Robin and Carole used their own capital to set up their companies. Bank loans can be particularly hard for creative companies to secure and startups may often rely on their own money or loans from family or friends. However they may also be able to apply for funding from **enterprise or arts and culture schemes**, depending on their product or service and their target audience. **Venture capital** may also be available, but this tends to be more likely obtained in sectors with high growth potential, such as technology firms. What companies need the startup funds for will depend on the product or service they want to offer, but typically the aim will be to keep the startup funds low, to minimize losses in case of failure.

Maintaining the business

Since many creative businesses are project based, they will continue to seek finance for each new project. Creative producers in TV, film, or radio will pitch to commissioners or investors (we will learn more about this process in Chapter 9). Advertising agencies will pitch to clients, as will design companies (we will learn more about this process in Chapter 10). Writers will try to sell their books or their scripts or their articles, and agencies, such as Blake Friedmann, will try to sell them on their behalf and gain their commission. As Carole says: "We only make money if the writer makes money... it focuses the mind beautifully" (Carole, 2011).

As a business grows more established, however, it should be able to recoup enough profits to provide a cushion of finance to use for contingencies and to plough back into the business in the form of research and development, expansion, etc. Businesses may also seek capital investment to fund strategic developments such as these from the same sources as mentioned above.

CONTRACTS AND RIGHTS

When you take up a job as an employee within a company you sign a contract of employment. If you are taking up a position in a creative business and will be involved in generating content, then your contract will require that you assign your **intellectual property** to the company. Once you have done this, every product you create belongs to the company. If, on the other hand, the company engages freelancers, it will enter into a contract with them for each particular project they are working on. For example, when Kevin, the radio drama producer we met in Chapter 3, casts actors for a radio play, each of the actors' agents will negotiate their contract for the production with the contract department at RTE. However, institutions will tend to develop a stand-ard contract template for writers, actors, etc., which they will use for each project. While this saves time for both parties, actually establishing the template may involve lengthy negotiations. Carole recounts how she spent two years in negotiation with a publisher to establish the typical **boilerplate** contract that they would use with all her authors. Similarly, in 2012, UK public broadcaster, the BBC, and directors' trade association Directors UK brought four years of negotiation to a close when they announced a directors' rights deal which would form the basis of future directors' contracts at the BBC (Campbell 2012a).

All parties involved in a contract need to be very careful about exactly what rights are assigned to whom and for how long, and recent technological developments have made this an increasingly significant and tricky thing to negotiate. Both contracts and contract negotiations have become longer as a result. When Carole first worked as a rights and contract manager for a publisher, she says their author contract was four pages. Now a typical contract may well be over 20 pages. Much of this is down to the wide range of new platforms available, to which rights may be assigned:

> "There's so much more to define... You have to describe in minute detail every single thing and many different versions have different royalty rates. And because that world is changing so much, take e-books for instance, we will only agree a set roy-alty for e-books for a period of two years. We then put into the contract the right to renegotiate. Because it's changing all the time." (Carole, 2011)

The 2007–2008 Writers' Guild of America (WGA) strike, which lasted 100 days and had a significant impact on television production, was over the fact that writers' con-tracts accorded no **residual payments** for online sales and rentals. Aware that digital distribution was likely to take over in the future, writers were determined to get their share of the revenue. As Miranda Banks (2010) explains, this was the latest stage in a history of struggle by screenwriters to receive remuneration from distribution on new media platforms. The WGA first successfully lobbied for residuals from replays of film and television series on television in 1965. However, according to Banks, they had been less successful in their efforts to obtain fair residuals from VHS or DVD distribution in the 1980s and 1990s. This strengthened their determination to get a better deal when it came to digital distribution (Banks 2010).

The number of platforms and markets for which it is now possible to license con-tent, has made IPR (intellectual property rights) an increasingly valuable asset and has significantly affected the way business is organized and how people make money out of it, as we will now go on to discuss.

BUSINESS MODELS

When you set up a company you have some kind of model in mind of how your company is going to work. Are you going to sell a product or offer a service? Who is your customer – other businesses or the general public? Is it a particular demographic or a community of interest? How are you going to make money? Will your customers pay per item or by subscription? Will you generate income through sponsorship or offering advertising space? These are all relevant questions to determining your business model, which includes, very importantly, your model of revenue generation, but also encompasses other aspects, such as the **business structure** and organization and its relationship with its customers.

Jansen et al. define a business model as being predicated on a value model (also called a value proposition), that is, "the values that are created for all participants, including partners, suppliers and customers" (Jansen et al 2007: 29). They point out that:

> Value involves more than one-way traffic. Managers should carefully consider the reciprocal value that is expected from the customer in return for the provided products or services. One of the common reciprocal values obviously is monetary, but information and communication technology offers organisations the possibility of receiving several different, very interesting values from the customer, such as customer profiles or knowledge. (Jansen et al 2007: 31)

Certainly these latter values are becoming more and more important to contemporary business models in the creative industries.

One of the most salient points about business models is that they do not necessarily remain static over time. While all businesses may not be growth businesses, all businesses need to change in response to internal and external pressures. One of the

Business structures: there are different legal structures which govern the organizational structures we encountered in Chapter 3. Each legal structure determines the rules the business needs to follow, with regard to tax and employment.

Self-employment: If you are **self-employed**, you own your own business and are your own employer, rather than being employed by another person or company. Being a **sole trader** (also called **sole proprietor**) is perhaps the simplest form of self-employment. When someone is a sole trader it means that 'the owner is the business' (Stokes 2002: 107). Freelancers — e.g photographers, journalists, actors, designers — operating alone and offering a service to clients on finite projects, have the legal status of sole traders.

Being a sole trader is the simplest and cheapest way of setting up a business, since it does not involve paying any registration fees or auditing or publishing of accounts. It is generally lighter on paperwork than other forms of business formation, although it does require you to register with the tax office, to keep books and to submit tax returns each year, since your tax is not deducted at source.

However, sole trader status does mean you personally have unlimited liability for any losses you may incur in your business, meaning that, if things go badly wrong, your non-business assets, such as your house, might need to be sold to settle business debts. This is in contrast to the limited liability status of a limited company (see below).

In the last quarter of the twentieth century and into the twenty-first, self-employment increased and sole trading was its most common manifestation. In 2005 at least 73.9% of all firms in the UK were sole traders (Burns 2011).

A **partnership** is another form of self-employment, in which two or more people set up jointly in business and share the profits. Partnerships most typically consist of two or three people, but they can go up to 20 partners, or more, in the case of law and accountancy, in which a partnership is the standard business structure. As with being a sole trader, it is fairly simple to set up as a partnership and it carries unlimited liability (unless the partnership is a limited liability partnership, a more recently introduced form of business structure). Many SMEs and microbusinesses in the creative industries operate as partnerships. Partnerships are often, but not exclusively, found in talent agencies, production companies, firms of architects, designers and other forms of creative business where the founders may each have their own client list.

Although **self-employment** may mean that legally you are your own boss, in practice it often involves working for somebody else. Builders, electricians, designers, screenwriters, producers, consultants all apply their skill and creativity to fulfilling a brief set by their client. The amount of autonomy they have in doing this will depend on the project, the client and the relationship they have with them.

Self-employment is often a necessity rather than a choice in creative production. If you want to work in film or theatre production, or as a writer, photographer or actor, to name but a few occupations, there is little alternative. However, not every job in the creative industries can be undertaken on a self-employed basis. Certain criteria will need to be met, as defined by the national tax authorities. The UK government, for example, offers the following general guidelines on the HM Revenue and Customs website (www.hmrc.gov.uk/):

> If the answer is 'Yes' to all of the following questions, it will usually mean that the worker is self-employed:
>
> Can they hire someone to do the work or engage helpers at their own expense?

key areas of transformation in recent years has been in the area of intellectual property, as Carole discussed above. With many more **platforms** on which to license the use of their intellectual property, the value of IPR has risen, leading to the increased use of the term 'content industries' to designate those industries which produce and license content, such as publishing, film, TV, games, etc. Significantly, it is a term that ignores traditional media-specific industry divisions, acknowledging their actual or future convergence.

A company, whose approach to content creation and licensing has moved beyond traditional boundaries in the development of a particular value proposition is Pearson PLC. Pearson owns the well-known **imprint** Penguin (as part of the Penguin Group) and the *Financial Times*. In the 1990s it expanded from print publishing into audiovisual media production and broadcasting. However, it then sold these interests in the early years of the twenty-first century to focus instead on education. As well as owning a number of textbook imprints, Pearson also owns education testing and assessment technologies and offers a cross-platform range of teaching and learning resources to teachers and students. In 2012, its main company website was promoting education as its core provision, the mission statement on its home page stating that:

Pearson Publishing provides schools, colleges and other educational settings with a wide range of products and services using a combination of print, fixed electronic media, online technologies and face-to-face delivery. (Pearson 2012)

Thus, although the company still calls itself Pearson *Publishing*, Pearson is in fact positioning itself as a provider of **platform-agnostic** content, independent of any one platform, medium or technology. Media platforms and technologies may come and go, but the demand for education is not reliant on any one of them. It is, however, a potentially high growth area, offering much scope for both technological enhancement through new media platforms and technologies and international expansion.

Pearson's business model has thus evolved substantially over the last 20 years, with digital technology a significant factor in its evolution. Indeed, digital technologies have had a great impact across the whole of the creative industries and facilitated new business models, such as those of social media companies like YouTube, Facebook and Twitter, which provide platforms for sharing content, rather than content itself. Recognizing and exploiting the reciprocal value of customer information that Jansen et al. discuss above, these companies have evolved the TV and print media revenue model of selling audiences to advertisers into a far more fine-grained exercise of data-collection, data-mining and selling, which is still emergent and controversial.

As we will also go on to discuss in Chapters 10 and 11, digital technologies have equally revolutionized distribution of creative products, inspiring creative producers, particularly musicians, to operate direct-to-customer business models, cutting out traditional commissioners and distributors.

Do they risk their own money?

Do they provide the main items of equipment they need to do their job, not just the small tools that many employees provide for themselves?

Do they agree to do a job for a fixed price regardless of how long the job may take?

Can they decide what work to do, how and when to do the work and where to provide the services?

Do they regularly work for a number of different people?

Do they have to correct unsatisfactory work in their own time and at their own expense? (HMRC 2012)

Details vary from country to country and more detailed criteria will be available from the relevant tax authority on request. But even these general guidelines make clear that junior positions, such as runner, production assistant and other assistant roles are not legally recognized as open to self-employment. Workers in these positions can only have employed status. This means that their income will be taxed at source and they will not be able to claim expenses and other deductions against income.

A **limited company** (**corporation** in the US) has an independent legal entity from its owners, which means that, unlike sole traders and most partnerships, the owners of a limited company do not have unlimited liability for its debts. Their liability is limited to the value of the shares that they have in the company and does not extend to their personal assets.

When the founders set up the company they determine the **share** that each holds in the company. Since shares are created by dividing up the total capital of the company, their respective share will often be determined by the amount of capital each has put into the company. However, it may equally be that a founder brings another kind of value to the company, such as skill or contacts, and this will be translated into monetary value to determine their share. The value of the ownership of these shares is known as equity. Many SMEs, as well as larger companies, choose to operate as limited companies.

In small companies the shareholders may be one or two people, the original founders. The owners/shareholders may also be the company directors, who are responsible for the management of the company. However, the shareholders and the directors may equally be different people. Whether or not the directors are also the owners, the company, as an independent legal entity, will employ the directors as employees. They will not have self-employed status.

As a company grows, it may raise finance for expansion by selling shares to investors. Investors will invest in a company because this will earn them a percentage of the company's profits, based on the shares that they hold. This income is known as dividends. In a large company there may be many shareholders. Very large companies may also choose to become publicly traded companies. This means that their stocks and shares are available for sale to the general public, usually through a stock exchange.

A limited company offers protection from unlimited losses and is more conducive to investment and growth, since it can widen ownership and raise finance through offering equity participation to investors. However, it is more costly and time consuming to set up and is subject to more regulation and scrutiny than sole trader or partnership structures and involves the filing of public records. Thus many creative businesses find operating as a sole trader or partnership better suits their aims and needs, despite the unlimited liability these structures carry.

However, as well as facilitating new business models, digital technologies also facilitate, indeed often necessitate, the evolution of existing ones and are of increasing strategic importance to all businesses. For example, Robin's business model has always combined mail order with retail, but now, with online selling, the mail order element has become much more central to the business and has been its main engine of expansion in the last couple of years. Robin says that this has been a welcome but also necessary development, allowing him to both meet the changing expectations of customers and also ride out a global recession by expanding his international reach and managing to grow, rather than shrink, his customer base.

PEST: POLITICAL, ECONOMIC, SOCIAL AND TECHNOLOGICAL FACTORS

Technology is not of course the only factor affecting creative businesses and business models. It is one of four factors considered in the PEST analysis, which is often carried out as part of business strategy. Besides technological analysis, a PEST analysis considers how local and global Political, Economic, Social and Technological factors might impact on a business (Tench and Yeomans 2009: 21). These are all important to consider, although not always easy to predict. Robin's shoemaking and retail business provides a good example. He started the business in the 1980s in a boom period, subletting space from a clothes retailer in a popular shopping street of a vibrant university town that is home to many creative and media professionals. Both economic and social factors thus worked in his favour. Even the recession of the early 1990s had a positive impact, since it put rents down and allowed him to rent his own premises in the same street for a knock-down rent. The global tendency to relocate manufacturing from Europe to Asia was also beneficial, since it made shoe factories in Portugal – a big centre for shoe manufacturing, which suffered in the move – more ready to manufacture shoes for him at cost-effective rates. Now, on the other hand, Robin says, some of the manufacturing contracts are beginning to shift back from Asia to Portugal, making it harder for him to get good deals for his shoe orders and causing him to look elsewhere.

PEST factors do not stay still; they need to be constantly analyzed and strategy evolved accordingly (Fifield 2008). Furthermore, the different factors are hard to disentangle from each other. Politics and economics, for example, come together in government economic policy. As mentioned above, governments may, for example, subsidize or otherwise support certain industry sectors or decide to incentivize business in certain geographical areas. This has been very much in evidence in the creative industries, where national and local government policy has often focused on **regeneration** of former manufacturing towns or regions by encouraging new growth in the creative sector to replace the declining or defunct

Regeneration: The economic and social transformation of urban areas through investment, infrastructure (communication, transportation, etc.), building projects and new institutions. It can be seen as the development of post-industrial cities, where the local economy has stagnated after key industries have failed or moved out of the area. Regeneration is about finding something else for entire cities to do, and helping them do it. *How* that help might work has been controversial, with many different approaches adopted by governments (Evans 2003, 2009; Pratt 2007). The creative industries have sometimes been seen as a driver of such regeneration projects, for example in the way that the BBC's operations have been relocated to regional centres such as Glasgow or Salford. However, the risks of regeneration (itself often measured in rising real estate values) include loss of affordable housing and increased gentrification (in which well-off professionals move into improved areas, leaving the less-well-off to move elsewhere) (Oakley 2006). See also **Creative clusters.**

Creative clusters: The concept of the creative cluster is based on the more general concept of business clusters (Porter 2005), and its application to the creative industries, for example media clusters (Karlsson and Picard 2011). The fact that particular and related industry sectors tend to cluster together is seen to offer advantages, such as a ready labour pool and supply chain, an established customer base or lower business-to-business (B2B) transaction costs. Furthermore, as both Pratt (2004, 2009) and van Heur (2009) have pointed out, other benefits, such as social networks and informal sharing of knowledge may be equally important advantages.

The idea of the creative cluster has come to be closely associated with **regeneration** initiatives, in that government economic policy has often been to attempt to establish creative clusters to replace the manufacturing clusters that have either declined or relocated from inner-city areas. This approach mimics the phenomenon whereby artists, attracted by large spaces they can use as studios and low rents, have tended to gravitate to former industrial quarters as places to work and live. In cities such as New York (Zukin 1982), Chicago (Lloyd 2010) and London (Pratt 2009) this led to a rejuvenation of these areas, attracting galleries, restaurants, bars and other business investment, as well as the arrival of the 'creative classes', as defined by Florida, as residents.

However, there are problems with this approach. One is that such policies may well be over-ambitious or optimistic in what they can achieve. In the UK, for example, the tendency has been to promote creative clusters as both an engine of economic growth and a force for social regeneration. Taking as a model the artist-driven regeneration examples cited above, creative clusters are seen as a way to generate community well-being and cohesion as well as wealth and employment. However, where such clusters do achieve a high level of investment and growth, the evidence is in fact that this drives up the price of rents and property, meaning that the arrival of the creative classes actually means that low-income residents and businesses are forced out, a process known as **gentrification**. Successful creative clusters, such as Silicon Valley in California, Wicker Park in Chicago, or Hoxton in London, might be seen in fact to be associated with economic and social inequality, since, while they generate wealth, they do not spread it across the wider community (Evans 2009; Pratt 2009; Lloyd 2010).

manufacturing base.[1] Florida's concept of the creative class, which was discussed in Chapter 1, has been influential in much government policy and regeneration strategies, although it has generated sharp criticism. So too has the concept of **creative clusters,** which focuses on the way that related businesses tend to cluster in particular areas, turning them into centres of production and consumption for particular industrial sectors. Although both these concepts have been extensively critiqued (Pratt 2004, 2008, 2009; Evans 2009; van Heur 2009), they still have currency in government policy for the creative industries, for which many examples of both success and failure can be cited.

CLUSTERING AND THE SENSE OF CREATIVE COMMUNITY

While government policy tends to focus on the potential of the creative industries to drive local, national and international wealth and job creation, not all creative activity is market facing. Creative practitioners may in fact value creative clusters as environments in which it is possible for them to operate in an alternative economy, different from that of monetary exchange value (van Heur 2009; Pratt 2009), for example, enjoying the community, inspiration and support of fellow practitioners. Rachel is a writer and storyteller whose

---

[1]In many cases the manufacturing base may have moved to a region or country with lower labour costs, rather than disappeared altogether. At the end of the twentieth century there was a large-scale shift of Western manufacturing operations to the developing world, particular Asia.

creative practice encompasses both paid and unpaid activities. She has lived for over 10 years in what she calls a "vibrant creative community" (Hackney, East London – see Pratt 2009 for a detailed case study of the Hoxton creative cluster, based in the borough of Hackney), which she says facilitates both these aspects:

> "It's quite a loose community but it's part of a wide network of artists and creatives who live and work in that area who are my friends socially but who I also work with and collaborate with and to be honest it's quite a seamless relationship between social and professional work because you work with your friends and friendships grow out of work situations. The more projects you work on the more people you meet, the wider the network becomes. The greater the spectrum of creatives you're meeting and the more people you meet the more you get approached to do things the more it feeds into your own ideas. You're definitely being fed... you know you're putting into it and you're getting out of it. It's a constant flow of exchange, creative exchange... I think one of the benefits of being part of a community of artists is back to this idea of skillshare and collaboration. And I think that's where, if you're not working in isolation, it's easier to get together with a bunch of people and put on an event than work on your own and everybody's wanting to do interesting, exciting creative things." (Rachel, 2011)

Here Rachel is invoking the kinds of social networks and informal knowledge transfer associated with business clusters, which is particularly vital in the development of **creative clusters**. This kind of environment means that it's possible to get artistic projects off the ground, without always needing to make a profit from them or secure private or public funding. While cheap

Critics have also argued that the focus on creative clusters has oversimplified the complex relationships and networks that link creative organizations. This has often engendered a 'build it and they will come' approach, in which the assumption has been that if an area is developed as a creative quarter, it will automatically fill up with creative individuals and businesses and make money, no matter when or where it is built. Such an approach ignores the particularities of history and geography of country, region and industry sector, as well as the different structures, networks and cultures that characterize them (Pratt 2004; Evans 2009; van Heur 2009; Lloyd 2010). Hoxton in East London, for example, which emerged as a creative cluster for music, visual arts and then new media in the 1990s, had a long history of marginality from the City of London authorities and had been a site of "various 'undesirable' activities (social, economic and environmental) from noxious manufacturing to illegal trading and prostitution" (Pratt 2009: 1045). As well as being a site of social deprivation, it was also one of entertainment: "prostitution, drinking and the establishment of England's first theatre" (Pratt 2009: 1053). Pratt argues that Hoxton's particular history as a liminal space of unregulated and marginal activity was crucial to its late twentieth-century incarnation as a location first for punk music and then the visual arts. He also points out that the development of the area as a centre for artists to live and work was effected through social networks that "were not self-generated but migrated towards it" (Pratt 2009: 1055). In particular, he cites the Royal College of Art and Goldsmith's College, whose networks of graduates were looking for cheap space. Thus the development of the area as a creative cluster was both related to its particular history and location and to factors external to the area.

Van Heur (2009) also relates a complex web of factors contributing to East Berlin's development as a music industry cluster. In his view, the term 'creative cluster' is an attempt to define and regulate creative activity in purely economic terms, which, since it ignores the more complex networks at play, is unlikely to provide a successful basis for economic policy. In short, while most commentators agree that the phenomenon of creative clusters can be empirically observed, there is wide disagreement about what causes them, how they might be encouraged and sustained and what social and economic benefits they might bring. Recommended reading: Charlie Karlsson and Robert G. Picard, *Media Clusters: Spatial Agglomeration and Content Capabilities* (2011); Terry Flew, *The Creative Industries: Culture and Policy* (2012).

space and proximity to central amenities may have attracted the first artists to East London, those who followed came also because it offered them both a community and an audience. The people who put on the exhibitions and performances are the same people who come and see them – because they have a creative interest and because they also want to make sure that others attend their own events. Thus a lively arts scene of free or low-cost exhibitions, performances and other creative activity can sustain itself outside the commercial marketplace. A **gift economy** is in operation in which creative practitioners will give their time, attention and sometimes money freely to others, without expecting to receive something immediately in return. Instead a culture of mutual responsibility and indebtedness is established, strengthening the bonds felt between each member of the community and their commitment to the community as a whole.

For Rachel, participation in this community is about "living and working as a creative," which cuts across boundaries of art and commerce and paid and unpaid activity, but necessitates living in a creative environment full of likeminded people who are taking the same approach. Echoing Lloyd's (2010) perception of the interrelatedness of bohemia and commerce, she doesn't see it as impossible for these economies to co-exist, in fact she sees it as both inevitable and productive:

> "You know where the art is the money follows... the idea of art and culture being a commodity... it's inevitable. You can't be too purist about it... So, when you're working on a commercial project you know that you're doing it for the money. When you're working on your own project you know that it can be quite pure. And rather than see the two things in conflict, see them as part of the bigger picture which is living and working as a creative. So you might spend weeks doing largely commercial work, which are going to pay your rent but which might also take you in interesting directions in terms of your art practice and introduce you to other people who it might be interesting to collaborate with or who bring new ideas.... You're shifting between creative contexts and commercial contexts, but the idea is to try and do it on your own terms where possible.... The fact is you're operating in an area of great flux and uncertainty and change. And that's part of the creative practice. You don't want to get too comfortable to be honest. So it's about developing ways to manage that and I think there are various approaches you need to find the approach that suits you. But I think it's about managing the flux, rather than trying to impose a kind of balance or equilibrium on it." (Rachel, 2011)

For Rachel, participating in this creative cluster offers the possibility of both economic benefit and personal creative fulfilment, which sometimes overlap but sometimes are separate. Commercial paid work enables her to pay the rent and other necessities, while the artistic gift economy enables her to realize less commercial creative projects. Her writing practice is wide-ranging:

> "I have written a novel and I'm involved in a number of other kind of creative writing projects. I occasionally write essays on art, usually on commission.... I've also been commissioned by the advertising agency Mother to write a series of essays on contemporary ideas in culture. So writer encompasses novelist, essayist and other creative writing projects. In addition to being a writer, I'm also a curator. I curate children's literacy programmes for literature festivals. So that means curating programmes of storytellers and children's authors to do reading. Also curating workshops and interactive storytelling games and interactive activities, which the children participate in.... I've got my own storytelling project, which is kind of the umbrella I operate under. It's called 'Don't tell stories' and Don't tell stories encompasses my own practice, which is doing performative readings of my own work, in collaboration with artists and musicians to create theatrical storytelling spaces for adults." (Rachel, 2011)

She has observed a change in the area:

> "It's becoming more affluent and the irony being that rents are becoming prohibitive and artists are less able to afford cheap studio space, especially because of the Olympics as well, that's driving up costs in the area. Also, I guess once you get any kind of art movement you get hangers on, which does kind of dilute it.... But I think it's easy to be cynical. There are so many interesting projects, community projects, art projects happening in East London. I think it's a very credible and exciting place... there are positives and benefits and I would say the positives outweigh the negatives." (Rachel, 2011)

Rachel has not yet found herself priced out by **gentrification** and it would seem that, for her, market-oriented and non-market-oriented creative activity are actually co-constructive. This is made possible by the particular creative cluster in which she lives and works. Its culture is one that sustains her in different ways. The significance that particular cultures can have for people working in the creative industries is something that we will go on to explore in more detail in the next chapter, when we will investigate work cultures in the creative industries.

SUMMARY

In this chapter we have examined some of the ways in which individuals and organizations make money and build businesses from creative activities and products, and considered the main legal frameworks in which these businesses operate. We have also investigated similarities and differences between creative businesses and businesses in other sectors. In particular, we have considered the prevalence of microbusinesses, the overlaps between culture and commerce and the importance of IPR in creative business practice. We have considered the concept of the creative cluster and the significance of location to creative business success, and also investigated the way that political, economic, social and technological factors can impact on creative businesses and business models. The creative professionals that we have heard from have all emphasized the fact that the business environment in which they operate is subject to both local and global change and that creative businesses need to evolve and find new and innovative strategies to respond to this change. As well as producing creative products and supplying creative services, creative businesses, large and small, also need to be creative in the way that they develop their business model and manage their business operations.

RECOMMENDED READING

Burns, Paul. 2011. *Entrepreneurship and Small Business: Start-up, Growth and Maturity*. Basingstoke: Palgrave Macmillan. A lively and informative introduction to small business and entrepreneurship.

Caldwell, John Thornton. 2008. *Production Culture: Industrial Reflexivity and Critical Practice in Film and Television*. Durham, NC: Duke University Press. Focused on the US film and TV industries, highly informative and well researched.

Intellectual Property Office website (www.ipo.gov.uk). Good resource for entrepreneurs and professionals on issues related to patents, trademarks, copyright and design.

Karlsson, Charlie and Robert G. Picard. 2011. *Media Clusters: Spatial Agglomeration and Content Capabilities*. Cheltenham: Edward Elgar. A study of how and why media firms tend to cluster together; international in scope, with detailed studies of national contexts and media markets.

Lloyd, R. 2010. *Neo-Bohemia, Art and Commerce in the Postindustrial City* (2nd edition). New York/London: Routledge. A detailed and insightful case study of Wicker Park, the Chicago West Side music and visual arts creative cluster, which expands on many points of general relevance to the relationship between art and commerce in the creative industries.

Powdthavee, Nick. 2010. *The Happiness Equation: The Surprising Economics of Our Most Valuable Asset*. London: Icon Books. An accessible introduction to "happiness economics" and how it applies to everyday life.

Pratt, Andy C. 2009. "Urban Regeneration: From the Arts 'Feel Good' Factor to the Cultural Economy: A Case Study of Hoxton, London." *Urban Studies* 46 (5–6):

1041–1062. An informative, critical case study of the recent history of Hoxton, a London neighbourhood currently associated with a range of creative industries, from arts to advertising.

Sandel, Michael J. 2012. *What Money Can't Buy: The Moral Limits of Markets*. New York: Farrar, Straus & Giroux. The value we place on things, places, people and relationships as distinct from economic values.

5

Work Routines and Work Cultures

From the business of creativity we turn our attention to the work routines and practices of creative workers. In this chapter we consider the differences between the work cultures experienced by *employees*, whose stable, enduring relationship with an employer is different from that of *freelancers*, who work on a short-term basis, usually on a specific project, and most typically have a relationship with a client rather than an employer. It is, of course, possible to be both an employee and a freelancer at the same time, as with *portfolio workers* who combine short-term or part-time employment with freelance project-work – instead of having a single job, they have a portfolio combining a job (or jobs) with other projects or "gigs".

Whether one makes a living through a job, projects or a mixed portfolio of work, certain skills and activities are important for all. We consider the importance of teamwork, collegial networking, and the crucial question for newcomers of how to get "a foot in the door". Therefore, we look at key aspects of creative industries culture: *networking*; building a professional *profile* for oneself: and *internships*, work experience and other forms of "free labour". These practices underline the fact that experience tends to be valued over formal qualifications in many sectors of the creative industries. Finally, we consider the question of whether the creative industries offer their workers *equality of opportunity*, with an eye to the role of work cultures in relation to this question.

EMPLOYEES: STAFFERS, IN-HOUSE WORKERS

We start by considering employees in creative businesses who have stable "standard jobs" (Osnowitz 2010: 6) which involve an ongoing, long-term contractual relationship with an employer, possibly even a whole career spent within one company or institution. This is, in other words, the established sense of "having a job", going out to work at a specific workplace which is separated from one's home.

Cultures of the workplace

As we've seen in the previous chapter, location, involvement in a creative cluster and being part of a particular cultural community can be important to the success of a creative business. Culture also plays a role *within* each company, since creative businesses establish their own individual workplace cultures as well as participating in wider sector, regional, national and indeed global cultures. Such cultures play a vital role in attracting workers to the creative industries. Perhaps the most obvious example is the reputation for glamour and excitement that attaches to the creative industries – the "glamour industries" (Frederick 2003). The glitzy world of show business and the high status awarded to artists, musicians and other creative people exerts a strong attraction. Many well-qualified graduates compete to pursue a career in the creative sector, despite qualifications that might possibly earn them higher salaries and higher status work in other professions, as Carole explains:

> "These days every entry level person that comes in has got a degree. Every single person who works for me, even the most junior, is practically over-qualified because it's a business that people think is glamorous. I can tell you right now it isn't. There are glamorous bits to it, but those are add-ons and the working day isn't 9–5… You know I left here at seven o'clock last night and my contracts manager was still here. That's not at all unusual. I think everybody here likes the product that we work on – books. It's not the highest paid industry." (Carole, 2011)

In publishing, as well as across the creative industries, it is the norm to work for long hours, and most workers do not receive high levels of pay. Freelance rates tend to be higher than employee rates, but this is because freelance work is seasonal rather than guaranteed 52 weeks of the year.

Consequently, in Carole's business, as in many others, level of pay is not what primarily motivates and satisfies workers; rather, the creative and cultural benefits that they perceive in the work keep them in the job. Even if you are not actually a celebrity – an actor or a rock star or a famous writer – a little bit of their aura seems to rub off on those who participate in the world that they inhabit (Rojek 2001; Turner 2004). Even if you have a low-paid, low-status job, you are part of a high-status, glamorous industry, where money is lavished on parties, festivals, previews, etc. and some people do actually attain fabulous wealth – what Caves (2000) calls the "winner-takes-all" character of many creative activities. Many entrants to the creative industries may aspire one day to be one of those people. Others may be satisfied with making a living from something they enjoy both personally and socially. As Carole points out, people want to work in the creative industries because they love the products and want to be involved in their creation, a perception borne out by Hesmondhalgh and Baker's (2010) interviews with workers in TV, music and magazine industries, for whom the enjoyment of the autonomy and freedom associated with much cultural work is mixed with anxiety and even a sense of victimization because of the way pleasure and obligation blurs together – as we shall see later on when we consider the role of sociability and networking for creative workers.

We might say that this aura of glamour and status is part of the global culture of the creative industries. However, local cultures are also significant to people's experience of work. As we saw in the last chapter, Carole sees staff satisfaction as crucial to her business success and she puts a lot of time into arranging social events to encourage a sense of collectivity:

> "We're always thinking up ideas of what shall we do for our next company outing… We went on the London Eye once, which was just a very short precursor to a five-hour lunch… There are groups of staff who've become very close friends with each other. They go to each others' houses for dinner and things like that. So I like that. I think you have to try and run a happy group. We're all working on top of each other." (Carole, 2011)

Robin also emphasizes the role of workplace culture in motivating and retaining staff at his shoe business. He explains how there are various landmarks that are part of the rhythm of the business year, which become social as well as business occasions.

> "There's all these things throughout the year, which are little traditions… part of the fun of working in a small business… the free shoes in February and we have Summer of Love in the summer, which is like a summer Christmas meal. We have the stock take, which is… I think, it's fun, it's a bit different… we all get to eat junk food and it's kind of a fun day." (Robin, 2011)

For Robin, it's important that his company is "a nice place to work". He believes that the sense of belonging is very much related to the small size of the business:

> "Being this size is family. There's eight of us who work here… in total. All part-timers. Bigger isn't better… I guess you get that in any organization… you get your immediate circle. But I think once it gets bigger than a certain size, you have to sort of divide don't you… [This company] it's a nice little cell to be in and I don't want to make it bigger." (Robin, 2011)

As we learnt in Chapter 4, in Robin's case the company's ethos is a work-life balance in which working long hours are not in fact the norm. Robin himself only works four days a week, and one of the reasons why people want to work at Robin's business is that it gives them the freedom to pursue other things in their life apart from work.

"Good work" and "bad work"

The concept of job quality, or simply the difference between a "good" and "bad" job, is not as simple as it looks. We might be tempted to equate a good job simply with measurable attributes such as earnings, benefits (e.g., holiday, sick pay, pension), and the educational level required for the job. However, there are elements that are far harder to measure that matter a great deal: the variety of tasks involved, the level of personal initiative possible, the degree of participation at work, opportunities for personal and professional development, as well as job security (Sengupta, Edwards, and Tsai 2009: 28). Creative workers value the autonomy, creativity and excitement that attach to "cool jobs" that can be as different as fashion modelling and web design (Neff, Wissinger, and Zukin 2005). This question of what counts as a "good job" matters a great deal in the creative industries, not least because the personal and professional identities of creative workers are so intertwined, as Hesmondhalgh and Baker point out in their book *Creative Labour* (2011). Several key characteristics that they enumerate in their discussion of the concept of "good work" match those listed by Carole and Robin as important to their employees' job satisfaction and as part of the culture of their business. These include interest, involvement, sociality, and work-life balance.

"Bad" work, on the other hand, tends to be characterized by features such as monotony (a lack of variety, doing the same tasks over and over), boredom, isolation and overwork (Hesmondhalgh and Baker 2011: 39). Such features are clearly not dependent purely on the content (i.e., what it is that the workers make) or the specific industry sector they work in, but also on the way that the work is organized. While Carole and Robin each emphasize different features, both have definite views on what constitutes good work and how they try to develop a work culture that achieves this. The work cultures they describe emphasize both the importance of feeling part of a community and sharing a common experience and of feeling valued and fulfilled as an individual.

Advertising director, Chris, is also very clear about the particular kind of culture he wants to create in his company. He says of himself and his partners in the business that: "We only want to work with people we like to work with and have a good time. We want to be small and keep them (i.e., their directors) all working" (Chris, 2011). He contrasts this with the larger company where he himself worked previously as a contract director. This company had a huge 'stable' of freelancers on standby, each of which might not get work for months. Chris says his company motto is to "take the work seriously but not ourselves" (Chris, 2011). In order to foster a sense of community, Chris and his partners in the company order lunch every day to the office, which everyone eats together. He says he wants to create an informal workplace culture, which does not require people to clock in at 9am: "Everyone knows what they have to get done in what time frame, they have autonomy in how they do that" (Chris, 2011).

Autonomy is another of the key characteristics of good work (Hesmondhalgh and Baker 2011). This kind of work culture offers people both more freedom and more responsibility. It is not the kind of workplace where you can while away the work day on social media sites, planning your weekend, organizing your holidays, etc. What is required of you is not to be in the workplace a set number of hours each day, but to achieve a particular brief in a particular time frame. Autonomy therefore does not mean less work, but rather more flexibility in how you execute it.

The people we have heard from so far are all from small businesses, and they tend to extol the particular small business culture they belong to, each of which is quite distinct and yet shares with the others the particular benefits of being small. However, large organizations also actively seek to create a sense of shared culture and community, as well as personal and professional development, among their employees. Ian, a web applications development producer in BBC Learning, says that the BBC's programme of talks, workshops and events for staff is something that he appreciates. They are internal events, usually featuring speakers from within the organization, and may cover a huge range of topics, including a wide variety of creative or technical skills, specialist equipment or aspects of programme making. Ian says that "every other week I go to a lunchtime talk" (Ian, 2011). He values the chance to develop his professional knowledge and skills and also to meet other BBC workers, outside his immediate team, expanding his social and professional knowledge and reach within the organization. Similar, more sustained advantages are offered by the BBC's system of attachments. These are temporary internal secondments, advertised internally, which BBC staff can apply for and which are intended to "cross-fertilize ideas and develop careers" (Ian, 2011) within the organization. Ian recently spent eight months on an attachment at the BBC World Service working on a web project with them.

Many large organizations, both public and private, will tend to commit some of their resources to similar activities. These ideally achieve the multiple purpose of strengthening employees' loyalty, ensuring cohesion and communication of best practice across the organization, and developing the professional skills of their staff. One of the things that workers value highly in an organization is the sense that it offers them room to develop personally and professionally – to "keep up" with developments in their field (Kotamraju 2006). As well as the attributes of "good work" we looked at earlier, it may be equally important to workers that they can move on from their current position to gain higher skills and knowledge, to achieve promotion to more senior positions, or perhaps move sideways into a position that allows them to use or develop different skills. Radio producer, Kevin, describes how his broadcasting company allows producers what he calls "internal sabbaticals" where they are released from working full-time on the regular daily programmes to work on their own programme idea, which they are passionate about. Kevin sees this as an important practice for both the broadcaster and the individual producer, in that it allows the producer to make their creative mark and develop their career and profile and also encourages innovation and new ideas in programme-making for the organization.

In a large organization, this kind of personal and professional development is often discussed and planned as part of a staff appraisal, in which an employee will discuss their performance and their progress with their **line manager**. An appraisal is meant to have the dual purpose of making sure that the employee meets their manager's expectations and also that they are achieving their own goals. Its success in achieving both aspects is likely to be dependent on the approach of the individual manager and the workplace culture as a whole. Many employees might feel that appraisals largely focus on whether the employee is meeting managerial expectations. However, in Kevin's case, he is clear that the appraisal puts a lot of emphasis on his own personal development and fulfilment:

> "Basically, there's a formal process where different aspects of your performance are graded... but what seems to be more active in a small tight-knit environment like this is the conversation with your line manager where they would say are you happy with what you're doing now, are you happy that you're managing to strike a balance between work and all of life outside work? Do you need specific training that would help you do your job more efficiently? Are you bored and is there some new challenge you'd like to take up, and is there some idea that you've been holding back? Would you like to write it up and send me a page about a new series?" (Kevin, 2010)

Kevin clearly sees it as very much part of the culture of his workplace to focus on the personal and professional development of its employees.

Sometimes it may be easier for larger organizations to offer their employees professional development and career progression than it is for small ones. Large companies can afford to provide external or in-house training and secondments, which smaller companies may not have the resources for. They also may offer more opportunity for promotion or a change in job role. As Carole explains:

> "I've had to accept that in a small company there are some jobs that can't change. So our previous contracts manager left after three years, which was about the period I would have expected... She went to a much, much bigger agency, where she could be given a selling role as well. Now our contract manager's job here is and always is going to be just doing contracts. We can't change it because the company isn't big enough." (Carole, 2011)

However, in other cases, small companies may themselves offer more flexibility and variation in job role than larger companies, as Chris described above in relation to his ad agency. There are no rules set in stone, but there are clearly going to be differences in organizational cultures between a company of eight employees and a company of 800.

Corporate culture

Most organizations see it as important that employees understand and buy into the corporate identity of the organization that employs them, since alienated employees are unlikely to excel in selling the organization's products or services to the customer. Nor are they going to be motivated to give their all to any other aspect of the business. In some sectors, of course, monetary incentives are used to motivate employees. People in sales often work on commission, for example. However, in the corporate strategy of large organizations, "employee engagement" beyond financial incentives is increasingly seen as an important factor in the productivity and success of an organization.

Consequently, corporations seek to define and manage not only *what* people do in their jobs but the *meaning* of what they do and to promote "self-actualization within the attitudinal framework of the company" (Julier 2008: 198). In other words, the most successful attempts to build corporate identity manage to imbue the experience of working at the company with particular values and succeed in collapsing or at least blurring the distinction between personal and corporate identity, so that the employee feels that their personal identity is actualized through the company that they work for.

We have already seen that this is what is going on in the businesses that we looked at above: Carole mentions how her employees are close friends as well as employees; Robin stresses the sense of family and how quality of life and work-life balance are part of what makes his company a nice place to work; Chris stresses the importance of fun and personal freedom as core experiences of the workplace. The experience of self-actualization is also present in the accounts given by Ian and Kevin of the way that they are able to achieve personal and professional development as part of their job.

However, can Kevin and Ian, working for large organizations, in which they cannot know everyone, possibly feel the same sense of collective identity as those employed in small businesses? The analogy of the family, which Robin uses, cannot apply. Even with the built-in advantage of the glamour that automatically attaches to the creative industries, compared to other business sectors, achieving a strong and positive collective identity among all the employees of a large national or international organization is a complex undertaking. As Julier explains, large corporations address this by building their **brands** internally, among their own employees. The various elements of the material environment of a company – its location, office layout and décor, its dress code, down to its logo and typeface – act as signifiers of this identity. A company's management style, working hours and other aspects of its culture are also signifying practices, which form an important part of this brand identity. Through such strategies a company will seek to engineer the relationship of the employee to the brand in the same way as they seek to engineer the customer's relationship to it:

> Internal brand building draws a closer relationship between the employee and the products or services it purveys and ultimately a closer relationship to its audience. It may therefore put the employee in the shoes of the consumer. Put otherwise, it aspires to inculcating an emotional investment in, as well as intellectual knowledge of, what it is hoped that the consumer eventually experiences. (Julier 2008: 192)

Teamworking

One of the reasons why organizations in the creative industries want to create a sense of collective purpose and engagement is that they are important to successful teamworking. While "creative originals" such as artists and writers tend to be either individuals or small teams, most of the output of the creative industries involves the coordinated efforts of large teams of people. Whether the aim is to produce a newspaper or a film, develop an advertising campaign or a computer game, the work is done in teams.

Within large organizations in the creative industries, workers will often identify most closely with smaller collective identities – that of their particular department or workgroup or team. As radio producer, Kevin, explains, a collective purpose and/or identity and strong bonds of trust are often vital to the successful outcome of a project.

> "In a media organization you have to respect deadlines first and foremost. That means that very often, getting ready for a live show or whatever, you're in such a complex tangle of cooperation that it requires that the dialogue over the desks is informal. It's at the speed that friends talk to each other… people work so fast on things together that equality seems to be a precondition of getting the work done." (Kevin, 2010)

This kind of high-speed collective working relies on the team knowing how each other think:

> "The team at first learns how to collaborate… they learn that the word black might mean different things to five different people and once that's overcome people are much more able to cooperate with each other, they kind of assume the best of each other… It's basically just that some of the words you use mean different things to different people. And then when that trust is built up the team becomes way less formal and capable of solving problems much faster because they spot things that are like a mistake of two months ago early in the life of the programme and they basically cut off that problem before it becomes any worse… or the flipside of that is that they've learned you can do a really excellent programme exploring a different theme each week with music, say, which sounded like an outsider idea at the start but it worked well and it didn't take too much work so that's sort of part of their repertoire of winning formulas… and also a shorthand as well… you know 'will we do the music thing' will be what's said and it will denote 'will we bring a guest in to discuss a certain theme in the human condition using music to illustrate what they're talking about?'… The team then finds it way easier to deal with the stresses and demands of serving up a programme everyday." (Kevin, 2010)

However, Kevin acknowledges that there may also be a downside to a team becoming too comfortable in working together:

> "There might be some kind of atrophy where the team isn't so open to doing crazy things because they think that they've written a recipe… But what you learn is that that plateau is actually something to be afraid of because you're in some sort of coma of suspended animation, thinking everything's going great and you've maybe lost your perspective to see how things are stale." (Kevin, 2010)

But people need to feel secure in a creative team in order to take creative risks:

> "The radio producer is not kind of availing of some kind of hierarchical status. It's more like they're good at saying things that put people at their ease… so [creating] a genuine group brain that is generating ideas so people aren't fearful of how they'll sound." (Kevin, 2010)

Like Kevin, TV drama executive producer Anne emphasizes the importance of collaboration both for successfully making a product and for the job satisfaction of those involved:

> "Behind every drama there's a team. It's never down to one person. It is a very, very collaborative process. Whoever comes up with the initial idea, whether it's the writer, the executive producer, the director, you know, whoever it is, it is always a very collaborative process and that's part of the joy of being involved in it I think." (Anne, 2011)

Successful teamwork produces the sociality that we discussed earlier as an element of good work, even without the kind of organized social events that Carole mentions. Strong bonds are created between people when they share an intense and challenging experience and these bonds are an important part of the joy of collaboration of which Anne speaks. Creative workers also testify to the fact that such work relationships can also lead to long-lasting friendships outside work (Hesmondalgh and Baker 2011: 152).

As producer and executive producer, both Kevin and Anne have managerial roles in the team. Their job involves steering the workflow of other team members, as well as making creative decisions on the product itself. However, they both choose to downplay their place in the hierarchy. The emphasis they put on collaboration and consensus is characteristic of managerial styles in the creative industries. It is not that hierarchies are absent in the creative industries, but that the management style tends to be one of negotiation, rather than command and control. Within highly skilled and self-motivated teams, the authority of those in managerial roles (such as producers, directors, editors, etc.) often rests on their ability to understand and participate in the creative process and "to form administrative systems that impinge as lightly as possible on the labour process" (McKinlay and Smith 2009: 30). Since team members retain control over their specialist knowledge and skills, their work cannot be too tightly monitored and regulated. Managers are likely to get better results from their team through according its members trust and autonomy, rather than enforcing rigid and hierarchical lines of command.

In some sectors of the creative industries this kind of collaborative participation in and understanding of the creative process may be aided by the fact that managers may have arrived at their position through a career as a "creative". In radio or television, for example, many, though by no means all, senior managers in the production division will have arrived at their position through a career in programme-making. However, managers' perspectives on their role may not always perfectly coincide with those they manage. Hesmondhalgh and Baker cite an executive producer of a TV talent show whose account of her relationship with the production team "portrayed a democratic relationship" which was not shared by the production team (Hesmondalgh and Baker 2011: 169). Hesmondhalgh and Baker make the point that workers whose work involves a high level of autonomy, as in the creative industries, tend to have "a very uneasy relationship with managers" even though they may exercise a certain amount of power within that relationship (Hesmondalgh and Baker 2011: 31). They also report the views of some managers that their own specialist activities – such as problem solving, organizing, securing and liaising with clients – were as creative as practices such as writing, designing, composing, and the like. These managers seemed to be effectively contesting the unique special status accorded to "creative personnel as the basis of their relatively autonomous working conditions" (Hesmondhalgh and Baker 2011: 111). Nevertheless, while the reality may not always live up to the ideal, many managers, and indeed the rest of the production team, will tend to describe the manager's role as ideally being that of an informed and engaged collaborator rather than a supervisor from on high.

Both Kevin and Anne's teams will be made up of permanent and temporary members. If Kevin is working on an arts feature, the team may consist only of in-house staff. However, if he is producing a drama, his team will expand to include many freelancers in key roles, such as the writer and the actors. Anne's core team consists of Anne, her producer and other key team members, such as director, editor, production designer, director of photography. Anne's producer may be in-house or freelance; the other heads of department will all be freelance. This newly created team will need to establish strong bonds of trust and understanding very quickly in order to work together. The same will be true in the production of a video game, a theatre play or an advertising campaign, to name a few other examples.

Since teamworking is a strong ethos in the culture of the creative industries, creative workers will put a lot of effort into making the team work successfully on each project they work on. Not only is feeling part of a successful, supportive team personally and professionally rewarding, but, in a high-stress, high-cost, time-limited production environment, a dysfunctional team will cost dear in both financial and creative terms. The trust and understanding necessary for successful teamwork will obviously be easier to establish if team members have worked together before. As Kevin has explained, a prior relationship (as long as it was a good one!) facilitates fast and effective communication. It is therefore unusual for a project team to consist entirely of people who have never worked together before. Rather, a producer or project manager, who is in charge of putting together a temporary project team, is likely to bring on to it people they, or other trusted members of the team, have worked with before on other projects. As Smith and McKinlay explain, such "networks of friendship and shared experience" create a sense of community and a shared culture which makes it possible for "labour to cope with highly fragmented labour markets," in which creative workers do not form permanent teams within one organization, but move from one temporary team to another, working for different organizations and each time needing to establish "fast trust" and effective modes of teamworking to ensure the success of the project (Smith and McKinlay 2009: 29).

Given the importance of effective teamwork, if communication breaks down, or one member of the team isn't pulling his or her weight, the consequences can be severe. In the intense environment of a film shoot, for example, punctuality is vital and lateness, even by a few minutes, can result in dismissal (with exceptions for principal actors, directors or others whose position gives them more leeway). This is not only because such under-performance by one team member affects productivity, but also because it damages trust and morale within the team, which could spiral into serious conflict.

FREELANCERS AND PORTFOLIO WORKERS

What about freelancers, who usually do not belong to any particular organization? Do they have any sense of belonging to a particular culture, or of having a collective identity? They may well do. As we have discussed, when freelancers are engaged on a project, teamwork can give them a strong sense of community. Another way freelancers might achieve this is through the creative clusters that we investigated in the last chapter and the kind of supportive and stimulating local culture that freelance writer, Rachel, described in Chapter 4. However, freelancers may also gain a feeling of belonging to a particular community through other factors than where they live. Trade unions and associations play an important role in giving creative workers a collective identity. As well as lobbying and negotiating on behalf of their members, these organizations provide them with advice and contacts. They run schemes and events to support and inform their members and provide them with networking opportunities. Creative workers may also participate in other formal and informal professional associations, such as WIFTV (Women In Film and Television) and also online communities.

The rhythms of creative work

Another way that creative workers sustain their connection with their sector and its culture is through attending the key events, such as festivals and trade fairs and exhibitions which punctuate the year and inform its work patterns.

In agricultural communities, the rhythm of human life tends to be regulated according to the seasons: sowing the seed in the spring, tending the crops in the summer, harvesting in the autumn, clearing the ground in winter and preparing it for the following spring. The different sectors of the creative industries also work to their own particular rhythms. In Chapter 3 we discussed the rhythms of activity associated with different stages of production. These rhythms relate to the particular internal dynamics of each project. However, there are wider rhythms also at play. In part this may also be to do with the seasons: late spring, summer and early autumn is when film and television productions tend to shoot on location, for example, since the daylight hours are at their longest and the weather most accommodating.

Beyond this, however, there are key events in each sector which regulate the year. One such type of event, to be found in nearly every sector, is trade fairs and festivals. These provide particularly rich opportunities for networking, marketing, pitching, buying and selling products, developing one's client base and many other crucial business activities. The lead up to and aftermath of these events lends a particular rhythm and pattern to activities. For example, in the publishing industry book fairs play a pivotal role, as Carole Blake describes, when talking about the annual Frankfurt Book Fair:

> "We get there three days before it starts because in those three days we have meetings with all of our agents in different markets, so that we can be well briefed for going into meetings with publishers. During the five days of the fair, four of us have totally filled schedules from 8 till 6. We have a meeting every 30 minutes, each one of us... We then go to several parties each evening and have a dinner and then go to a bar and then go to bed far too late and get up the next day and do the same thing all over again... so we go for about eight days in all. But for about three or four weeks before that there's a constant stream of overseas publishers coming through these offices – all trying to get a head start on their competitors... So while you're trying to get ready for the fair, you're nevertheless having meetings all day long with foreign publishers... And then when we come home we have to type up our meeting notes... I think this year it was just under 100,000 words. That's the outcome of four of us having meetings there for a week. Following all of that up will probably take us until the London book fair next spring. Then we do it all over again." (Carole, 2011)

Robert, a film distributor, describes a similar situation with film festivals:

> "Our year is built around film festivals, which is extremely active times for us, so the whole year is mapped out for us... In January we've got Sundance, which is mid to late January... I'll watch about six films a day for a week, which is great. It's great fun. However, you still have to assess each film commercially. Who will be the audience? How will you market it? Will it pop? And then that's followed by Berlin in February... the bigger budget movies coming on to the market... Then there's Cannes, which is the focal point of the year... You move at a real pace there. I think last year we closed 18 deals in a week.... Then the next one is Toronto... And then the final one of the year is the American Film Market, which is in November." (Robert, 2012)

As with Carole, Robert's time before and after each festival is spent first preparing for and then processing the deals that have been done:

> "Before the market they'll send you the scripts for you to assess, with the key elements and directors and then, if it's a hot project, before Cannes you start negotiating on it and then you try to close a deal there... After the festival there's going to be this period of consolidation, where it's the contractual work.... There's about a month afterwards that's spent on that, but what we're going through now is that we're seeing a lot of films that are going to be in the Toronto film festival and might be early

award contenders. We're screening a lot of cuts of films that we've got and we advise on the edit, whether cuts need to be made or whether you need to add some more clarity through **ADR** or other fixes. Music is also a big concern." (Robert, 2012)

As soon as one festival is finished, he's preparing for the next and this provides the rhythm of his working year.

Along with these communal rhythms, freelancers in particular experience their own individual seasonal rhythms according to the cycle of projects beginning and ending, with fallow periods in between. Freelancers in film and television production tend not to be employed the whole working year. Estimates of how high their "utilization rate" actually is range from approximately 50% of the year (Sengupta, Edwards, and Tsai 2009: 42) to 77% (Skillset 2011: 28). This might be described as a cycle of feast and famine, since the workflow is not usually even, but more usually follows a pattern of intensely busy periods, perhaps even an excess of work offers that cannot all be taken up, interspersed with periods when projects fall through or nothing is on offer. These seasonal rhythms shape the sector cultures of the creative industries in a similar way to that in which the rhythms of nature shape the culture of agricultural communities, except the arrival of spring tends to be more predictable than the next *Harry Potter*.

NETWORKING

Working in any creative industry involves looking for work through informal channels, more often than not friends and acquaintances in the business. As discussed above, most creative teams are put together from a network of contacts. So in order to find work, it's important to be part of other people's networks, knowing what you want and need, identifying the people who might be helpful, and then contacting them. This comes up again and again in the stories of creative professionals, as we shall see below.

In a wide-ranging survey of the labour market and conditions of employment in the UK media-production sector, Skillset (the sector-skills council for the creative and media industries) suggests that networking is not as important for new entrants as it is for more established professionals. There are some formal "ways in" for new entrants – work placements, internships, graduate schemes and other arrangements that do not rely on contacts. Therefore, the old cliché that "it's not what you know, it's who you know" is only partly true. However, as Skillset points out, "less formal recruitment methods become more prevalent once individuals are moving around within the industry than when they first entered it" (Skillset 2011: 38). In short, creative professionals tend to rely more on their networks of contacts the more experienced they get.

The compulsory sociality of freelancing

Whatever the career path, some networking is essential for both starting and furthering a career in the creative industries. Judy, the games writer we've previously met in Chapter 3, describes how she got her first job as a story editor on a video game from a European company. The client was looking for a native English speaker and approached her because she had given their game a good review when she worked as a games journalist. Later, when asked to pitch for a job on another game, she had met both the creative and business directors of the company before at various industry events and, although it was still a competitive pitch, she feels, looking back, that it "gave me a bit of an edge as they sort of knew who I was coming in the door" (Judy, 2010).

Going to study at a particular educational establishment can also provide networking opportunities, as well as teaching you skills. More established institutions will tend to have industry links, such as **agents**, who will keep an eye on students' and graduates' work. Clive, the screenwriter, went to the National Film School and got an agent on the basis of his student work. Another way of making contacts and getting a foot on the ladder can be through becoming involved in the creative fringe of low-budget or no-budget projects, for example, through resource-sharing websites such as *Shooting People*, *Ideas Tap* or *The Unit List*.

The reason it's necessary to network, according to games writer Tom Jubert, is because **informal recruitment** is so prevalent. Paying jobs are filled by informal means, through the social networks of the practitioners: "[It] doesn't matter what route you come into the business through, getting jobs – particularly writing jobs – isn't always a case of seeing an ad and sending in your CV. Go to events, buy people beer, bum a cigarette, blog, twitter, remind people you exist" (Jubert 2011). This is echoed by Shalane, a film editor based in London. At the time of the interview, she was transitioning from a period of stable employment at a post-production facility to freelancing:

"I've done freelance before but I've always been working full-time at a facility. This is the first major freelance thing I've done where now, in a month's time, I don't have a job. So for

Informal recruitment: Recruitment through informal channels such as friends and colleagues, instead of formal channels such as job adverts in newspapers or the trade press. In labour markets characterized by high rates of freelance or short-term contract work, the majority of positions tend to be filled by informal means – through word-of-mouth or asking a colleague if they can recommend someone (Skillset and CCSkills 2011: 36). Informal recruitment is common for a number of reasons: large amounts of money spent on projects; the uncertainty about what products are likely to sell; the intensity and skilled nature of the work involved, and the importance of being able to work in a team. For all these reasons, a large number of jobs in the creative industries are not advertised, but filled through word of mouth. Networking both helps you find out about these opportunities and, by initiating relationships with people, helps you to establish a level of trust, which is a crucial element in every successful project.

me, personally, that's actually quite a scary thing. But it's all about networking and meeting all the other assistants, because film and television is actually quite a small world. You meet the same people over and over again. So networking with other assistants and other editors is really important, so that when they think, 'oh I've got work going, I think I'm just going to call that one from the last film 'cause she was really good,' or they'll call someone they trust to recommend somebody. So building up those kinds of relationships is really important." (Shalane, 2011)

Therefore, becoming "established" is a matter of building contacts and a track record, finding work through networking and repeat custom. As one independent producer puts it: "We really do prefer to work with people we've already worked with... Our greatest success has been where we've taken people where there's been some recommendation. You know they've worked with somebody that we know and we can be sure of getting a completely frank reference about them" (in Holgate and McKay 2009: 159).

Networking is not something that comes naturally to all people. Some of us are uncomfortable with the idea of dealing with other people in a strategic fashion for professional, rather than personal, ends. A recent survey of UK artists shows that "attitudes to both the need to network and its effectiveness are complex. Networking is seen as necessary, but people may personally find it uncomfortable. But some see it as the only way to get on" (Oakley, Sperry, and Pratt 2008: 33). This is not something confined to freelancers in the creative industries. Short-term, flexible labour makes "Friday night drinks" (Gregg 2010) effectively compulsory for workers, both in terms of office politics and maintaining a network – it is useful for the next job search. In short, there is little choice in the matter for most creative professionals. Rosalind Gill, in a highly informative book of interviews with "web workers" in Amsterdam, points to this pattern of compulsory sociality among freelancers who work on a project-by-project basis:

> People in new media move rapidly between different kinds of employment – sometimes freelancing, sometimes working for a company, and at other times setting up their own business. Some people also combine these, dividing their weeks accordingly. The informal nature of the field is central to understanding individuals' work biographies. Only 2% of jobs/work opportunities discussed in these interviews were achieved via traditional means (e.g. responding to publicly placed advertisements). The remainder were obtained through personal contacts in the guise of teachers, students, clients, friends and networks. This led to a kind of 'compulsory sociality' in which networking was the norm, and people could lose out by dint of not having the right contacts. (Gill 2007: 6)

Another way of looking at this is that the economic realities of agencies and small companies only allow for a minority of long-term jobs. These businesses survive on projects of varying sizes that come in as and when the clients put them out to brief.

David, an executive producer at a London-based interactive agency describes his studio as composed of a small team of full-time staff, with freelancers joining them on a project-by-project basis: "We have a locked number of full-timers, just a core and then we scale up when we need to, rapidly, and then we release." His studio recruits in a largely informal manner, through contacts and personal recommendations:

> "[Recruitment is] a little bit scattergun to start with. We get people back who have done brilliant work and we get people based on recommendations. Have they come in [before]? Do we get on with them? Are they easy to work with? Do we like them? For a lot of [the freelancers] it's a lifestyle choice. They want to work hard on a project for a while and then they want to take a month off." (David, 2012)

For David, who oversees recruitment at his agency, the challenge from the employer's side is to find people with the right skills and talents for the jobs that come in, when they come in. That means that he has to attract talent both through remuneration and by offering interesting, challenging work:

> "So we're finding that more and more there's a lot of people – especially people that used to be at digital advertising agencies, who were working in their coding or development departments who were just doing Facebook apps, are going "I don't want to be doing that, this is really boring" so they're just leaving to go freelance to come and do *interesting* work at places like us." (David, 2012)

Therefore, it's not just the freelancers that have to network actively; the employers themselves are subject to the same compulsory sociality in having to maintain a network of skilled freelancers and looking out for fresh talent. Employers, therefore, use the same networks, events and social opportunities that the freelancers do, in order to maintain and expand their pool of contacts.

Building a profile

The notion of "personal branding", treating oneself as a brand, may seem pretentious and "fake" for creative practitioners. But think about how important it is for potential collaborators, producers, project managers and potential employers to find your portfolio easily and quickly. How would such people verify that you've done what you say you've done in your CV or in person? They will use the same tools we all use online: search engines, social networking sites and professional networking sites for specialists.

    Personal branding involves crafting and communicating an identity for oneself – for example, as a professional or as an artist. Anyone who uses social media (which for freelancers means simply everyone) is pushed, to some extent, to become a marketer for themselves, of their personal brand, as Clara Shih argues in *The Facebook Era* (2011). Even commonplace social media like Facebook demand a certain level of personal brand management. For example, most of us make sure that our Facebook profiles are only visible to friends, so that random strangers who happen to search for us online are not treated to the full collection of photographs that make sense to our friends and family, but might raise eyebrows if viewed by a potential employer. "It's becoming increasingly common for hiring managers and recruiters to perform due diligence on candidates via social networking sites. (They used to just Google candidates.)" (Shih 2011: 178).

Derek, who works as a planner specializing in digital media at a London advertising agency, emphasizes the importance of building a profile, and an online presence. At his first agency interview he quickly realized that his interviewers had already looked him up online, and were interested in what else he could bring to the table. "When you work in advertising in the UK you're competing against everybody." Therefore, getting noticed in the first place is a real challenge:

> "You see people out there, they've built their profile on Tumblr, LinkedIn, Twitter, blog, Flickr, entering all the competitions. What else did I do? It's all about building a profile. I was a very active blogger when I was a student, because I was analyzing something that was out there and giving my own thought to it. It's very easy to write an essay for university because you just follow the rules – you're not doing it with your own creative and critical mind. That's how I felt, and the guys I work with. By writing your own blog, even if nobody reads it, you put your own words to something." (Derek, 2012)

Derek emphasizes that building an online presence is not about becoming famous as a blogger or photographer or visual artist right away; it's more important for beginners to use their online presence to find their own voice and build up a collection of material that potential employers can find once they do a search for the applicant – to have something for them to find: "When I walked into an interview, they had already done the research on me by clicking on my name in Google." What Derek had done was to establish a community of bloggers within the university he studied at:

> "I didn't want to write all the blog posts myself. I wanted the whole community to contribute inside the university. I set that up without anyone telling me to do so – which shows a bit of initiative, which then gets somebody's attention, which then put me on the map. So it's not just about setting up a blog. The point is to be a bit strategic about [whatever it is that you do, creatively] and being a bit strategic about how you set up your profile, who you are – to define yourself." (Derek, 2012)

In short, Derek's advice is not simply "blog, and you'll be noticed". In his experience, it matters less whether a graduate has organized events, written, created images or videos than the fact that they've *done something*, demonstrated initiative and independent thinking and doing – and documented it online for potential employers to find later.

Denise, a freelance writer and editor, makes a similar point for journalists and writers. She says that it's vital to pay attention to one's online presence, making sure to build a portfolio of work that is immediately accessible online when needed. She advises writers to keep their work in one place online (for example, using a LinkedIn profile or a similar service for professionals): "If you're ever in an interview or in a situation where they'll want to see your work you can show them with just one link. Editors don't really want to take on someone who's never written anything before for anyone. They want to see examples of work, and variation if possible" (Denise, 2012).

Networking strategies

> "'Networking' sounds so cold. It's just about hanging out with people, enjoying life. Also, as an artist you can't work or deal with people you can't stand. Stick to your principles and enjoy yourself. Life is too short for boring people and boring projects." (Mary, artist, 2012)

Building a portfolio of work goes hand-in-hand with networking. For Tom Jubert, a writer for computer games and interactive media, there's no way around the necessity to network. In a blog post titled "10 Tips on How to Become a Professional Games Writer," three of Jubert's tips involve networking. First, he advises the aspiring writer to build a portfolio by doing anything that comes along, so long as it's relevant to games development – reviewing new titles, QA (quality assurance) testing, or "get in with the indies" as he did: "Working on something amateur is very easy to get into (by comparison to, say, writing a novel). Do it enough and one of them might turn pro. Congrats – you've got your first professional writing credit! Now go network!" (Jubert 2011).

It's important not just to network, but to network *strategically* – "creating, maintaining and extending a network of contacts in order to maximise the opportunities to work" (Randle and Culkin 2009: 111). What Helen Blair, who has studied the film labour market extensively, calls "active networking" means to regard certain types of socializing as part and parcel of one's work and professional development and to conduct "job search activity, purposefully using network connections to source and transmit job information" (Blair 2009: 120). Therefore, developing techniques of one's own is an essential element of becoming a professional. They vary across sectors and roles – networking is different depending on whether one is a film editor, writer, online community manager or a TV producer. However, most creative workers use one of the following tactics, consciously or not.

First, through family, friends and other people in our lives we *already have a network*. Audrey, an experienced portfolio worker who has combined journalism and magazine editing with writing books and screenplays, suggests that "If you're a student or graduate you already know some fellow students, you have friends, you have relatives, teachers, lecturers. The first step is to *ask* the people around you."

Second, it's important to *research your professional sector*. Every specialism in the creative industries has trade publications (magazines, blogs and associated job sites) that cover developments in the field. Find out what the professionals read and how they keep up. Take notes after conversations, jotting down names of people, businesses, organizations, publications, websites, and so on. Professionals are not born with long lists of names of companies, organizations and important people engraved on the inside of their foreheads. They learn over time, through training, experience and networking.

Third, having a *business card* is essential for professional networking. In a world of smartphones and online profiles, a business card may seem almost redundant. However, when you think about it, a card, preferably a well-designed, beautiful one, is a physical reminder of you that the recipient carries away from your meeting. Paul, a veteran marketing professional, says that one of his best networking tools is an oddly shaped business card – a square – that does not fit neatly into a stack of normal-shaped rectangular business cards. "It sticks out. Maybe it's a little awkward, but that's precisely the point" (Paul 2011). Denise, whose work as a freelance journalist depends on keeping in touch with both her sources and commissioning editors, recommends not only having a business card, but also making good use of the ones you get. Keeping them in order and accessible is just as important as passing them along to people who might find them useful: "Networking is brilliant; it's absolutely key to journalism. I've got to a point where I had to buy myself a Rolodex" [a round stand for storing and retrieving business cards] (Denise, 2011).

Fourth, being socially *generous* is an important way to grow one's own network of contacts. "You might often know someone who will tell someone else, pass it along that way. You can do someone a turn like that, who can often come back and do you a favour" (Denise, 2011). For example, Denise helped a friend she had worked with before to pitch to a fashion magazine by giving her the online editor's contact details. "If she goes and works somewhere else at a different publication and becomes an established journalist there, then I'll have an immediate contact there and I'll also have a favour on my side" (Denise, 2012). In a similar vein, Audrey suggests: "Be kind, and be generous. It keeps you front of mind with your contacts, and it encourages others to reciprocate" (Audrey, 2011). This is what Malcolm Gladwell calls being a "connector" in *The Tipping Point* (2000).

Fifth, our interviewees frequently mention *socializing* as an important activity. Facing a roomful of strangers is a daunting prospect, but it's also a situation filled with potential. Some of the conversations could be interesting, some of the people might be pleasant, well connected and useful, but that's impossible to know in advance. Going out and meeting people is about opening oneself up to possibilities; it is very rarely possible to predict exactly what might happen or who you might meet at an event or a party. Often, meeting someone by chance can have extensive results for one's professional life, but this is not about random luck. It's just as much a matter of positioning oneself at the right time, the right place with the right people. In other words, there is a big difference between "chance meetings" and random encounters:

> A core element [of networking] is being able to "open up and talk to people". One respondent who works in the music industry says: "I found that any kind of breaks I did get was through, not being pushy but putting yourself about, and being out

and about, and doing things and meeting people, not waiting to be discovered. But then, that's music isn't it?" (Male, 1970s graduate quoted in Oakley, Sperry, and Pratt 2008: 35)

Furthermore, it's important to make good use of such encounters. Following up from face-to-face meetings, whether they are routine or happenstance, is essential – particularly for freelancers and portfolio workers.

Internships, work experience, unpaid labour

A recurring theme that comes up in conversations with our interviewees is that building a portfolio, networking and experience all go hand-in-hand. Often, people will take jobs not for the money involved but because they offer opportunities to make new contacts, learn new skills, and gain experience (Blair, Culkin, and Randle 2003; Randle and Culkin 2009). Audrey, remarking on her work as a magazine journalist and editor, puts this bluntly: "The work you do is owned by the company you work for. Your contacts are your own" (Audrey, 2011). In other words, some jobs or roles within media and publishing companies are valuable because of where they might lead:

Online networking: Social media play a key role in networking (Shih 2011). LinkedIn, for example, is a social network for professionals, which is particularly helpful for keeping track of people when they change jobs or employers or have new projects coming up. Twitter is also used, in a more open and accessible fashion, to curate updates and maintain a professional persona visible to others. Denise, whose work as a freelance journalist relies on building and maintaining contacts, mentions as an example that people she used to work with two years ago have now moved elsewhere:

> I'm really up to date with people because I have them all on LinkedIn or I've got them on Twitter. I know when jobs have changed, when people have left, when there are new editors. This is important because you don't want to be emailing someone who doesn't work there anymore. Also, if someone does leave it's quite interesting to work out where they're going to. Say someone leaves *Mixmag* to go work for *NME*, and they've gone from being a reviews editor to being *the* editor, then suddenly you have a stronger contact in a different publication who already knows you. (Denise, 2012)

> "Internships and 'menial' positions can get you in contact with your desired network. So does freelancing outside your own comfort zone – I've done web, copywriting, voice-overs. Think of a transferable skill and use it." (Audrey, 2011)

Peter makes a similar point about getting a foot in the door with media organizations, not just for the experience and skills, but also to get a sense of the culture in-house and how things work:

> "When starting out, if you can get some work, but it's not exactly what you want, it doesn't matter – you're in the door, you're in the canteen, you see how the system works. Once you're in you can find out who people are and what they do in the organization. You're on the inside." (Peter, journalist, 2012)

However, getting inside in the first place, even for no pay or low pay, can be a hard slog. Shalane describes her path into film editing as leading through a series of unpaid, low-paid and menial jobs in post-production. Starting out, she had no contacts in London, having moved there in her twenties, and had not gone to film school either, which meant that she didn't have much of a network of friends already in the business:

> "How I got started was I did some charity work, just to build up some editing skills and that sort of thing – which doesn't pay enough money to live in London, unfortunately. So then I started to run, or what they call running, at a television facility in Soho. Running is something that even if you've been to film school *everybody* has to do, or almost everybody – some people are quite connected. I suppose they don't have to, but everyone I've ever talked to, even the ones who are connected, had to run. And running is what it sounds like: you're getting things for people, you're delivering things to places, you're making tea, you're getting lunches. It is at best mildly degrading; at worst, people are just shouting at you all the time and blaming you for things that could in no possible way be your fault. It's something that hopefully you don't have to do for that long." (Shalane, 2011)

An aspiring filmmaker and editor, Shalane graduated from unpaid work for charities to paid work as a runner for two years, to finally gaining a foothold as an editor for film and television. She describes the transition from running to being an assistant editor on a feature film as a combination of luck and hard work:

> "Somebody just came into my facility who I'd worked with before and said, you know, 'Hey, I know you want to be an editor. This friend of mine, he's looking for a trainee – you should call him.' That's how I got this job, like, and that's the importance of building a network of people who trust you. If you're a good runner, then you're going to be a good assistant, because it's all about your attitude towards work and not necessarily your skill level." (Shalane, 2011)

As Shalane and the other interviewees all point out, *experience* tends to be highly valued in the creative industries, more than formal education – although having some degree-level qualification is often a basic prerequisite, particularly when employers are filling entry-level jobs that are commonly seen as stepping-stones on the way somewhere else within the industry.

A runner doesn't need a degree to fetch tea or keep someone's schedule up to date; it's where the running might lead to that matters. This notion of doing something for free in order to gain some other benefit than simple remuneration is not specific to the creative industries, and is not isolated to new entrants or those who are looking to establish themselves in a new career. In April 2011, a lawsuit was filed against the *Huffington Post*, an online news and blogging aggregator, seeking $105 million in damages for over 9,000 writers who had contributed to the site without compensation. The filing followed the sale of the *Huffington Post* to America Online for $315 million, which returned a considerable profit to Arianna Huffington, the site's founder, and her business partners (Peters 2011). Reacting to the lawsuit, David Plotz, editor of *Slate* magazine, remarked that it could be seen as a testament to the way in which the idea of work is changing: "There are now categories of work where you do something which used to be paid for, but you now do for free in anticipation of some future benefit that you will get elsewhere" (Bazelon, Dickerson, and Plotz 2011). This case, which the writers eventually lost, was about the legitimacy of online *visibility* as a form of compensation. The basic provision of the US Fair Labor Standards Act is that "labour contributing to the wealth of someone else must be compensated" (Fredrick 2003: 311). Interestingly, in the *Huffington Post* case, this was the principle that the plaintiffs sought to uphold in the face of the counter-argument that they had already been compensated in a different coin – that is, with visibility, links to their blogs, and a boost for their personal branding.

In the UK, interns have contested unpaid internships on the grounds that they violate UK minimum wage laws when interns are paid nothing or expenses only. The UK minimum wage is £6.08 per hour for workers over the age of 21. Intern Aware, (backed by the National Union of Students and the trade union Unite) along with Graduate Fog, a graduate careers website, launched the Interns Fight for Justice campaign to get compensation for unpaid interns in spring of 2012. With union backing and legal support, they assisted current or recent unpaid (or expenses only interns) in taking employers to an employment tribunal for minimum wage back pay owed to the interns. One result is that in June 2012 TalkbackThames paid four interns who had worked for three months as assistants to a freelance stylist, employed on the popular *X-Factor* programme up to £3,000 for work they performed as interns in autumn 2011 (Greenslade 2012; de Grunwald 2012).

As we have seen earlier in this chapter, the glamour attached to many areas and jobs in the creative industries has an attraction that goes far beyond money. This leads to a serious problem of access to these glamorous professions, essentially "giving people who grew up and still live in London – often with parental financial support – a better chance than the vast majority of young people across the country" (Haddow 2012). If an industry demands that all new entrants work for free or for very low wages for an extended period of time in order to be offered living wages after this period of "apprenticeship" is over, then that industry is effectively barring the gates to anyone who does not have the resources to pay for food, housing and transportation in the busy urban areas where the "glamour industries" are based. "The expectation that new entrants will have to work without remuneration at the start of their careers adds to the disadvantages faced by workers from lower-income backgrounds" (Holgate and McKay 2007: 7).

Beyond the creative industries, this culture of "free labour", unpaid internships and serial work experience stints has been seen in government and much of the public-interest sector, as well as among private corporations such as banks, business consultants and law firms. In addition to organized campaigns such as Intern Aware, this has been critiqued by journalists (Malik and Syal 2011; Perlin 2011) and policy-advocates (Heath and Potter 2011), as well as activist groups such as the London-based Precarious Workers Brigade, mainly focusing on the arts, and the Carrotworkers' Collective, who have mounted protests against exploitative practices by cultural organizations and galleries that receive public funding. The latter have also published the illustrated, sharply humorous *Surviving Internships: A Counter-Guide to Free Labour in the Arts* (Carrotworkers Collective 2011), aimed at informing students and aspiring new entrants of their rights.

EQUALITY OF OPPORTUNITY?

Some scholars have argued that there is widespread reluctance among practitioners to acknowledge the inequalities and forms of exploitation that persist within the creative industries. As Rosalind Gill argues in her article "Life's a Pitch", equality and inequality among media workers is papered over by what she describes as:

> the increasing unspeakability of structural inequalities. This unspeakability of inequality could be seen in relation to race and ethnic minorities, too. In my research it was clear that interviewees had a deep attachment to the notion of the field as "diverse" and "egalitarian" with success based solely on merit. This led to a reluctance, even a refusal, to see or speak of inequalities. (Gill 2011: 258)

The most visible and glamorous parts of the creative industries are also the most white, middle-class and male of all occupations. As Jim Frederick puts it when describing the ethnic composition of magazine publishing in the USA in the late 1990s: "One of the glamor industries' dirtiest secrets: There's not a black face in the joint" (Frederick 2003: 309). In the UK context, in its wide-ranging research, Skillset points to significant problems with social mobility, gender equality and ethnic diversity in the creative sector: Black, Asian and Minority Ethnic (BAME) groups are under-represented, at 7% of those employed, as compared to 9% in the overall workforce. For women, the numbers reported by Skillset are even less encouraging: 38% of those employed are women, as compared to 47% in the UK workforce overall (Skillset and CCSkills 2011: 33). Other parts of the UK labour force seem to offer greater opportunities for female and non-white workers, including better chances of landing a paid job, building a career over the long term, adapting to life changes (e.g., having children) and finding opportunities for advancement (Skillset 2011: 33–35).

Internal barriers?

Film director Yousaf says that he feels that it is more socially acceptable for him to openly claim his minority ethnic identity than his class identity. Having grown up in extreme poverty, he defines himself as coming from an underclass rather than the working class. He feels that this remains a taboo identity, not one that you can openly acknowledge:

> "Class has become taboo. The working class aspire to middleclassdom and actually perceive themselves as middle class now because their wage level has increased… and then there is an underclass, who basically are of a taboo class where they can't even themselves acknowledge that they are a member of that class. What do you say to that question that sometimes comes up in conversations with people, particularly if they've offered their family identity you know, and then they're asking you… what do you say? We're on benefits? Not when you read the *Daily Mail* and you read the vitriol that comes out about people who draw benefits." (Yousaf, 2012)

Yousaf sees this "taboo identity" as acting as an internalized cultural barrier, which is one of the factors that may stop people from achieving a career in the creative industries. First, he explains, because it is rarely found in cultural representations. While music is an area in which disenfranchised communities do recognize themselves as being represented, he argues that this is less true of other media, particularly film and television:

> "A lot of people who have something to say in film are in conflict with the status quo. And so they're sort of in conflict with the symbols of the status quo… you know, the high creative products of that community." (Yousaf, 2012)

Thus, even before people meet and have to overcome the kind of gatekeeper barriers we discussed above, they may have to overcome these internalized barriers. Yousaf says that, in his own case, he worked as an advertising photographer and then as a photographer documenting development projects in India, before returning to set up a gallery and picture-framing business in the UK. However, he never considered film as a career because it seemed to belong to another world, one to which he didn't belong. It was not until a friend suggested that documentary filmmaking might be a good fit for his interest in both creative activity and politics that he considered it. "But I thought but how do you do it? How do you enter it? When I grew up there wasn't an idea that there was an access path into it" (Yousaf, 2012). His route was to take a film course as a mature student. He says that this was important for him, in order to enter the industry:

> "I don't really come from a background of film culture. Now the effect of that is two-fold. One is educational and one is an access route into the industry… understanding it from the maker perspective allows you to, with the help of the people that you know, to find a way in… it's not just about contacts, it's about being able to walk the walk and talk the talk." (Yousaf, 2012)

New technologies have made production and distribution without access to the official media gatekeepers much easier to achieve and Yousaf acknowledges that online video platforms such as Vimeo, YouTube and the like enable small filmmakers to use social networking sites to reach an audience that was previously inaccessible. "YouTube does level the playing field in a way," but he stresses that larger scale projects cannot be achieved by lone filmmakers "largely because it does involve finance, and attracting finance means understanding the industry – the culture of the industry and the film society and being able to access that. Not just understanding it but somehow fitting in" (Yousaf, 2012).

Fitting in – how do you "join the club"?

Here, Yousaf is not only talking about gaining technical and aesthetic skills, but also what is sometimes called **cultural capital** – a concept drawn from the work of Pierre Bourdieu (1990). This is both a matter of formal education and a broader cultural "fluency" in being familiar with a range of recognizable and highly valued cultural references, and having the vocabulary to talk about them. The concept of "the old boys' network" provides an illustration of some of the issues at stake here – how inclusion and exclusion operates culturally as much as economically. This term originates in the UK and has been used to describe the informal network of former (male) pupils of public (i.e., fee-paying) schools, such as Eton, Marlborough and Westminster – "old Etonians", "old Marlburians" and "old Westminsters" – who went on to university together (typically Oxford or Cambridge) and then moved on into politics and elevated positions in government and the professions. In the latter half of the twentieth century many such positions were within media organizations, both public (primarily the BBC) and private. The "old boys'" natural instinct as employers was to employ other people like them, who had come up through the same system, had the same values and were the kind of people they would be happy to socialize with.

However, it is important not to exaggerate the influence of such barriers to entry; while they exist, they are not absolute nor insurmountable. As Holgate and McKay report, in a study of institutional barriers to recruitment and employment in the audiovisual industries, research in this area consistently points to the importance of good contacts in securing employment: "Informal recruitment methods are still widely used in the industry, adding to the perception that old boys' networks operate to the benefit of some and the detriment

Cultural capital: Education, knowledge and a confident familiarity with cultural references is a form of wealth – it is an asset that we invest in through formal schooling, degrees, and also through experience, connections and social skills. In fact, Bourdieu distinguished between four kinds of capital: *economic capital* (command of economic resources such as cash, assets or credit); *social capital* (resources based on group membership, networks of support, and "contacts"); *cultural capital* (knowledge, skill and education); and *symbolic capital* (accumulated prestige, honours, and the like). Each of these types of capital invite different forms of "investment" – in education to build cultural capital, and in networking to build social capital, "that network of contacts and influential friends so important to a successful career" (Lane 2000: 152).

of others." However, this is not to say that there is no way in without knowing a few of these "old boys". Holgate and McKay found that "more BME [black and minority ethnic] workers than white had used friends (35% to 28%) and word of mouth (27% compared to 18%) for finding their current jobs" (Holgate and McKay 2007: 6). More recent research into the Film and TV industries by Grugulis and Stoyanova, on the other hand, shows that, although BME workers do use their social networks to find work, these networks tend to provide access to less high level jobs than do the networks of non BME workers (Grugulis and Stoyanova 2012).

Discrimination appears to operate in subtle ways. Georgina Born quotes a senior black employee at the BBC, interviewed in 1996, who notes that with equal opportunities policies coming into place in the 1990s, and overt racial, ethnic and gender-based discrimination becoming both illegal and socially unacceptable, a different, subtler form of inequality crept in:

The BBC tradition of the old boy network has become the culture of the whizz-kid, equally elitist and exclusionary. The clubbishness is about having certain favoured skills; when you write a report, for instance, do you write it in landscape with bullet points as Birt [Director General of the BBC at the time] and the management consultants prefer, or do you write something worth reading in portrait? A lot of work has been done on this aspect of corporate cultures in the equal [opportunities] field, the way people are comfortable with others who lock into the same references

Class, in this sense, is not simply about money, the "haves" and the "have-nots". Instead, class is a complex manifestation of distinctions among people, places and things. Some of these distinctions are economic, for example, being able to afford to shop at certain supermarkets, drive a certain type of car, or live in a certain neighbourhood. Social and cultural distinctions have to do with our knowledge, education and skills, as well as whom we know and don't know. We might not necessarily be aware of the social and cultural distinctions we draw; instead they come out in our sense of fitting in or not fitting in. Often we only notice these distinctions consciously and on our own skin when we "feel out of place" somewhere. Conversely, we mark our social place through lifestyles, expressing ourselves through our tastes and activities (Bourdieu 1985; D.B. Holt 1997; Prieur and Savage 2011; Savage and Gayo 2011).

The name that Bourdieu gave to how we navigate such social and cultural distinctions, and how we learn where we "belong", is *habitus*. "Sometimes described as a 'feel for the game', a 'practical sense', habitus conceptualises agency as being the inclination of people to act in a particular manner in certain circumstances as the result of socialisation" (Blair 2009: 121). To simplify a bit, if cultural capital is like a language, *habitus* is the fluency with which you speak it and your ability to fit in among other speakers. Cultural capital has relative value, depending on the context, a bit like knowing how to use a particular tool. A good grasp of programming languages would be important for someone working as a games developer, while an extensive knowledge of contemporary cinema and television would be necessary for someone working as a broadcasting commissioner. However, having those qualifications, knowledge and skills says nothing about how an individual would put them into practice, either personally or professionally. This is why the concept of *habitus* is so useful for identifying social practices that include or exclude, allowing some dancers on to the floor while leaving others standing by, or possibly not admitted to the venue by the doorman. Recommended reading: Jeremy Lane, *Pierre Bourdieu: A Critical Introduction* (2000).

without long-winded explanations, cultural references that are really about their own ethnicity and gender. (Born 2004: 207–208)

Born's interviewee points to something very interesting about how class distinctions register at this subtle level, namely that something so incidental as the *style* in which a document is presented can affect how well it is received (or whether it is read at all). Grugulis and Stoyanova have also found that cultural and social "middle-class signals", such as education, manners, habits and tastes, raise a significant barrier to entry for the most sought-after jobs in broadcasting (Grugulis and Stoyanova 2012).

Yousaf mentions that seemingly small cultural differences can have highly damaging consequences for new entrants who run afoul of them, particularly those whose habitus is different from the prevailing one. As an example, he mentions the delicate politics of informal recruitment: it is necessary for freelancers and portfolio workers to make sure they keep their contacts happy. If you turn down work for whatever reason, usually because you have other work already booked, you find someone in your personal network who can do the job instead of you. Then your contact is likely to come back to you with more work. As Yousaf puts it, "it's about not leaving any debris behind that could hurt you". He says that he has seen some new entrants struggle to grasp this:

Soft skills and hard skills: A distinction sometimes drawn between skills that are broadly useful, such as literacy, communication, problem-solving, organization and people skills and more technical, specialist skills, often closely tied to a particular industry or sector. Soft skills are therefore portable between many different jobs, and are valuable for very different specialisms. Various types of services rely on soft skills, especially those considered "emotional labour" – dealing directly with people in customer-facing roles, a form of labour that applies directly to many jobs in the creative industries (Hesmondhalgh and Baker 2008; Hochschild 2003). Hard skills, however, are often seen as more economically valuable, since they are directly related to specific jobs or types of employment, for example computer programming, accountancy, or flying a plane. However, as we see in this chapter, it is often, in fact, soft skills, which may make the difference between success and failure in the creative industries.

> "…Some of the young people that are trying to access it [the film industry] they burn bridges… People will generally not give you the time, if they think you're hard work…" (Yousaf, 2012)

Acting in a manner that says to colleagues and employers "I'm not hard work or difficult to get along with" is itself an important **soft skill**, in particular when it comes to entry-level positions or opportunities where first impressions count for a lot, and small infractions can easily lead to dismissal.

Status issues

One such soft skill, or asset, is to have enough social confidence to take on menial tasks without feeling diminished. People who already come from a position of acceptance, if not outright privilege, are usually able to set aside any sense of subordination or humiliation when taking on temporary menial positions. "You're getting things for people, you're delivering things to places, you're making tea, you're getting lunches. It is at best mildly degrading; at worst, people are just shouting at you all the time and blaming you for things that could in no possible way be your fault" (Shalane, 2011). For Yousaf, however, this was not easy to accept. Feeling that he was already coming from a position of low-class status, he would insist on a certain level of respect usually not available to someone in the position of a runner. According to Yousaf, if you have already accumulated cultural capital, either through education or family background or both, this is less likely to be a problem:

> "If you've got a degree, you've got self belief at a certain level. You've got the confidence and the assuredness to feel that you actually are capable of other things… but if you're not coming from that level of confidence and that level of achievement and status in society and you go running and someone says 'go and get that'… It is quite complicated because you end up in a status relationship… I never ran. I did once, you know, it didn't go down very well… I didn't like it." (Yousaf, 2012)

Of course, as the example of Yousaf himself as a jobbing filmmaker shows, the various inequalities of opportunity in the creative industries are not entirely intractable, and they do not systematically exclude everyone who aspires to make films, write screenplays, publish books or direct advertising campaigns. As a recent interview-based study of careers in advertising suggests, creatives who identified as "working-class" found themselves having to overcome economic, social and cultural barriers in entering the advertising business. However, once they were "on the inside", the influence of social class "was more subtle and less detrimental, due to the social capital they accumulated *en route* and the value of their distinctive brand of cultural capital" (McLeod, O'Donohoe, and Townley 2009).

Newcomers to any professional sector must keep in mind that they may encounter various hindrances and challenges. In glamorous lines of work, like many of the creative industries certainly are, there is an oversupply of new entrants, eager to try their luck, talent and skills. We have seen how industry and work cultures are an important factor in worker satisfaction and productivity. Our investigation of networking has also shown that they are, moreover, crucial in helping people to find work. These same cultures may also cause dissatisfaction and indeed deep unhappiness among workers, while unspoken codes of behaviour, tastes and style may limit their ability to progress, to move up the career ladder and indeed to find any employment at all. Nevertheless, while recognizing such structural inequalities at work in the creative industries, we must also remember that they are not insurmountable.

SUMMARY

In this chapter we have considered the cultures and routines of work in the creative industries. We have, in particular, looked at the differences between long-term employment and shorter-term freelancing or portfolio working, especially how they appear to practitioners themselves out in the creative labour market. One prominent feature of the work culture of the creative industries is networking – the building and maintenance of professional contacts, both for newcomers and seasoned professionals. Finally, we considered whether there are particular cultural or social barriers to entry into the working world of the creative industries, particularly with an eye to experiences regarding ethnicity, gender and class.

RECOMMENDED READING/RESOURCES

Ball, Linda, Emma Pollard, Nick Stanley, and Joy Oakley. 2010. *Creative Career Stories: Creative Graduates, Creative Futures*. London: University of the Arts. Interviews with recent arts graduates about their experiences entering the job market. Available for download at: www.employment-studies.co.uk/policy/report.php?id=477.

Carrotworkers Collective. 2011. *Surviving Internships: A Counter Guide to Free Labour in the Arts*. London: Carrotworkers Collective. A witty, polemical "guide" for potential interns in the arts. Freely available online at: http://carrotworkers.files.wordpress.com/2009/03/cw_web.pdf.

Gill, Rosalind. 2007. *Technobohemians or the New Cybertariat? New Media Work in Amsterdam a Decade after the Web*. Network Notebooks. Amsterdam: Institute of Network Cultures. An influential critical study based on interviews with "web workers" in Amsterdam, with extensive quotes from the interviewees. Available for free download at: http://networkcultures.org/wpmu/portal/publications/network-notebooks/technobohemians-or-the-new-cybertariat/.

Healy, Ros, Ewa Mazierska, and Georgina Gregory. 2008. *Careers in Media and Film: The Essential Guide*. London: Sage. Good reference for understanding the myriad different roles, responsibilities and job titles in media production.

Hesmondhalgh, David and Sarah Baker. 2011. *Creative Labour: Media Work in Three Cultural Industries*. London: Routledge. Drawing on interviews and participant observation, Chapters 5–7 are specifically about some of the difficulties faced by young workers in creative labour markets.

McKinlay, Alan and Chris Smith, eds. 2009. *Creative Labour: Working in the Creative Industries. Critical Perspectives on Work and Employment*. Basingstoke: Palgrave

Macmillan. In particular, see Chapter 7, "I Don't Know Where You Learn Them: Skills in Film and TV" by Irena Grugulis and Dimitrinka Stoyanova.

Rabin, Steve. 2010. *Introduction to Game Development*. Boston, MA: Cengage Learning. Industry professionals introduce aspects of games development, from design and writing to programming, business and production.

Richmond, Siubhan. 2012. *An Expert's Guide to Getting into TV*. e-book. London: Siubhan Richmond. Accessible e-book on how to get into TV, based on Richmond's own experiences. She also has a useful Twitter feed: @ShuRichmond.

Sharp, Elsa. 2009. *How to Get a Job in Television: Build Your Career from Runner to Series Producer*. London: A&C Black. A handy guide to roles, terminology and standard practices in the industry.

Shih, Clara. 2011. *The Facebook Era: Tapping Online Social Networks to Market, Sell and Innovate*. Boston, MA: Pearson. This book is about marketing, but contains some advice at the level of individual careers, self-promotion and the use of social networking services.

PART 2

Production and Circulation of Products

How does an idea become a creative product? How does it travel from the mind of a designer to the shelves of a shop, or from a conversation between a writer and a producer to the airwaves? How does the tune a musician hums to herself become a download on someone's mp3 player? What people, places and activities are involved in the production and circulation of creative products and what exactly do we mean when we say 'product' anyway? These are some of the questions we will try to answer.

In Chapter 6 we consider what it is that the creative industries make, the tangible and intangible products we encounter, and how they can be regarded as belonging to one of four key categories: creative originals, creative content, creative experiences, or creative services. Each of these categories is explained through examples ranging from designer fashion, Disneyland, *Vice* and *Monocle* magazines, to making dance music.

This sets the stage for Chapter 7, where we look at the complexities of creative research, development and production from the point of view of the makers themselves — designing a shoe without animal products, making a documentary in Kazakhstan, adapting Dickens' unfinished final novel for television, and the perennial question of how musicians make money.

Finally, in Chapter 8, we look at circulation — how creative products and services are marketed and distributed. It's a long way from the ideas and craftsmanship of the creative to the eager hands of the mass-market consumer.

6

Creative Producers and Products

What is it that people working in the creative industries make – or *create*? First, we must remember that not all productive labour creates *tangible* physical artefacts that we can touch, hear, see or taste. The designer Jonathan Sands offers a succinct definition of what a job in the creative industries entails: "At the end of the working day, there should be something there that didn't exist when you arrived in the morning" (Wright et al. 2009: 79). This new something can be an individual creative expression of some kind, but it can also take the form of a more complex, collaborative effort that takes a long time to create (e.g., a film or a computer game), as we will see in Chapter 7, or it might be an experience of some kind, or a creative service that someone performs.

CREATIVE GOODS AND SERVICES: TANGIBLE AND INTANGIBLE

There are different ways of defining and understanding both what the creative industries make and who can be said to work in the creative industries. It's important to note that these taxonomies are not fixed in stone – they are attempts to better understand an economic sector that is constantly undergoing change and development. New technologies, trends, fashions and businesses come along all the time, making the creative industries an evasive object of study.

There exists a great diversity of creative and cultural activities that can be gathered under the broad umbrella of the creative industries. This is a challenge for governments, policymakers and international organizations such as the United Nations. It is important to understand that the professions and products of the creative industries are not simply luxuries of the rich, developed economies of the world; quite the reverse, they are an important area of economic development across the world, as we have already seen in Chapter 1. This great variety is one reason why the UK's National

Endowment for the Sciences, Technology and the Arts (NESTA) has suggested a taxonomy for the kinds of work performed within the creative industries. Instead of looking at the end-products (e.g., a film, a guided tour), we follow NESTA in dividing the creative industries into four different styles or ways of pursuing creativity (NESTA 2006: 54–55): creative *originals* producers; creative *content* producers; creative *experience* producers; and creative *service* producers.

CREATIVE ORIGINALS PRODUCERS

In this category we find anyone who creates, makes or trades in original, rare and unique objects: "Producers of creative originals typically include crafts makers, visual artists and designer-makers (for example, of clothing)." The work of creative originals producers is valuable because others see it as having creative or cultural value – it is exclusive and authentic. These are small-scale productions, one-offs or limited production runs – making them is the work of artists or artisans.

Creating a designer fashion collection

Christopher and Hannah run a small, independent fashion label based in the East End of London. They produce two collections a year – spring/summer and autumn/winter – doing the patterns and designs themselves, while outsourcing the manufacturing. They design women's clothing, positioned in "the upper end of the contemporary market".

Christopher doesn't know exactly who buys the clothing that his company makes because his company does not retail the clothes directly. He imagines their typical client as a professional, someone who appreciates design and is willing to invest in a distinctive item: "The girl who would buy our clothes is probably someone working in the creative industries or in an office, and it's a piece that she would save up a little to buy, but definitely not the very rich… well maybe. This is tricky, figuring out our brand positioning, because stores buy our clothes and [because] we're not doing direct retail ourselves we don't get to meet the customers. We get some feedback about who it is that buys – like Rhianna has bought pieces, some pop stars, some actors, and then it's all the way down to the girls who would save up to buy something special that they've seen on a blog somewhere" (Christopher, 2012).

The process, from original design idea to a finished garment on sale at a fashion store, is dictated by the seasonal cycles of the fashion business, a collection of clothes appropriate for either autumn/winter or spring/summer. In some ways, the "product" of a fashion designer is the *collection* rather than individual items of clothing.

Each collection begins with a research phase, says Christopher – an activity that in other areas of the creative industries might be called *development* (see Chapter 7):

"We go through images, things we like, something we feel strongly about. Then it's fabric research, finding the right fabric mills to work with, finding where we can get the various things we're interested in. After that there's the design phase [where we start to create] the concrete shapes and looks of the collection, the rough sketches. From there you go [on to] do more detailed drawings of the pieces that you want to make, the looks, what could go with each other, and how to make a coherent collection. Then it goes into sampling, where patterns are made, and patterns adapted from previous seasons we might want to reuse. They get made up in simple cotton fabrics, and when we're happy with those they get made in real fabrics, or *toiles* (the plain cotton versions are called *calico*). Then we do a first sample where we see if the direction we're going in is actually working. It depends whether we need a second revision, but most often we get it right the first time. Then the collection steadily grows towards Fashion Week." (Christopher, 2012)

The autumn/winter collection is exhibited at the four main Fashion Weeks in New York, London, Milan and Paris in February into early March:

"We do a photo shoot before Fashion Week with a photographer where we style the looks the way we want to present them. Then either people do fashion shows or presentations, or take it straight to a trade fair or a showroom where they conduct sales. We do a presentation, and sales shortly thereafter. Stores come in for appointments, they make a selection and buy. They choose their numbers – five of that jacket, 10 of that jumper."

Only after the fashion buyers have selected individual pieces from the collection for purchase do they go into production.

"After the sales season is done you collect all the orders, start finding which manufacturers would be good for which styles, and depending on the quantities you have and the quality you need it in, etc. A tailored jacket goes to a different manufacturer than a sweatshirt. That is quite a long process – ordering fabrics, having them made up. When that's done, you get everything in from manufacturers, package everything, do quality control and ship it out to the stores that ordered."

This means that there are parts of each collection that never go into production. Christopher points out that this is not exclusive to fashion – there is a rule of thumb when it comes to bringing original designs to market: "Something like 6% of your product range should make up for 30–50% of your sales. Then the next 25% should make up for 30%. It's used all over the manufacturing industry. There are parts of your collection, around 30% that represents maybe 2% in sales. They are things you need to have for show, but they will never get ordered."

"The sales go on until the end of March, maybe, then you close the order books and start production – ordering fabrics, etc. Fabrics take usually a month to get in, so production takes place from the beginning of May until the end of June or beginning of July. There are always delays, things go wrong, so products usually ship by mid-July, and that's the autumn/winter selection you see trickling into stores at the end of July and the beginning of August."

While one collection is being shown and put into production, the next one is already being designed. In early September the Fashion Weeks start again for the spring/summer collections. Interviewed just after the Fashion Weeks in March, Christopher explained: "We're in the long season now, but the spring/summer is a short season, you have from the order books close mid-October, and then you have November to mid-December for production. Manufacturers are closed for Christmas and New Year holidays, and then you ship to stores in mid-January – so it's a much shorter timeframe. And meanwhile you have to start your new collection and have it ready for February" (Christopher, 2012).

CREATIVE CONTENT PRODUCERS

Comprising makers of content for various media, this category includes people work-ing in film, broadcasting (TV, radio), publishing, recorded music, and interactive media (games, mobile apps, online media). Enterprises that make creative content produce intellectual property. Usually this is protected by copyright and distributed on a large scale to mass-audiences. The revenue for these productions comes through sales, adver-tising or subscription, usually after a significant initial investment. Creative content producers "invest capital upfront in order to develop creative projects prior to any rev-enues. Creative content enterprises typically include film, television and theatre pro-duction companies, computer and video game development studios, music labels, book and magazine publishers, and fashion designers" (NESTA 2006: 54).

Creative originals and creative content both involve the generation of new intel-lectual property and the use of existing intellectual property, often through a laborious process of development (see Chapter 7). Some enterprises will work on a project-by-project basis, starting from scratch in each instance (e.g., a TV production company will work from a new screenplay for each project). Others build on their existing body of work, drawing on a body of intellectual property that they own, for example when fashion designers rework previous ideas and production lines into new iterations.

Magazine publishing: *Vice* and *Monocle*'s big bets on content

At first glance, it seems difficult to find more dissimilar media properties than *Vice* and *Monocle*. One is a youth and fashion brand that embraces a rough-and-ready aesthetic of street photography and DIY fashion alongside journalistic reporting that eschews mainstream subject matters and reporting styles. The other is beauti-fully designed and presented, with all photography produced in-house, a network of correspondents around the world, providing updates on current affairs (commerce, transport and infrastructure, in particular), fashion and style for the international businessperson. However, the similarities between the scrappy punks of *Vice* and the well-groomed grown-ups of *Monocle*, are striking: setting aside their differences of style and presentation, we notice that these media brands both focus on content – delivering print, audio, and video both online and through broadcast channels.

Vice and *Monocle* illustrate how *content* and a strong *brand*-identity is the key to cross-platform media businesses. Founded in 2007, *Monocle* magazine should, according to conventional wisdom, not exist. Printed on multiple paper stocks, weighing more than a small laptop or tablet computer, and priced in the range of a mass-market paperback book, *Monocle* appeared at first to be an expensive folly, and was initially not predicted to last long (S. Rushton 2008; Bell 2010). By investing in a print brand, the owner and editor-in-chief, Tyler Brûlé, swam against the currents of digitalization by publishing a magazine. Global in scope, *Monocle* has correspondents (or "bureaux") across the world, with a strong focus on style, business and current affairs – occupying a niche between *GQ* and *The Economist*.

Despite the editorial team's commitment to ink and paper – even down to the smell of the printed magazine (Larocca 2010) – *Monocle* produces content that goes far beyond conventional notions of what a magazine does. Unified through its website, *Monocle* offers Monocle 24 web-based radio programming (which grew out of its Monocle Weekly podcast) with interviews, reportage, music and news – often featuring in-house writers and editors. Monocle TV on the Bloomberg network is an hour-long weekly programme, which Brûlé described at its launch as "gentle, good, informative viewing," featuring magazine-style reports from correspondents around the world, delivered in a tone of leisurely analysis, distinguished from the breathless pace of television news channels: "I hope it will be a return to more *elegant* television" (Larocca 2010). Alongside the magazine, Monocle retail shops can be found dotted around the world, often near the local Monocle offices, offering accessories and designer travel goods promoted in the pages of the magazine itself. Finally, alongside publishing, radio, television and retail, Brûlé is chairman and creative director of the branding and advertising agency Winkreative, which shares offices with Monocle in London, New York, Tokyo, Zurich and Hong Kong. "Winkreative is a wholly owned subsidiary of Swiss holding company Winkorp, which Mr. Brûlé founded in 2002. Monocle is 70% owned by Winkorp; the remaining 30% is held by five wealthy European families, who so far have been more than happy to indulge Mr. Brûlé's quest to turn Monocle into a multiplatform global brand" (Dumenco 2011).

Vice began life as the community-oriented *Voice of Montreal* in 1994, part-funded by the local government. After a change of title and ownership in 1996, it grew into an international magazine, distributed for free through fashion retailers, and became an established guide to trends in music, fashion and culture for the young, hip and fashionable, as described in an *Observer* profile of the publishers: "'Vice' is practically a definition of the magazine's content. All off-kilter life is here. Skaters feature alongside interviews with the likes of Abu Hamza. And its take-no-prisoners approach has captured the imagination of what marketing people call 'trendsetting metropolitans' aged 21 to 34" (Wilkinson 2008). From its roots as a printed magazine, *Vice* has grown into a "globe-strangling youth media company that includes publishing, events, music, digital television, marketing and feature film divisions," according to the appropriately irreverent Vice UK Media Kit (*Vice* 2012: 2). *Vice* makes no secret of its core strategy: To be a hub for original media content aimed at young people.

The *Vice* brand pulls together a variety of content, across multiple platforms – magazine, video, books, music publishing, etc. – and distributes this content both through its own media assets as well as partnerships with other media brands, most notably having a dedicated slot for its current affairs documentaries on CNN (Carr 2010). Alongside this extensive and expanding content-production, *Vice* operates a marketing agency (appropriately named Virtue) and the newly established AdVice Network – an advertising distribution network operating in partnership with a variety of popular, youth-oriented media brands ranging from *The Onion* to *The New York Times* (*Vice* 2012: 5). For more staid corporate sponsors, unwilling to associate themselves with the more risqué content offered by *Vice*, separate sponsored outlets have been created, such as Noisey, Motherboard, and The Creators Project (in partnership with Intel), each offering curated content on music, technology and creativity.

As media businesses, *Vice* and *Monocle* are betting heavily that quality content (albeit for rather different audiences) can be profitable. In the first decade of the century, established media companies, such as Viacom and News International, found themselves in competition with new entities, some of which dominated the new online media platforms (e.g., Google, which owns YouTube). They responded by investing in competing platforms such as MySpace (News International) and Last.fm (CBS), often with mixed results. As Shane Smith, CEO and co-founder of Vice Media, puts it: "Everyone was spending all their money on platforms but none of it on what you put in the pipe. So we said, Okay, eventually the market's going to catch up, and everyone's going to need content" (Bercovici 2012). Both *Vice* and *Monocle* have been successful in getting investors on board with their content-focused strategies, *Monocle* through Winkorp, as we've seen, and the Vice Media Group through raising investment for an expansionist push into new markets such as India and China, with advertising giant WPP, and the media merchant bank The Raine Group on board, among others (Bercovici 2012). These two media groups have taken the familiar model of content commissioning from magazines, and adapted it for delivery across multiple media platforms: editorial oversight; commissioning of content from external parties (freelancers, **independent** production companies); quality control and editing; and distribution through branded channels.

CREATIVE EXPERIENCE PROVIDERS

People who create experiences include performing artists (actors, dancers, musicians) and anyone working in spaces that offer particular experiences, such as museums, galleries, libraries, music venues and those working in tourism and heritage – all of these make experiences happen for their audiences and clients.

Disneyland – the place that was also a TV show

Historically, the idea of the "creative experience producer" owes a great deal to Walt Disney and to Disneyland – "the place that was also a TV show" (Marling 1996). Struggling to fund the construction of an amusement park (originally to be named Disneylandia), Disney eventually made a deal with the ABC network – a weekly TV series in exchange for investment and loan guarantees so that construction could be completed:

> *Disneyland*, the weekly series, premiered in October of 1954. It played on Wednesday nights at 7:30, the children's hour, and within three months it had reached the top ten. *Disneyland* became a family institution: homework was deferred; sales of TV dinners soared. [...] "I saw that if I was ever going to have my park," [Walt Disney] admitted, "here ... was a way to tell millions of people about it – with TV!" And so, every week, the program format introduced the audience to the principal themes of the park. One Wednesday, the topic would be Fantasyland, with the content made up of clips from animated films. Adventureland evenings recycled footage shot for the nature documentaries. (Marling 1996: 122)

Disneyland, the park, opened in July 1955, with the opening broadcast on live TV. Disney's decision to unite the TV programme with the park under a single name proved highly influential, creating "an all-encompassing consumer environment that he described as 'total merchandising.' Products aimed at baby boom families and stamped with the Disney imprint [...] would weave a vast,

Spoiler alert! Try this for an experiment. Go see a thriller you know your friend has been looking forward to seeing. Catch it before your friend has a chance to go to the cinema. After the screening, phone him up and proceed to discuss in detail every twist and turn of the film's plot, especially the ending. Make sure to tell him how much fun you had. If you're still on speaking terms after this, he'll probably tell you that you've "spoiled" the film for him, that is, diminished the pleasures of surprise, anticipation and delight that he otherwise would have enjoyed at the cinema, had you not spilled the beans in so much detail. Films are experience goods, and audience members are largely unaware of the specifics of each film in advance of seeing it. We may know about the genre of the film, the stars, the reputations of those involved (e.g., the director or the writer), which other films this one resembles ("It's *Die Hard* meets *Bambi*"), and what the reviews have been like, but we don't want to know *all* the details.

commercial web, a tangle of advertising and entertainment in which each Disney product—from the movie *Snow White* to a ride on Disneyland's Matterhorn—promoted all Disney products" (Anderson 2000: 4).

There is not a clear-cut distinction between creative content and creative experiences, just as there isn't between the Harry Potter films and the experience of visiting the sets on a Harry Potter Studio Tour. After all, these products are "experience goods" (Caves 2000). That is to say, the experience of the creative product is what the user pays for – whether that's watching a film, playing a game or visiting an amusement park.

CREATIVE SERVICE PROVIDERS

Services are a major part of the creative industries, particularly in specialisms such as advertising, architecture, graphic design, public relations, promotion, production facilities, and the like. Creative service providers earn their keep by "devoting their time and intellectual property (IP) to other businesses and organisations" (NESTA 2006: 54). Many agencies, large and small, are creative service providers – marketing agencies, advertising agencies, architecture practices, design agencies, interactive agencies, and the like.

While it's easy to see architects, software makers and graphic designers as "creative", the inclusion of advertising agencies and media agencies in this category might perhaps make some of us pause. However, far from being an extraneous component of the creative industries, there are strong arguments for seeing media agencies and advertising agencies, or simply *marketing* in general, as an important part of the creative industries. Creative service providers, in their various functions, make creative content visible to consumers at large – taking products to a mass-audience:

Branding: A great deal of creative work goes into the design, development and maintenance of brands, brand identities and brand recognition. Branding is, at its core, about differentiation: the American Marketing Association defines it as "a name, term, sign, symbol or design, or a combination of them, intended to identify the goods, or services of one seller or group of sellers and to differentiate them from those of competitors" (Moore and Pareek 2010: 12). More broadly, branding is about the creation and maintenance of a brand, its presence in the public eye (and mind, which is why some marketers use the notion of "mindshare" to describe what it is they acquire for their clients), its affiliations, contexts, and the connotations (or "brand associations") it evokes for consumers.

> Over the past 20 years economic, technological, social, and cultural changes have conspired to devalue cultural content and place a stronger emphasis on the services and systems that convert raw symbolic goods into meaningful and valuable experiences for consumers. Consequently creativity is closely linked to the management of cultural production and cultural distribution. (Bilton and Deuze 2011: 34)

One important way in which raw symbolic goods are turned into meaningful experiences for consumers is **branding**. A brand is a good example of how the mixture of tangible and intangible characteristics of creative products plays out in practice. It is a symbolic good that conveys meaning and even carries emotional associations that are not inherent in the physical manifestations of the brand, such as the products, the logo, the visual identity of the brand, or individual advertisements. In branding, such important but abstract elements as "brand values" are translated into material form (Moor 2008).

Taking music to market

When a musician or a band attempts to reach a wider audience for records and live performances, managers, record companies and other creative professionals come into the picture. Simon is a freelance A&R (artists and repertoire) manager who works with musicians on developing their songs, sound, performance and other aspects of their craft.

When asked what it is that he actually *makes*, what qualifies him as a *creative* practitioner, he sees himself as making music – as part of the creative process. However, the picture immediately gets more complex when he starts to describe how the musicians he works with actually make a living. Rather than seeing the sales of recorded music as the primary source of income, he suggests that a certain levelling has taken place among "the different things that make you money":

> "The physical products selling music in a CD or a download is a smaller part of the income you'd look at getting. It would be less than the other areas where you can earn money: live, merchandising, sponsorship, specific fan experiences, etc. It's more about creating value and having multiple ways of exploiting that. [...] Taking the piece of music to market [is] part of the chain of things that might mean that you make money from DJ-ing or exploit it in other ways. Like, for instance, a lot of urban artists that have given away free mix tapes, but then have made money from selling T-shirts. It's the music [that] – in commercial supermarket terms – becomes the loss-leader." (Simon, 2011)

Simon was previously employed by a record label until 2007, when it was sold for its back catalogue and almost all the staff were made redundant. When he was interviewed, he worked with musicians on a freelance basis, while maintaining a portfolio of other work, including spending around half of his time employed in education.

Simon's career trajectory is an interesting example of what Leyshon et al. (2005), in a study of the musical economy after the internet, argue is a long-term development in the music industry that arises from the changing importance of music in people's everyday lives: "The problems facing the music industry have not suddenly been manifested overnight, or even in response to on-line digital file exchange, but rather have accumulated in time in response to a set of broader cultural forces that have changed the role of music within society, and relegated its immediacy and importance among many of its consumers." The chief reason for this, they argue, is that recorded music "is decreasingly valued for itself, but is, instead, increasingly valued more for the ways in which it is consumed in relation to other things," that is, as part of the background of other entertainment, as soundtracks for advertising, film, TV and video games (Leyshon et al. 2005: 181–183). In other words, music no longer occupies the cultural central stage for young people the way it did when fewer media and technologies competed for their attention and disposable income – with games emerging as a significant winner over other forms of physically distributed media (Arthur 2009). "Music is 'used' rather than 'owned'" in the digital environment, argues music manager Malcolm McKenzie (Smith 2008: 91). Therefore, the way Simon describes his work with musicians suggests that the various creative services that musicians previously relied on to get their recordings and live performances to a larger audience – promotions, advertising, music videos, radio play, etc. – are still important, but now these services have the purpose of locating music within other entertainment and deriving income from that integration, rather than selling music on a per-unit basis in the form of CDs or even digital downloads.

Collaboration and coordination: Simplicity and complexity are features of the collaboration and coordination involved in the making of a creative product. For a hypothetical example, the rock band Purse Snatchers compose a song together one evening, jamming in their rehearsal space. Having created the song as a band, they share the copyright evenly between themselves, each member having contributed something to the eventual composition. Then, after playing it live and releasing a recorded version, the Purse Snatchers are approached by a large computer games company who want to put it on the soundtrack of an action-packed snowboarding game. The Purse Snatchers' song is now one of the many components of a complex creative good called *Thunderslopes*, which is the result of the work of large teams of writers, graphic designers, software engineers, actors, motion-capture technicians, directors, project managers, and many more. This is what defines a complex creative good — it can only

FROM SIMPLE CREATIVE GOODS TO COMPLEX CREATIVE GOODS

Richard Caves distinguishes between *simple creative goods* and *complex creative goods*, depending on how many (and complex) contracts are involved in the making of the final product. The work of creative originals gives us the most straightforward examples of simple creative goods: painting a picture, composing a song, writing a story – these are simple activities by individuals or small teams involving simple contractual arrangements. But that's only the beginning of the story:

Artists of all types engage in creative processes and tasks that come to completion only with the collaboration of "humdrum" (or "ordinary") partners, and perhaps of other artists as well. The painter needs an art dealer, the novelist a publisher. The cinema film requires a number of actors, a director, screenwriter, cinematographer, production designer, make-up specialist, and many others who see themselves in some measure as artists (along with teamsters and accountants, who likely do not). These collaborations rest on deals and contracts – perhaps of the "handshake" variety, perhaps elaborately drawn. (Caves 2000: 1)

exist because of "activities that require complex teams of creative and humdrum inputs" (Caves 2000: 85). Complexity enters the picture when large teams have to be coordinated, there is uncertainty about the success of the project (nobody knows how well the game will be received, how many copies it will sell, etc.) and the intricate problems of time-coordination against deadlines (because *Thunderslopes* has to be ready in time for the Christmas shopping season).

Simple creative goods, from the point of view of the contracts involved, are creative activities in their simplest setting, as Caves (2000: 19) suggests: "One artist deals with a simple firm that promotes and distributes her creative work." This, however, can get quite complex quite quickly. A screenplay is simple, but a feature-length motion picture, with a budget in the millions of pounds and large teams of specialists working on different elements of the finished product, is complex, to put it mildly. It is also a good example of the project-based working so prevalent in the creative industries: a complex creative good is the end product of a production chain which involves not just many different teams of people, but also multiple projects that converge (Mayer, Banks, and Caldwell 2009). Each of the teams involved in a complex creative good has a specific set of goals within the overall project, many of which constitute separate subordinate projects in themselves.

Assembling a complex creative good: assistant film editor

Shalane, a London-based assistant film editor, was interviewed about her experience of working on a feature film in summer 2011. She emphasized the project-based character of her work: "Most editors work on a freelance basis so I've been hired just for this film. So, I work for a company who's funding this film, technically, but I'm only employed until the end of this film and then I'll need to find something else." While it's going on, with everyone working against a coordinated production schedule and deadlines, the work is quite intense:

"We [the editors] are on this film from the beginning, right from day one of the shooting. For that time, every day, they bring the dailies, the rushes, which is everything they shoot in one day. They bring it in the day after it's been developed, and you [the assistant] have to go through it, you separate it by every take of [every scene]. You sync the sound to it so the sound matches the picture – because the sound is recorded separately. Then you have to organize it all for the editor. So he'll look at the rushes all together but then he also wants stuff done so that he can see, you know, scene 1, scene 2, and he can see all the takes of things like that in the Avid [editing system]. So, he then goes through and he picks his favourites, he'll start to assemble the scene." (Shalane, 2011)

The film that Shalane worked on was shot over 60 days. By the end of shooting, the editor had a rough cut of the entire film ready.

"The director and the producer will watch that to make sure that there is a film and they've shot everything they need to shoot. Then the editor and the director will sit every day and just go through scene-by-scene: replacing takes with others. For us, the assistants, it's a lot of fixing the picture – you go through to make sure all the dialogue's in sync and add some temporary music so that the composer can hear, sort of, what the idea was for the way that scene is supposed to sound and they compose something. And then temporary visually effects, same thing again, so the VFX [visual effects] guys can know what you had in mind for what was happening there – temporary sound effects – all that will then get stripped out and done properly by someone who specializes in that. We just put it together." (Shalane, 2011)

The job of the editing team, as Shalane describes it, involves making sure that the work of various separate teams comes together seamlessly in the completed film, without the viewer knowing where the raw footage ends and the visual effects begin, or that the sound of footsteps was not made by the actor on the screen but by a dancer on a soundstage in suburban London. This is why the final stage of the filmmaking process is very demanding for the editing team:

"[We are] continually monitoring if anything changes, even the sound, or like this morning there were some frames that got repeated – honestly, I don't even know how he did that, but he did, and we had to go through and make sure that everything is exactly the way that it's meant to be so that nobody can get confused about anything." (Shalane, 2011)

Traditionally, the musical score is the last major creative element that is added to a feature film. In some films, a music supervisor will work with the director and editors, negotiating with composers and musicians, sourcing music, licensing it for use in the film – linking the music industry side of the project to the film industry side (Lewandowski 2010). Shalane was interviewed in the week when the score was being finalized for the one she was working on:

"Right now we've got a composer who's composed the score, but then there's also bits and pieces [in addition to the score itself]. In movies there'll be pop songs and that sort of thing. You've got to get clearance for all those things. If you've got someone who's going to sing a song for the end credits [you've] got to make sure that's happening, got to make sure the end credits are all correct and are sent out to the right people – that sort of thing." (Shalane, 2011)

SUMMARY

This chapter describes the different kinds of work people do when they produce creative goods and services, setting the stage for the stories of development and production in the next chapter. We borrow a handy typology of creative products that asks *how* a good or service is made, not what it is: creative originals, creative content, creative experiences and creative services are distinguished by the kind of labour they involve – the work that goes into them – rather than by what the end result is. This allows us to examine further the difference between what Richard Caves calls *simple* and *complex* creative goods – a distinction that turns out not to be straightforward because almost every creative good, once it travels beyond a writer's keyboard or a band's rehearsal space, becomes remarkably complex on its journey to reach a larger audience. Investigating how that works in practice, we draw primarily on the experiences of Christopher, a fashion designer, Simon, an A&R manager, and Shalane, an assistant film editor, to illustrate how these complexities play out in working life.

RECOMMENDED READING

Bilton, Chris and Mark Deuze, eds. 2011. *Managing Media Work*. London: Sage. An informative collection of essays on management and the work of creative producers.

Lash, Scott and Celia Lury. 2007. *Global Culture Industry: The Mediation of Things*. Cambridge: Polity Press. A look at certain material cultural objects (Nike shoes, *Toy Story*, global football, conceptual art) and how they move across national borders.

McRobbie, Angela. 1998. *British Fashion Design: Rag Trade or Image Industry?* London: Routledge. Groundbreaking study of the British fashion industry.

Passman, Donald S. 1994. *All You Need to Know About the Music Business*. New York: Simon & Schuster. A music manager dispenses tips and stories from a long career managing bands and helping musicians not to get fleeced by music labels.

Smith, Stuart James. 2008. *How to Make It in Music: Written by Musicians for Musicians*. London: Dennis Publishing. A short book featuring short interviews with jobbing musicians, managers and music professionals.

7

Research, Development and Production

RESEARCH AND DEVELOPMENT

Research and development (often shortened to R&D) is a crucial stage in the process of turning an idea into a product and often takes much longer than the production stage, since it can require a lot of time and effort to work on an idea and to find collaborators. To understand this process in practice, we look at research and development through four different case studies: the design of a shoe, the making of a documentary film, a TV adaptation of an unfinished Dickens novel, and the creation of a piece of dance music. The outcomes are very different, but in each case the research and development process is fundamental for what later happens at the production stage.

Case study: the creation of a shoe – from Japan to the UK to Portugal and back again

Robin, director of Vegetarian Shoes, says that it can take anything from a few months to a couple of years to develop a new shoe. As a designer and retailer of shoes, Robin's company has to both source materials and find factories which will make them up into shoes, before finally taking possession of the finished product, which they sell to customers through their shop and through online, telephone and mail orders.

The initial stage is to decide on the design. Sometimes it may begin with a sketch that Robin draws and takes to a shoe manufacturer, but he will also attend shoe exhibitions, where shoe manufacturers display their products, and will ask for a variation on one of their current designs. However, this is just the beginning of the process, what happens next can take all sorts of unexpected twists and turns, as Robin explains:

"Some people think we have our own shoe factories. We don't. I don't own a shoe factory. We go to a factory... they'll do you a **sample**. Oh you're on holiday, they're on holiday. They've got the wrong material... they made it wrong. They lost the thing [i.e., the *design* or *specification*]. You've got to send them the thing again. You're busy doing something else. You've got to leave it a month before you find the thing. They send it to you. Actually you want to change it. You send it back... they'll change the thing you asked and they'll change something you didn't ask about." (Robin, 2011)

Even though Robin's shoes are manufactured on a factory production line, the process is clearly not as simple as Robin saying what he wants and the production line producing it. The development process is rather one of trial and error and negotiation between people, as each party involved tries to understand their collaborators' requirements and capabilities. For Robin, working with a shoe manufacturer to produce shoes is not a quick or a casual transaction. It involves developing a relationship and investing in it for the long term:

"We got some shoes made in Poland recently and they weren't that brilliant at first but they had good prices... we worked with them for about a year before we had a shoe that was any good, but we built the relationship in that time and the shoe that was right. We sell hundreds of them now. So it's building that relationship and trust..." (Robin, 2011)

As Robin points out, this trust needs to go both ways: "You're selling your stuff as much to them as they're selling to you. You know... are you reliable, are you going to pay them?"

Robin's experience is widespread across the creative industries. When people invest time, money and other resources to collaborate on a product, it is not just the quality of the product they want to be sure of; it is the quality of their collaborators.

Negotiations between potential collaborators will also turn, however, on the relative strengths and weaknesses of each party's position in the market. Many of Robin's shoes are made in Portugal, which has a history of shoe manufacturing. Robin recounts how, shortly after he started his company, a loss of business to factories in Asia caused a lot of Portugese factories to close, making it easier for him to negotiate favourable deals with those that remained:

Their **minimum** was 200 pairs and I said can we get 100 pairs? And they did because they needed the work. And now we do thousands with them... We've had time to build that heritage and they know that that's what we're like. (Robin, 2011)

More recently, prices in Portugal went down again and business began to swing back from Asia to Portugal. Robin then relied on the strength of these established relationships and trust to help him maintain his supply chain in the face of competition from other, possibly larger, customers for the factories' services. He works hard to maintain these relationships as he knows they are crucial to the business.

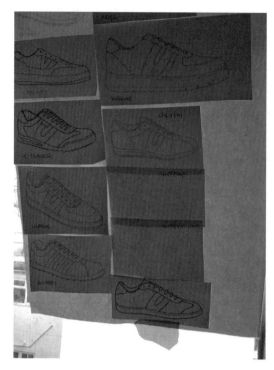

Figure 7.1 Shoe thumbnail sketches, courtesy of Vegetarian Shoes. Photo credit: Rosamund Davies

When a shoe design goes into production, the material is cut into panels to make up the finished shoe. Robin likens the process to cutting out pastry with pastry cutters. These cutters are called patterns and sometimes, if they have a new design, Vegetarian Shoes will need to pay for a new pattern to be made up from scratch in order to produce the sample. If they go down this route, they need to be sure that they can sell enough shoes to cover the cost of the pattern as well as the materials and manufacture and still make enough profit. However, if they have chosen a design from the manufacturer's current range, buying a new pattern will not be necessary. As Robin explains, it is quite standard practice in the shoe industry for different shoe brands, from high street to niche, to work with an existing pattern from the factory and to customize the design. Sometimes a particular brand will have paid the factory to make up a unique pattern and it won't be available for others to use, but often the pattern is generic and will be used by more than one brand, keeping development and production costs lower.

It is not only relationships with manufacturers that have to be developed and maintained, Robin also has to establish good relationships with the companies that supply the materials for his shoes. Indeed, it is the special breathable non-leather materials that go into them which constitute Vegetarian Shoes' **USP**. Problems recently arose for Robin when a supplier changed owners and suddenly a long-cultivated relationship reset to zero: "One of our [material] manufacturers changed hands and the material's gone from a super good business to someone who doesn't answer their emails." The company's tardy response threatened a break in the supply of material, which would hold up the rest of the production chain and ultimately result in empty shelves in the shop. To avoid this, once he finally got his order accepted, Robin ordered a much larger quantity than he used to in the past to make sure he didn't run out. This had a negative effect on his cash flow, making the company overdrawn for a while, but he felt it was a necessary strategy, not only to ensure the smooth running of the production line, but also to try to build the relationship up again: "To show that we're a serious customer, and maybe get a little bit of discount and maybe that it's worth answering our emails..." (Robin, 2011).

Robin's company devotes time and energy to making sure they have the best materials for their shoes from the best suppliers, shopping round the world, in Asia and Europe. More recently, in order to gain even greater control over the supply, they have started shipping in material to the UK in an unfinished state and getting it finished there: "We get it turned into our own material, which is kind of cool. Also, as we can control the quantities, we can get a small batch done in a colour that we like, because we're holding vast stocks of the base material" (Robin, 2011).

The process of developing a new shoe design demonstrates the importance of both keeping a tight control of operations and nurturing and relying on the collaboration of others. Success depends on maintaining a balance between them.

Case study: an international documentary

A fashion item, like a shoe, is one thing, but what about a less tangible product, such as a television programme? Does the journey from programme idea to transmission have anything in common with the design and production of a shoe? For Antony, co-producer and director of *After the Apocalypse* (2012), a documentary about the after-effects of nuclear bomb testing in Kazakhstan, the process was twice as long and even more torturous.

The idea for the project came from the original producer of the documentary. She brought Antony on board the project because he spoke fluent Russian and had experience of filming in former Soviet countries. The producer had raised some **seed funding** through the WorldView Broadcast Media Scheme (http://worldview.cba.org.uk), which is financed by the UK government's Department for International Development, and she used this to fund Antony's trip to Semipalatinsk in Kazakhstan. The idea was to **recce** the location and to carry out some preliminary filming in order to use the **footage** to raise production finance. However, when Antony got there, he found that the brief he had been given didn't quite match up with reality. The **working title** of

Commissioner/controller: A TV commissioner or controller for a particular area of programming or for a channel is the person who is responsible for deciding what programmes will be made for that strand or that channel and for committing the funds of the company to make them. See Chapter 9 for further discussion of TV commissioning and production.

Sheffield MeetMarket and other film festivals: Sheffield MeetMarket is part of the Sheffield Documentary film festival. As we saw in Chapter 5, industry events, like trade fairs and festivals, play an important part in the creative industries. Film Festivals act as central marketplaces where producers, financers and sales and distribution representatives gather in order to buy and sell content and do finance and development deals. (See Chapter 10 for further discussion of film financing.) Much of this business takes place informally, but many festivals organize a specific time and place for such activities. They range from a marketplace for finished products, such as the huge film marketplace at Cannes, where hundreds of sales companies set up stalls promoting their rostas of films, to pitching events, such as the Sheffield MeetMarket, which consists of two days of 15-minute 'speed-dating' type meetings between producers and commissioners. The feature documentary *Searching for Sugar Man* (Bendjelloul 2012), which opened the 2012 Sheffield Documentary Film festival and went on to win an Oscar in 2013, had originally found finance through the MeetMarket (Sparke 2012: 20). The BritDoc initiative, Good Pitch, which Antony also mentions, has run internationally in countries including the UK, USA, Canada, South Africa and the Netherlands (website: http://sheffdocfest.com/view/meetmarket).

the film was *Radiation City,* and it was meant to be about a town, in Kazakhstan, that was badly affected by radiation. But Antony says he couldn't find much evidence of radiation in the town itself and he realized that their information was not quite accurate:

> "Kind of lesson to learn in future is Wikipedia and trusting other people's information will only take you so far... you go out there and like reality just doesn't conform... That's not to say that there wasn't a big problem there, but the problem was a very different thing. So I was sent there to get one thing but I found that the story was another." (Antony, 2012)

What Antony found was that the real problem facing the area was that nuclear testing had been carried on the steppes outside the town, without the evacuation of communities living nearby. Antony calls them 'human guinea pigs'. The experiment caused birth defects in children born to people exposed to the radiation and was still causing birth defects in the present. A highly controversial policy was now being proposed by some doctors to prevent people who had been born with birth defects from having children themselves. He filmed interviews with some affected families and with doctors and scientists, and edited it together to screen to potential **commissioners**:

> "I took this footage then to the **Sheffield MeetMarket**. Basically that's a room full of broadcasters. It's a bit like speed dating, they go from table to table, seeing if they like what you're proposing... but nobody's interested... they couldn't decide whether it's history or current affairs... they want to stick things in boxes. And real life

sometimes doesn't fit into boxes... Everyone wanted the red line you know, what's the big narrative arc of the story? So this is always the problem with documentary...

if it's not a **formatted** or event-led programme, the **story** must somehow be in and of itself... I didn't have the main character... I originally thought this would be portraits of life after the apocalypse, just a bunch of vignettes. And I thought that would be enough, but it wasn't." (Antony, 2012)

All the broadcasters passed on the project at Sheffield and Antony and his producer were quite disheartened:

> "So we sat on the film for a year. I think three years had gone past now... there was nowhere else for this programme to go... So we were about ready to give up on the project at this point. There's only so long you can keep banging this stuff out without money." (Antony, 2012)

However, then the documentary was selected for another funding market, called Good Pitch. This was a different kind of event, organized by the Brit Doc Foundation (http://britdoc.org), a support organization funded by Channel 4 and other sponsors. Good Pitch brought together other organizations, besides filmmakers and broadcasters, such as NGOs, who might be interested in funding documentary projects because of the issues they explored.

Antony re-edited the film and pitched it once more. He recounts how, although no NGOs showed any interest in the project, the commissioner for the Channel 4 TV documentary strand *True Stories*, which had previously turned down the project, was also at the event. She saw the re-edited version and heard the new pitch, which was more story-oriented – focusing on one central character going through a pregnancy. This time *True Stories* commissioned the project. After a protracted development period, to which the producer and director had already committed extensive resources, the project could finally go into production.

Formats: Both factual and drama formats have become increasingly important in television over recent years. A significant proportion of international programme sales is in formats (Monks 2012: 13), much of it in entertainment and reality genres, with perhaps the most well-known being the Endemol format *Big Brother*, which first ran in Holland, before being exported worldwide. As Antony attests, many documentary makers are concerned that the popularity of reality TV formats has negatively affected the money available for other types of factual programming, including investigative and observational documentary. The focus on formats is part of a wider tendency in broadcast documentary towards branding and labelling content to make it more recognizable and so more appealing to audiences, hence the tendency to 'stick things in boxes', of which Antony complains. Another way that broadcasters brand documentary content and encourage audiences to 'make a date to view' is through the use of strands, such as the *True Stories* strand, for which Antony's documentary was eventually commissioned. Channel 4 head of factual programming in 2012, Ralph Lee, describes documentary strands as "a way of putting a quality premium across things that otherwise might not have that much in common" (Khalsa 2012: 24). Strands ideally allow one-off documentaries to benefit from an established relationship with an audience that has been built through the strand identity, meaning they don't have to find their audience from scratch. The flipside of this, of course, to which Antony testifies, is that filmmakers need to tailor their films to the identity of the strand, as defined by its commissioning editor.

Case study: solving a Dickensian mystery — a UK–US co-production

In-house production: An in-house production is one in which the same company develops, finances, produces and distributes the project, using its own resources. It is closer to the Fordist model of production that we looked at in the first section, than to the post-Fordist outsourcing model. This does not mean, however, that everyone involved in the production is permanently employed by the company. Freelancers will also be involved, whether the in-house product is a television production or a newspaper. In television drama production, the production crew will nearly all be freelance and temporary, even if key development personnel are in-house and permanent. Moreover, in the case of *Edwin Drood*, as we shall see, another broadcaster and a distribution company co-financed the project. (See Chapter 9 for further discussion of TV commissioning and production.)

Channel 4 is a publisher broadcaster and does not produce its own content. However, some broadcasters do produce programmes **in-house** as well as commissioning productions from **independent** producers and buying in content.

Even when a programme is being developed and produced in-house, there is still a pitching and commissioning process to go through, although it is a more informal process than the one Antony experienced. Anne and Lisa, in-house **executive producer** and producer of drama at the BBC, explain:

"'In development' can cover anything from the moment a producer thinks 'wouldn't it be great to do this book, I shall go and find a writer who would like to do this book with me'... any idea that you've just had tickling away... either because a writer comes in and says I'm passionate about this subject, I want to write about it... or the producer might go out and talk to agents... That's the initial stage of development... you do need to get permission from somebody else to go out and develop that thought a bit more. It's part of the **slate** that we collectively maintain here, for all of the channels... So I might, for example, pitch to the creative director and, if she was interested, she might take it to our head of department and the drama commissioner. And if they were interested then that begins to filter back down to me... then we might commission a **treatment**." (Lisa, producer, 2011)

As a producer, Lisa develops projects as well as takes them into production. However, executive producers and **script editors** are perhaps the people who are most centrally involved with developing projects.

"I will be juggling anything up to 10 projects in development... at different stages, from an initial idea, to a treatment, to a script that we may have revisited a few times, drafting and redrafting, before we feel it's ready... Every project has its own unique gestation period. You can never tell. Sometimes something is commissioned and goes into production very quickly. Sometimes something is commissioned and it takes the writer a fair bit of time to work out exactly what they want to do with it, how to get it right, or they go off and do other things and come back to it... There are many examples of shows that have been in development for quite a long period of time and then suddenly they have found their moment, so it really varies show to show.

"With *Edwin Drood* [an adaptation of an unfinished novel by Charles Dickens], Gwyn [the writer] had the idea quite a while ago... she brought me a good idea of finishing off Charles Dickens' last work, *The Mystery of Edwin Drood*, and all I really knew was that it was the last book that Dickens had started to write and that he had died before he was able to finish it. So of course I was immediately intrigued... We had it sitting on our development slate for quite a while and she had been busy doing other things, I had been busy doing other things and when the bicentenary came up, I was already doing *Great Expectations* for BBC1 and it seemed like a perfect companion piece to do on BBC2... I had the initial conversations with Gwyn and got her to the second or third draft script stage, which is when we sent the scripts to the controller of Drama and he liked it and felt that it was right for BBC2." (Anne, executive producer, 2011)

"It had been commissioned by the channel but it hadn't been financially greenlit. There's two **green lights** at the BBC. There's the commissioning green light and a

```
     MURDER REPRISE: Edwin, falling to the ground.

     Jasper's body sways, and his voice echoes in the empty
     vaulted space.

                         JASPER (CONT'D)
               No!

                                                    CUT TO:


2/05    EXT. CATHEDRAL - DAY 5                             2/05

     Revd Crisparkle and Durdles approach the cathedral door.

                         DURDLES
               Lost some lead from the roof too,
               sir. And the hands of the clock is
               all bent and twisted.

                         REVD CRISPARKLE
               Dear me. What a night. We must pray
               no lives were lost.

     They are almost floored by Jasper, running from the
     cathedral, in such distress he can barely see them.

                         REVD CRISPARKLE (CONT'D)
               Jasper? Jasper!

     Jasper turns a tear-stained face to them.

                         JASPER
               My bright boy is gone.
```

Figure 7.2 *The Mystery of Edwin Drood* (Screenplay) ©BBC 2011, Writer Gwyneth Hughes

financial green light, and you need both of them before you can properly proceed. They generally follow one after the other. It's not usually an issue at all, very unlikely to get the first without the second. But it's possible because to put together the money to make anything requires a few things to fall into place... There's BBC money and there's **co-production** money. You need both..." (Lisa, 2011)

In this case, as well as the channel money, the production was part-financed by BBC Worldwide (www.bbcworldwide.com) and by American public broadcaster WGBH (www.wgbh.org).

> "WGBH they're our partner on most of our period dramas... our drama plays very well for them and we have an intensely collaborative relationship with them... The person who heads up *Masterpiece*, which is the strand that tends to air our period dramas, might speak to the Drama Commissioner or the head of our department to say 'what dramas have you got coming up? What have you got in development?' And then she might earmark things that she felt would play well and come in on them... I will talk to her throughout the process... she will read the scripts and I will keep her informed about casting and obviously she watches **cuts**." (Anne, 2011)

In television drama co-production, just as in shoe manufacturing, it is clear that relationships are important. In the same way as Vegetarian Shoes has established relationships with suppliers and manufacturers, the BBC drama department has tried-and-tested relationships with writers and production partners and between its own in-house staff, through which trust and confidence have been developed. Established channels of communication and a track record of previous collaboration help the development process go more smoothly.

This does not mean to say that there is no room for new entrants. The BBC has a dedicated unit, The Writers' Room, to encourage, support and commission new writing talent. It also runs schemes for new talent in other areas, as do other television channels (see Recommended Reading at the end of this chapter). But, as we heard from Antony, it is inevitable that new entrants will have to work harder to get an idea commissioned, either as a writer or a producer, until they have established a track record and developed those relationships.

Case study: the local and the global — dance music

Simon (who we met in the previous chapter) has been involved in the music industry for 27 years. Having worked as a DJ and in a record shop, he became an A&R (artists and repertoire) manager, specializing in dance music, for a major music corporation, before going to work for independent labels and freelance. In that time he has seen many changes in the industry:

> "There was definitely a time when music as a physical product, through vinyl and then CDs, became a business and a business grew around it, and then for a while it seemed to people that music was something to invest in, and music was a thing that

had unbelievably exponential earning potential... I think the problem the industry's having now is coming to terms with that there's not endless growth, and actually there's diminishing returns." (Simon, 2011)

Digital technologies have dramatically altered the parameters and reduced the revenues of the music business, although, as Simon points out:

"There are still companies in the world making money from music – the previous business models exist in some form. Most companies are still only selling a percentage of the music they sell digitally. But underlying that are trends and cycles that mean it's significantly different, peer-to-peer sharing of product and people's changing notion of value."

As far as Simon is concerned, this means a different understanding of what the product is that is actually being developed and produced:

"It's still music. What you may view more differently now is that rather than seeing music as the primary source of earning money, and other things as ancillary – now you would see that the hierarchy of different things that earn you money is all levelled now. The physical products selling music in a CD or a download, is a smaller part of the income you'd look at getting... proportionately it would be less than the other areas where you can earn money: live, merchandising, sponsorship, specific fan experiences, etc... you no longer control things and you hold the product and you sell it. It's more about creating value and having multiple ways of exploiting that."

The relationship that Simon puts the most emphasis on then is the one he develops with the potential audience for these products:

"You're still trying to create music and you're still trying to get to fans, but you're trying to do that in a direct way and you're trying to build a relationship that at points you can monetize. The problem is you can't necessarily monetize it straight away because acts need to be developed and, if you try to monetize a relationship too early, sometimes the communication doesn't work." (Simon, 2011)

In the context that Simon is working in, development means developing the act and the relationship with the audience as well as the music itself. Marketing and distribution thus become part of development and production, as we will explore further in the next chapter. The relationship between them is not a linear process from one to the other but a constant feedback loop. This is possible partly because the barriers to music production are much lower than they used to be in the past.

PRODUCTION

Broadly, when something goes into production it moves from the research and development-stage of ideas, sketches and plans, to investing time, labour and resources in turning those plans into actions and things. As we'll see, this isn't a clear distinction – sometimes development and production happen almost simultaneously – but it's useful for understanding the point in the process at which a creative product or service is made and delivered.

The bedroom studio

Digital technologies have not only changed the way that people obtain and listen to music, they have also changed the way they make it. The studio fits on a laptop now, as Simon points out, and it is fairly easy for aspiring musicians to make and record music:

> "Now with the means of production, that is, bedroom technology, and the means of distribution seemingly easier, that you can put something up on the net tomorrow... you can create something quite easily, quite good, quite quickly. Whereas before there would be more obstacles in the way of that creation... I think sometimes those obstacles made for more substantive [work] – or a learning curve that meant that artists, when they got to that point were more ready. So, I think it *has* changed the creation – technology's changed the way people create music, the way they think about music, the way people write music, the way people make music... And maybe I shouldn't say it's better or worse – it's just *different*." (Simon, 2011)

Simon's suggestion is that, when music is produced and consumed much faster in the way that he describes, then this leads to an abundance of content, where each individual track is less valuable in itself than it used to be, and what matters is the overall relationship of the musicians with their audience. Not only has the whole process of development and production got much shorter and more immediate, so has distribution:

> "And obviously it's also affected circulation in an enormous way, in that before there would be gatekeepers to circulation. Now there are less gatekeepers, but the issue is how do you get attention. So, in theory it's been democratized and it's more open, but what that means is that there are many, many, many competing voices seeking attention." (Simon, 2011)

The model of production and circulation that Simon is describing is most evident in the music sector but it is becoming more and more common across the creative industries.

From prototype to product

In the more traditional development and production paradigm, once what we might call the prototype (be it product sample, script or pilot) has been fully developed and tested, and finance has been secured, the project can finally go into production. Compared to the stop-start process of development, the rhythm of production is very different. It is typically a much more accelerated and intense stage of the process and is completed in a much shorter time than the development.

> "When you finally get it right, I give them the order the day the sample arrives... It's a way of communicating without using words. I give them the order straightaway,

as if to say 'if you'd done this two years ago, I'd have given you the order for this two years ago'... Also it means that the sooner you put your order in the sooner you get the shoes that you know you're going to sell. It's normally two or three months is the lead time for shoe making." (Robin, 2011)

"I'm on set every day. I don't produce it from the office. And it is difficult when all those immediate decisions are being made every day about how to stay on budget, stay on schedule, stay on story, all of that... to also be developing different shows... when you're in post-production, it's easier to pick up your development again." (Lisa, 2011)

The actual shoot of the drama *Edwin Drood* lasted five weeks. However, film and television production schedules include another important stage before production and after development, which is pre-production. Pre-production is the stage, after the project has been greenlit, when the schedule is drawn up, the locations are secured, and the cast and crew are hired: in short, it is when all the practicalities and logistics are addressed, and large-scale finances and other resources are committed to actually make the production happen. In the case of *Edwin Drood* there were six weeks of pre-production before the shoot. During this time an awful lot needed to be achieved.

Pre-production: planning and organizing

"The director [who had already been brought on board by the executive producer] and I sat down together with two scripts, we knew they'd change still, but we felt reasonably confident that this was the basic structure of what we wanted to do... We brought on the first of the HODs (heads of department). And the first people you bring on, under these circumstances would be locations and design, because they've got to create your world for you..." (Lisa, 2011)

Lisa and the director had already decided on the interior location they would use for the central setting in the story of the cathedral, which Lisa calls their '**hero** location'. In fact, the cathedral that appears in the drama is made up of several different locations, each used for different areas of the cathedral, such as the exterior, the main interior, the crypt and the cloisters. These are all cut together in the edit to look like one location. Sometimes the practicalities of location can impact significantly on the story and the script. For example, on *Edwin Drood*, another main location that the location manager was asked to find was a weir (a water feature like a small dam), which was at that time a significant setting in the story. However, as script development and budgeting continued, it became apparent that this might need to be rethought. Not only was the writer finding it quite difficult to choreograph the events of the plot between the weir and the cathedral, but it became apparent that a weir setting would have big budgetary implications. The cathedral exterior was being shot in Rochester, a town with Dickensian connections, which was also near London and in travelling distance for the London-based production team and crew. However, there was no suitable weir location nearby. Any other possible location would involve travelling further, taking more time and involving accommodation costs:

> "We realised that was actually going to be very difficult to try and pursue on the budget we had because all this inevitably necessitated overnighting and that's a big chunk of any budget. So we began to realize that actually it wasn't going to be an affordable way to do it... Eventually, we had to say the only way we can do this is to abandon the water as a major element of the storytelling... Some water was necessary. But we couldn't make it the beginning and end of episode 1, the beginning and end of episode 2... That's producing, that is completely producing." (Lisa, 2011)

For Lisa, being a producer involves three main things: "It's your job to get the best scripts out of the writer. When you've got the best possible scripts and you've been greenlit, then it's your responsibility to hire the best possible team... And then, lastly, it's your job as a producer to create the conditions for them to do the best possible work."

In order to achieve these goals Lisa needs to work closely with writer, director, casting director, executive producer and **line producer**, juggling budget requirements, script developments, cast availability and other logistics, all of which impact mutually on each other, as we have seen in the case of the weir location. A change in script may necessitate a different location, as may a change in budget. The schedule has to be built around practicalities such as actors' bookings and location proximity, to try to be as economical as possible with both time and money. Preparing for a shoot is consequently a complex and detailed organizational challenge.

Other HODs who need to be recruited include the cinematographer, or DOP (director of photography), the editor, the sound recordist, costume and makeup. The first step is for director and producer to draw up a shortlist of people, who they think might be right for the project, based on their track record of previous work. These positions are not advertised in the press or other media. Candidates or their agents will be contacted directly and they will be invited to a meeting. The shortlisted candidates will read the script and discuss their ideas with the director and producer: "You look for something... some exciting flavour you haven't thought of... You want them to understand what your starting point vision is, but also for them to bring something of their own" (Lisa, 2011).

Each of these HODs will recruit their own team to work with them on the project. Another important crew member is the first AD (first assistant director, there are also second and third ADs). The first AD draws up the schedule for the shoot and, once the programme goes into production, he or she will organize the set and make sure the production stays on schedule.

The schedule is drawn up based on the scenes and locations detailed in the script. But, as Lisa explains, script editing and revision may well still be going on at this stage:

> "Your shooting scripts are almost always a little bit late... but you can't really do a proper schedule until you've got your shooting scripts in. And, until you've got a proper schedule, you can't properly cast your actors, because you don't know when

you're going to need them... In an ideal world, for a five weeks shoot you would book your whole cast for the whole five weeks, for maximum flexibility of how you schedule. Obviously you can't do that. It's very expensive... a bit of a jigsaw puzzle to make the schedule and the actors' bookings." (Lisa, 2011)

So although the casting was carried out quite early on in pre-production, the final bookings of actors had to wait until the schedule could be confirmed. Once the actors were confirmed, makeup and costume then came on to the production a couple of weeks before the shoot:

End Day # 9 07 September 2011 – Total Pages: 4 7/8						
--						
Day 10 – Thurs 8th September 2011 (0800-1800)						
SR-0623 SS-1932						
N/A – Minor Canon Road						
Rochester						
1/4	Day 1	EXT	CATHEDRAL	DROOD DOOR	2/8 pgs	1
			Jasper hurries through the quiet old town to the cathedral.			
1/17	Day 2	EXT	CATHEDRAL – GRAVEYARD	GRAVEYARD	7/8 pgs	10, 100
			Durdles shares his lunch with Deputy.			
1/55	Day 4	EXT	CATHEDRAL	MEMORIAL YARD	2/8 pgs	1, 2, 3
			The couple both have something serious to say.			
1/62	Day 5	EXT	CATHEDRAL – GRAVEYARD	GRAVEYARD	1 5/8 pgs	3, 13, 100
			Princess Puffer warns Drood that he is in danger.			
2/12A	Day 5	EXT	CATHEDRAL – GRAVEYARD	GRAVEYARD	1/8 pgs	100
			Deputy picking through the graveyard mess.			
2/13B	Day 5	EXT	CATHEDRAL – GRAVEYARD	GRAVEYARD	1/8 pgs	100
			Deputy finds the ring.			
2/16A	Day 5	EXT	CATHEDRAL – GRAVEYARD	GRAVEYARD/MEMORIAL	3/8 pgs	2, 5, 9, 10, 100
			Deputy hands the ring over to Durdles.			
2/28	Day 7	EXT	CATHEDRAL – GRAVEYARD	GRAVEYARD	7/8 pgs	10, 100
			Months later. Deputy and Durdles hum along to the choir.			
2/5	Day 5	EXT	CATHEDRAL	CASTLE DOOR	3/8 pgs	1, 4, 10
			Jasper flees from the cathedral.			
TITLE	Day	EXT	CATHEDRAL	CATHEDRAL	1/8 pgs	
			Titles. Steadicam shot of cathedral.			
2/45	Day 8	EXT	CATHEDRAL	CATHEDRAL	1/8 pgs	
			Establisher. The cathedral looks doomy now.			
End Day # 10 08 September 2011 – Total Pages: 5 1/8						

Figure 7.3   *The Mystery of Edwin Drood* (Schedule) ©BBC 2011

"Once you've offered them the job, they can be thinking about it in terms of the look and they've got to put it forward to you. But they can't actually do anything until they've got the actual actors in front of them. So there's always a pressure in the last few weeks of prep to get all your actors booked as solidly as you can, so your costume and makeup have somebody to work with." (Lisa, 2011)

Production: putting the plan into action

Once the drama goes into production, Lisa continues to work with line producer and first AD to manage the budget and schedule. Revisions and rethinks will often still be needed and scenes may need to be cut in order to stay on schedule and on budget:

"We'd pretty much completed the second week of the shoot when we realized that there were a couple of days that were just a little bit too tight. We were trying to shoot an average of five pages (of script) a day... With contemporary drama you can get away with it... but period drama there's more time taken for hair changes, makeup changes, clothes changes. We're doing five pages a day, with a really good cast... and with a crew who were incredibly fast and incredibly on the ball... If you're on a location for a few days, you can begin to get... you move things on a bit, you know, 'we've dropped that scene off today but we'll get it here tomorrow'. But as you move around different locations, there comes a kind of hard deadline and after the end of tomorrow we'll no longer be here. So, in order to avoid us having a situation where we were constantly dropping scenes off, I did want to go into the script again in week 2 and say 'actually, what can we do to make all of this more achievable for the rest of the shoot?' If you make those changes in the second week, in our case, and issue a revised script that takes account of them, then everyone knows they're working to an achievable thing, because what everybody hates, and I hate on their behalf, is every day looking at a **call sheet** that's got too many scenes on, too much to do and feels oh we're not going to achieve it. Nobody wants that... so I really, really try to avoid that." (Lisa, 2011)

While the shoot is going on, the **rushes/dailies** will be going to Anne, the executive producer, who will view them and pass comments to the director and producer, who are also viewing them daily. They also go to the editor, who is employed from the start of the shoot and cuts the footage together into a first **assembly**.

Post-production: putting it all together

Once the shoot is over, post-production begins and the director will join the editor in the cutting room to view the assembly and work towards a **fine cut**. On *Edwin Drood*, the producer and editor had three weeks to fine cut each episode. After three weeks, Episode 1 was **locked** and went into the next stages of post-production, **track laying** and **picture grading**.

Before an episode can be locked, however, it needs to be viewed and approved by several people:

> "The way that this team in particular tends to work is that the director will have 10 days on his own [+ the editor] with it and then he quite likes me to come in, saying 'I think I've got this as far as I can, without an extra pair of eyes.' So now we both look at it and we get it to a place where we think that we're fairly happy to give it to the **execs**, who then come in with their thoughts on it and so on and so on until you get to a point where it's not that everybody has to be happy because that's almost impossible, but you want to have ironed out as many of the bugs as everybody can see... editor, director, producer, executive producer and writer, head of department, drama commissioner, in that order, everybody sees it. And everybody feeds notes back into it. By the end of the third week we have decided that we're happy with what we have and we're locking it." (Lisa, 2011)

> "It's a creative question of how do we make this show the best thing it can be?' How do we position the scenes in relation to each other? How do we edit performance to get the best nuance and the best resonance from that particular actor and that particular piece of writing?... This is called the picture lock of the show and then it has to go off and we start track laying, we start **sound spotting**, we grade... You have finite periods of time, by which things need to be decided upon and accomplished...

> "I would go to a grade review... to see if that was in keeping with the show... I would get a sense of the music... and then I would sit through the final mix, which is when everything's all mixed together: the sound, any additional dialogue recording, effects etc... Once the final mix has been done, the show is ready." (Anne, 2011)

Expecting the unexpected: completing *After the Apocalypse*

As we have already seen, in Antony's documentary project the various stages of development and production were less distinct from each other than in the drama production described above. This was partly because, as with the music production Simon discussed, the resources needed to shoot and edit 'taster' footage for the documentary, although considerable, were still more feasible for director and producer to self-fund than they would be for period drama. It was also because, since Antony was part of an independent new director and producer team, it was much less likely that his project would be commissioned on the basis of a paper treatment alone. For a documentary in particular, seeing actual footage is evidence to a commissioner that the production team has the access and the skill to deliver the programme. Thus, when Antony's project obtained a commission and officially went into production, some of the key material had already been shot. He is doubtful, nevertheless, whether he and his producer will fully recoup their costs, even with the money they received from the television commission:

> "So bear in mind that we'd spent probably... if we include our time... it all depends how you cost your time, but we'd put in our own money and everything. So this £40,000 was for past, present and future. As you can see it is not a lot of money." (Antony, 2012)

This is not an uncommon situation for independent producers to find themselves in, particularly if they are new entrants to the industry with international projects such as this one. As Antony says:

> "There are so many filmmakers going through similar experiences and we're all competing... these kind of passion projects, it's tempting to think that they will make money, but they don't. You're effectively having to work for free... the market is for formatted stuff... a lot of people just don't realize how hard it is... But I think that sometimes you have really no choice if you believe in something... A lot of them [the productions] will make money eventually. But I don't think they're very sustainable from the director's point of view. For every one you see on telly there are loads that never make it to TV. That's the problem." (Antony, 2012)

Antony says that one of the things that the broadcaster stipulated to him and his producer, as part of the commission, was that the production worked with an experienced documentary maker as executive producer, who would oversee the project. Although this took up quite a bit of the budget, it was an understandable requirement since they were fairly new to the industry. The money also paid for Antony to go out to Kazakhstan again and film the central spine of the documentary – the

Figure 7.4   Antony on location in Kazakhstan

story of a pregnant woman, herself a victim of radiation, who was facing opposition to her pregnancy from doctors who worried that her baby would also suffer birth defects. However, before the child was born, the money ran out. Antony had to return to England and shortly after that the producer's production company went bankrupt.

Although the original idea was not Antony's, he explains that he had become very involved in the project as a director and couldn't bear to see it fail at this point. However, the producer was not in a position to continue and it was the production company which owned the rights to the film. In the end, Antony managed to put together the money to buy the **rights** to the film from the production company's receivers. He went back to Kazakhstan and shot the final footage for the film. However, at the end of the process both the executive producer and the editor were owed money from the production and Antony, who was now the co-producer on the project as well as director, had to settle the bills. The way he did this was to give his collaborators a share in the profits:

> "I had to dilute my share. And of course the actual distribution is being done through a distributor so they're taking 40% (of distribution revenue). So, even though I own the underlying rights, I only get 30 or 40% of the money. So you still own all the rights, but you've given the share of the profit from it... you've parcelled it out to all these different people." (Antony, 2012)

We will look at this distribution process in a bit more detail in the next chapter.

At the end of the production, Antony was very pleased with the result and with the experience of making it, but also feels very wary of putting himself through such an experience again:

> "I've seen things that most people will never ever see in their lives... I'll always the rest of my life remember riding a horse on a nuclear bomb crater, drinking vodka with mad herders... So you've got the beauty, but I've paid a dear price for it." (Antony, 2012)

As a former financial analyst, Antony left finance for documentary production because he wanted to live differently:

> "Working in finance, you're aware that you're the elite of the capitalist system, aren't you? Top of the global tree... And you realize that even though you're an elite you're wasting money on all the idiotic things... girls, expensive nightclubs, stuff you don't need... I felt there was more to life than just wanting to earn money..."

However, he is also keenly aware that, as a filmmaker, he is also an entrepreneur and, in order to make a living out of media production, you need to find a way of making it profitable:

> "If you want to be a freelance filmmaker, you're a businessman. You're offering a product... you've got to go where the money is... The problem is this is effectively

like starting up... making films is like starting up many different businesses in different sectors... each one is like a little entrepreneurial company. So it's not like you make a model for making a pancake shop or a coffee shop. With *After the Apocalypse* it's not like a coffee shop... I'm an expert on making films about radiation but, guess what, there's only one nuclear test site like that in the world. So now forget about it and do something entirely different... which is really interesting but also like a nightmare, because you just have to become an expert at something else." (Antony, 2012)

Antony, like Simon, is starting to think that perhaps developing a direct relationship with his potential audience, rather than with a broadcaster, may be a model he would prefer to follow and is developing a few projects that he aims to finance through **crowd-funding** (we will look at this approach in more detail in the final section of the book):

"If you engage with your target audience first, and then ask them if you're willing to pay for it, that's the way I'm doing things now... The broadcasters are not in the driving seat any more, the audience are... It's all about finding the audience, saying you're offering a value proposition... It requires you to be a marketer." (Antony, 2012)

SUMMARY

Having examined the development and production of some different types of creative product, we can see that each project has features unique to its sector. However, we can also perceive many similarities between the processes involved in each case. Creative producers from different sectors describe the metamorphosis of an idea into a creative product as involving a mixture of passionate enthusiasm, careful calculation, stamina and perseverance.

In discussing the many things that can and do go wrong, they highlight the fact that their activities take place in a landscape of shifting sands, in which nothing can be taken for granted, big or small. Good and bad luck will always play its part, but equally, quick thinking and resourcefulness are crucial skills for success, as plans may have to change at short notice. It is not surprising then that creative producers also stress the importance of developing and maintaining relationships and relying on trust and shared histories in order for a creative product to get made and find an audience.

RECOMMENDED READING

BBC Writers' Room: www.bbc.co.uk/writersroom/

Bernard, Sheila Curran. 2007. *Documentary Storytelling: Making Stronger and More Dramatic Nonfiction Films*. Oxford: Elsevier. A helpful guide to story development and design in documentary filmmaking.

Cury, Ivan. 2006. *Directing and Producing for Television: A Format Approach*. Oxford: Elsevier. An overview of who and what is involved in television production.

Katz, Steven Douglas. 1991. *Film Directing Shot by Shot: Visualizing from Concept to Screen*. Michael Wiese Productions. A detailed guide to visualization, production design and staging for screen drama directors. It contains a workshop element exploring the many different ways in which a scene can be choreographed and shot, to achieve different dramatic effects.

Kerrigan, Finola. 2009. *Film Marketing*. Oxford: Elsevier/Butterworth-Heinemann. A concise how-to guide to marketing a film, from no-budget shorts to big-budget features.

Mayer, Vicki, Miranda J. Banks, and John Thornton Caldwell. 2009. *Production Studies: Cultural Studies of Media Industries*. New York: Routledge. Essays on studying media production, focused on Hollywood and the USA TV industry.

Passman, Donald S. 1994. *All You Need to Know About the Music Business*. New York: Simon & Schuster. A veteran music manager distils the tricks of the trade in book form.

Stradling, Linda. 2010. *Production Management for TV and Film: The Professional's Guide*. London: A&C Black. Step-by-step guide to managing a TV or film production with real-life examples.

8

Circulation: Marketing and Distribution of Creative Products

When we think about creative labour and the creative industries, we tend to focus first on the activity of *creating* things. Making something new is of course the first step. However, once a product is produced, it has to be sold in order to make a return on the investment put into it. The same goes for services, events, experiences – in short, anything that will generate revenue or other benefits. How will a film get seen, a book read, a game played or an exhibition attract visitors?

CIRCULATION

It is cultural distribution, not cultural production that is the key locus of power and profit. (Garnham 1990: 161)

Let's think back to the basic idea of what creative labour involves (see Chapter 1): the *creation of novelty*, the generation of *intellectual property*, and interaction with an *audience*. Circulation, then, is what happens after something new has been created, when it's time to find an audience who will enjoy it, talk about it or use it.

Marketing, publicity and distribution are important for creatives for two main reasons: First, it is important for creatives to understand where the fruits of creative labour go next, once they've seen the light of day. Second, marketing and advertising businesses represent a significant portion of the creative industries – they employ large numbers of creative people and generate vast amounts of creative products, either directly or indirectly (for more on this, see Chapter 10). Therefore, the aim of this chapter is to give you a sense of what is at stake in the space between creating something and the audiences out there in the big world noticing, enjoying, talking about and doing something with it. As David Hesmondhalgh (2007: 28) argues, *circulation* covers the marketing, publicity and dissemination of creative products. In this chapter we will consider circulation not just as a separate stage that follows the creation of a cultural product – when the seriousness of business takes over from the fun of dreaming up and making cultural products – but also as a form of creative labour in itself, including the creative work that goes into marketing and advertising.

Lisa, the film producer we met in the previous chapter, sees her job as encompassing the whole journey of the work from inception to distribution. According to her, "the producer's job is you are the godparent for this baby all the way through. So you can't just walk away from it. Somebody has to take overall responsibility... somebody has to love it onto the screen... In this case the executive producer and I will share that" (Lisa, 2011). Similarly, Simon, who has worked as an A&R (artists and repertoire) manager at various music labels for almost two decades, sees it as his role to both discover new talent and help it out into the market: "A&R has two roles: finding the talent, whether they write stuff themselves or other people collaborate as co-writers or producers. Secondly, you help take that creation and you build a vision for it so that the company you're working within then begins to build its other marketing and distribution plans" (Simon, 2011).

THE MASS MARKET MODEL

While production costs tend to be very high, the reproduction of the original, and its distribution into the market tend to be comparatively cheap. For games, films, music, therefore, the model has been to invest in a few 'big' products and then reproduce and sell as many of them as possible – this is the mass-market model as it operates in the content-producing creative industries. It can also be seen at work in design, although the mass-production of a physical artefact such as a piece of jewellery or a handbag is very different from making multiple copies of a film or music recording – in the business jargon, they "scale" differently. Conversely, designers can capitalize on the cachet and exclusivity of a unique or small-run product in a way that translates less well to the media sector. This is exclusivity born of scarcity. It can be replicated in mass-markets through artificial means with "limited editions" and "special editions" of films, music and games.

The long tail: This is a simple metaphor for how online retailers can offer a (hypothetically) near-infinitely large selection of products (Anderson 2006, 2009). Physical shops can only accommodate so much stuff within their walls. Amazon, by contrast, has successfully combined an easy-to-use web-storefront with cheap warehousing, sophisticated databases, and efficient stock-management systems to offer a vast range of products for home delivery. When the products are digital, as in the case of music, films and TV shows, an online retailer like Apple's iTunes Store can exploit the vast back catalogues of recorded music decades into the past. Digital copies are easy to store and transmit, and sometimes old records can even become hits again (Weeds 2012).

Mass-production goes hand-in-hand with high expenditure on mass-marketing. However, other models are evolving – with digital production and reproduction, lower production costs mean narrower distribution can still make money. Distribution and marketing over the internet also means that sales can happen over time, in a trickle, rather than all at once – essentially the sales of few copies of many items over a long period of time, rather than the conventional mass-market sales of many copies of few items in as short a time as possible. The editor of *Wired* magazine, Chris Anderson, dubbed this characteristic of online retail "**the long tail**" (Anderson 2006).

CHANNELS OF DISTRIBUTION AND MARKETING

Every type of creative product or service will have its own specific channels of distribution and marketing. For example, broadcast radio is still a very important medium for musicians to gain attention and recognition, and to connect with an audience who might pay to see them live, buy CD or downloads, or just share their YouTube videos with their friends via social media. How a product is distributed depends on what channels are utilized in each instance to get it to consumers, recoup the investment and potentially make a profit on it.

Although the documentary that we looked at in the previous chapter was commissioned for television broadcast, this is not the only distribution channel for the film. It was also screened at documentary festivals and, because the documentary raises awareness of biomedical issues, the producers secured funding from the Wellcome Trust for a theatrical release. The way this works is that the Wellcome Trust buys all the seats for each screening of the film for a short run of a few days. The cinema then pays the Trust back the money from the ticket receipts they get. The Trust thus makes back some but not all of its investment. However, the Wellcome Trust's funding of the theatrical release is not an investment for direct financial gain, but a form of sponsorship, which raises its profile as an organization.

Screening at documentary festivals raises the film's profile within the industry. This is important, not only for the film itself, but also for Antony's future career as a director, since producers, commissioners, financers and other key industry figures attend film festivals. Meanwhile, as Antony explains, the theatrical release also has an important marketing role for the film, as only films which obtain a theatrical release will be reviewed by the press:

> "The only reason why the *Sunday Times* reviewed it is because it was an official cinema release. *Empire* and *Total Film* would never have reviewed it if it wasn't released in the cinemas; if it had just been on telly it wouldn't have got reviewed. Ultimately, you want to be in a position where many more people have heard about your film than have actually seen it. So, actually, this film was reviewed all over the place and I've been on radio three times now." (Antony, 2012)

This media coverage will generate further awareness of and interest in the documentary, raising its international profile, and that of the director and production companies involved. Thus, although these distribution channels do not make the film any money, they have a marketing function for both producers and product (as well as sponsors such as the Wellcome Trust). The increased profile they provide may contribute positively to international (television) sales of the film. These international sales are managed by a sales company, who take 40% of the income generated.

WHAT IS MARKETING?

Marketing acts to stimulate demand (for a product, service, etc.). The most basic definition of marketing is that it is essentially any activity that serves to stimulate an appetite which did not already exist among the consumers, users or audience of a commercial product. Marketing is often seen as being a matter of *transactions*, such as how to price a product, how to promote it, where and how to distribute it, and so on.

At the BBC there is a dedicated marketing department, which managed the promotion of *The Mystery of Edwin Drood*, which we discussed in the last chapter. They worked with executive producer, Anne, and producer, Lisa, to arrange interviews and photoshoots with actors during the shoot, and then used these materials as part of the promotional **campaign**, promoting the programme with listing magazines and other media. They also manage media enquiries, talking to journalists and possibly organizing interviews with the writer and other key crew members.

Marketing can also be about *relationships*, for example, building and maintaining customers' trust in a particular brand or loyalty to particular products. This is why some marketing scholars argue that the "fifth P" of the marketing mix is *people* (Moore and Pareek

The four Ps: Marketing is often summed up as a combination of four key factors: Product, Place, Price, and Promotion (Russell 2010). From this point of view, marketing can be said to address four basic questions every time: What is being sold? Where is it made available? At what price? How will potential customers learn about it?

Campaign: An organized effort concentrated on a mutual goal or outcome. The word comes from military use, a campaign to achieve a particular aim, but in general use it can refer to a variety of organized, goal-oriented courses of action. Marketing is usually structured around campaigns, of varying lengths and scope, depending on what is being marketed. The marketing calendar is seasonal, following annual cycles in which the creative work, media planning and media buying takes place long before a campaign goes public at certain key periods during the year – the Christmas shopping season, the spring/summer and autumn/winter seasons in fashion, the school season, and the like (Baines 2008; Fill 2011). Marketing campaigns are therefore often quite territorially specific, taking into account the cultural specificities of each market – festivals, gift-giving holidays, religious traditions, etc.

2010). For example, Simon, the A&R manager, regards the creation and circulation of music as being closely related activities: the music cannot be easily separated from the associated performances and merchandise that will eventually bring in revenue. For him, circulation involves far more than simply making music and distributing copies of it. Instead, it involves working continuously over a long time to build a profile for the artist, to establish contact with important circulation channels, such as radio stations, music television, and events programmers who select performers for live events.

In popular music, as Simon points out, promotions or marketing communications are activities that are less and less confined to specialists. Instead, they are increasingly done by the creative practitioners themselves or those working immediately with them. This is also the reality of organization structures in small or microbusinesses, as distinguished from large organizations. For example, although Channel 4 will take care of publicity for the broadcast slot of *After the Apocalypse*, beyond the television screening, Antony (see Chapter 7) looks after the marketing himself, as co-producer and director of the film. In other words, do-it-yourself marketing with little or no budget, using cheap online tools, social media, and one's own professional and personal networks of contacts is now a routine element of creative practice.

Case study: DIY marketing

Jeremy, a director of research for a London-based media agency, points out that in the space of a few years, much of what used to be left to professionals in the areas of marketing and public relations (which are not the same thing) is now possible for anyone with a laptop and a broadband connection:

> "Marketing is much more a DIY business than it used to be. By that I mean that, say in 1992, if you were a local company wanting to promote, for example, a travel business. The only tools you really had at your disposal were advertising in the newspapers, which you'd need [a media agency] for because they got discounts, and they had better negotiation power. Or you would do press releases and perhaps liaison and try to encourage journalists to write about you. Again, that's a relatively specialist thing. It's much easier to get traction if you're ringing up from a company specializing in these sorts of things, because in 1992 there was no Google, there was no paid search, there was no internet, effectively, so nobody really bought their own advertising. But also, it was before social media, so it was pretty hard to actually connect to the end user, let alone people like journalists. In 1992 nobody had email addresses, while now a lot of newspapers will print an email address at the end of the story and you can get in touch with the journalist directly. So, if you see that somebody's written an article about something that may have relevance to you, it's easy to get in touch with them and say 'well actually my company does this, would you be interested?'" (Jeremy, 2010)

Jeremy sees online social media like MySpace, Facebook and later Twitter as having caused a major shift from professional PR and marketing to enterprising individuals doing it for themselves: "This is why it's much easier for people to do things like public relations, and to a lesser extent advertising, on their own than it used to be. Now, with a lot of things such as organizing parties or art shows or band nights – a lot of things that students do – many of them are probably doing marketing without actually realizing it, or at least thinking about it in those terms" (Jeremy, 2010).

SELLING STUFF: RETAIL AND ITS DISRUPTIONS

A street market is possibly the simplest kind of distribution there is. You show up in the morning with your stall and your goods, set up the display, people pass through during the day, buy what they fancy, then everyone goes home in the evening. Market stalls are often the first sales channel that young, enterprising creatives make use of when finding buyers for their wares. Designer-makers of clothing, jewellery and accessories can be found at street markets all over. When he first started out, Robin, who we met in the last chapter, sublet space in a friend's clothes shop to sell his shoes, later moving into dedicated space on a popular shopping street.

Shopping is an *experience* as well as a utilitarian necessity. From medieval markets to the department stores of the nineteenth century, the trade in goods has provided entertainment and excitement in public spaces. We go shopping not necessarily because we need something specific, but as a diversion, a form of social entertainment. As Michael B. Miller writes about the Bon Marché in Paris, the world's largest department store until 1914, the display of goods was a spectacle in itself:

"Part opera, part theatre, part museum, [the Bon Marché] did not disappoint

Disruption: The name of a process by which a product or service is introduced at the "low end" or bottom of a market, and then quickly spreads "upmarket" to unseat the established competitors or ways of doing things. Introduced by Clayton Christensen in his book *The Innovator's Dilemma* (1997), the term quickly caught on in business and management, and has become a great favourite among commentators and journalists. For example, the technology news site *TechCrunch* runs regular events titled *Disrupt* in various key cities like San Francisco, New York and Beijing, as a forum for new technology startups. Some have argued that "for the Net, disruption is a feature, not a bug" (Naughton 2012: 43). Originally, the idea of "disruption" in business arises from a rather mundane context – the analysis of steel mills and heavy industry. It turns out that new technologies that often put established companies out of business are not necessarily better or more advanced at the outset – often they are worse. Hydraulic backhoes, for example, were quite weak when they were first introduced in the 1960s; they were no match for the powerful steam shovels they eventually replaced. For a contemporary example of a disruptive low-end technology, consider how mobile phone cameras have replaced conventional cameras. Inferior in all aspects, phone cameras are nevertheless convenient, cheap, and they are always on hand (MacFarquhar 2012).

those who came for a show. Merchandise heaped upon merchandise was a sight all its own. Bargain counters outside entryways produced a crush at the doors that attracted still larger crowds, thus creating for all the sensation of a happening without and within." (Miller 1994: 168)

If the Bon Marché established shopping as a form of spectacular mass-entertainment, that was only the beginning. With Disneyland and the invention of "themed entertainment" in a contained space, retail, entertainment and public space converged on a scale that was far greater than that of the department store (Davis 2001). Around the same time as Disneyland was opened, the invention of the mall extended the retail environment from the space of the shop to the space of a neighbourhood or city – an all-encompassing environment mixing shopping with other attractions. Such branded, themed environments are replicated in shopping districts, shopping centres and individual stores, which remain destinations in their own right for tourism and amusement (Vanderbilt 1997; Moor 2003; Couldry and McCarthy 2004).

Retail trouble: disintermediation

Despite the deep social roots of shopping as entertainment, all is not well in the world of physical shops. Retailers, previously the most visible and immediate intermediaries between producers and consumers of creative products, are now vulnerable to what is sometimes called *disintermediation*, the removal of previously important links in the value chain that have become redundant or easily bypassed, for example when book-stores, record shops and other vendors of physical media find themselves in competition with the long tail of online retailers like Amazon or Apple's iTunes Store which can offer far larger catalogues for home delivery or download.

One example of the speed with which this can happen is the evolution of home video rentals. In September 2010, the fate of the neighbourhood video rental was sealed when the company Blockbuster Video filed for bankruptcy. In the early 1980s, when videocassette recorders (VCRs) became popular, viewers didn't want to buy a copy of every single film they watched at home. Therefore the convenience of having a local video rental serving the immediate neighbourhood was self-evident: VHS tapes were relatively bulky and fragile objects, not easily transported by mail. Along the way, video stores made a significant difference to how consumers conceived of films as physical objects: with the invention of the VCR, films became tangible consumer goods whereas before they had been transient experiences only available in movie theatres (Greenberg 2008). This was, historically speaking, an important change in the way viewers related to films and television.

Thirty years on, rental stores such as Blockbuster have almost entirely vanished. Instead, consumers either get their rented DVDs delivered physically by mail or electronically over broadband (streamed or downloaded). Mail-order DVD rentals disrupted the old business model of the local video stores by using DVDs, which are lightweight and sturdy enough to mail in an envelope, and abolishing the dreaded (and very lucrative) late fees. Instead of renting a movie overnight or for a set number of days, companies such as Lovefilm and Netflix would offer "DVD queues" online, where customers could queue up a list of movies they'd like delivered to them. When each DVD was returned, the next one would be dispatched. Moreover, as the business journalist James Surowiecki writes in his obituary of Blockbuster, online services such as Netflix added a new level of service that the chain's staff could not hope to match:

> There was a time when customers had few alternatives, so they tolerated the chain's limited stock, exorbitant late fees (Blockbuster collected about half a billion dollars a year in late fees), and absence of good advice about what to watch. But, once Netflix came along, it became clear that you could have tremendous variety, keep movies as long as you liked, and, thanks to the Netflix recommendation engine, actually get some serviceable advice. (Places like Netflix and Amazon have demonstrated the great irony that computer algorithms can provide a more personalized and engaging customer experience than many physical stores.) (Surowiecki 2010)

Some remaining bricks-and-mortar video rentals survive by providing a specialist service, a face-to-face experience of browsing, discovering and talking about films, as Surowiecki points out. Because they cannot compete with online rental services on the breadth of their catalogue or the memoriousness of their recommendation engines, they distinguish themselves through *depth* – catering to a particular *niche*, such as horror, manga, sci-fi, and so on.

However, digital technologies do not always hurt retailers. They have had a very positive impact on Robin's Vegetarian Shoes business, for example, allowing him to greatly expand the existing mail order side of the company, which had always run alongside the retail outlet. Online orders allow his business to maintain a steady growth, without opening new retail outlets. Because he designs and manufactures a unique niche product, rather than simply supplying it, he does not rely on people coming to his shop, but can exploit digital technologies to expand the reach of his product all over the world.

The problem that physical retail stores face with selling books, films, music and games is essentially how to persuade people to buy things in physical shops that they can get online, often cheaper. In the face of this, some retailers have turned the question around to see how a high street location can be made an asset for retail. Independent bookstores and smaller chains have successfully competed with large chains and online retailers like Amazon by focusing on the retail experience: by selecting the stock carefully, hiring knowledgeable staff, and offering products relevant to the local context, retailers previously threatened with extinction have successfully refashioned their shops as destinations where the customer's experience in the shop itself becomes a primary reason for going there.

By offering locally relevant products (not competing with the large catalogues of online competitors) and having staff who know and understand the product – whether it is books, music or video games, certain retailers thrive by creating a social experience around their products. For example, gaming retailers can make use of their physical space as a social destination for gamers themselves, rather than trying to rival supermarkets or online retailers on price. Their unique selling proposition is to "delight the customer" (Hammond 2003: 81) who comes into the shop for trying out games with kiosks and games pods, discovering new games, and to pick up new games for their collection. As the video games journalist Keith Stuart puts it: "We are social, we still like going out, we still like sharing, we still like meeting each other, and I think games shops can still be part of that if they can get that whole social experience thing right" (Stuart, in Krotoski 2012).

After disintermediation, reintermediation

Disintermediation is not the only form of disruptive change that can happen in a value chain. *Reintermediation*, the introduction of new intermediaries, often from outside the current established value chain, can cause just as much upheaval. James Surowiecki points out that the most significant challenge to video rentals such as Netflix (whose business model, at the time, involved posting physical copies of DVDs in the mail) comes not from established competitors in the rentals business, but from Apple, Amazon and Google – technology companies that are well positioned to integrate the sales and rentals of all electronic media into their online platforms (Surowiecki 2010). Therefore, established cultural gatekeepers such as publishers, broadcasters and record labels have found themselves contending with software companies (Google), computer makers (Apple), mobile phone operators and internet service providers for influence over how films, music, TV and radio reach an audience.

This is particularly important when it comes to one of the trickiest business problems that content-producers face. As Matt Mason puts it in *The Pirate's Dilemma*, the question of distribution is fundamental to the viability of the creative industries worldwide:

> If our property can be infinitely reproduced and instantaneously distributed all over the planet without cost, without our knowledge, without its even leaving our possession, how can we protect it? How are we going to get paid for the work we do with our minds? And if we can't get paid, what will assure the continued creation and distribution of such work? (Mason 2008: 10)

Mason raises two very important business problems here, in relation to the circulation of creative products, and in fact all intellectual property: first, how to *get paid* for intellectual, creative work in the first place and, second, how to make such work *sustainable* for the future? In other words, this is not just a question of remuneration for creative workers, but also of whether we all can have access to the cultural commons of shared stories, sounds, images, music and so on – the food of our imaginations, as Lawrence Lessig suggests in his influential book on copyright, intellectual property and digital technology, *Free Culture* (2005).

With the traditional media formats (e.g., print, music, film and television) produced and distributed digitally, the content-producing industries find themselves using technologies that directly enable others to copy and distribute their products for free. This is sometimes called "online piracy", which is a simplified metaphor for a process in which companies and individuals produce something new, sometimes at enormous expense, but immediately when it gets distributed this content is copied and made available to anyone with a computer, broadband and a small amount of technological savvy to download at no charge. The question, in other words, is how do producers of paid content compete with those who insist on offering it for free?

Competing with "free"

Lester Bangs, the late, great early-rock critic, once said he dreamed of having a basement with every album ever released in it. That's a fantasy shared by many music fans—and, *mutatis mutandis*, film buffs as well. We all know the Internet has made available a lot of things that were previously hard to get. Recently, though, there are indications of something even more enticing, almost paradisiacal, something that might have made Bangs put down the cough syrup and sit up straight: that almost *everything* is available. […] Soon, we'll all have Lester Bangs' basement in our pockets. And it's just a matter of time that we'll be able to do something similar for film. (Wyman 2011a)

Simon, after almost three decades' worth of experience in the UK music business, argues that in the digital era the key issue for all content-producing industries (film, TV, music, etc.) is how content can retain its value. If that's not possible, then the challenge is how to build in different value so that consumers will be persuaded to pay for it:

"Everybody who makes content is trying to work out how to protect it – either in reactionary ways or by adding value. Online piracy is just part of the set of issues that's faced the industry. In the 1990s there was an enormous boom because the record companies began reissuing back catalogue on CDs. The music industry discovered a new identity for itself as a **copyright** industry. It was in possession of a large number of intellectual properties, copyrighted works of art, music, with which it had very favourable terms. In the 1990s they were able to persuade consumers to buy everything they already had on vinyl again on CD. Now, the record industry would argue that this is defensible, because probably 5% of the artists at a record label pay for the other 90% of artists that don't make money. Therefore, being able to exploit that catalogue allows them to invest in new artists." (Simon, 2011)

The greatest challenge for the digital distribution of music through downloading was initially negotiating **licence** agreements with music publishers. The first successful large-scale distribution platform for digital music downloads came not from the Big Five music labels, which had successfully shut down the file-sharing service Napster in 2001 through litigation, but from a technology company. In his biography of Steve Jobs, the CEO of Apple, Walter Isaacson details the personal effort that Jobs had to put into negotiating directly with reluctant music publishers to persuade them to license their music catalogues for sale through the iTunes Music Store, which opened for business on 28 April 2003 (Isaacson 2011). In Simon's experience, working at a London-based record label in the early 2000s, the problem that the music industry had in coming to terms with digital distribution was that CDs were far more profitable, and the industry had no incentive to move away from them, despite consumer demand for legal downloads:

> "Because [record labels] were making so much money from CDs, they couldn't find a way to attract the consumers that might want to pay for music if they'd give it to them at a reasonable, accessible rate. It wasn't about paying, it was about ease of access. Because they made it so difficult to access music for so long, they missed that opportunity, and a computer firm came in to provide the world's biggest downloading service, something that they could have done for themselves." (Simon, 2011)

In retrospect, it seems clear that Apple revolutionized the distribution of recorded music, with iTunes transforming the music industry as a whole, as noted by obituarists after the death of Steve Jobs (Markoff 2011). However, the music industry's reluctance to negotiate with Jobs, as Steve Knopper has argued in *Appetite for Self-Destruction*, may have been only one of many mistakes, most of which have less to do with internet-based distribution than the previous digital technology that the industry embraced: the compact disc. The success of CDs in the 1980s and 1990s, Knopper argues, caused the industry to grow unsustainably large, with staffing, overheads and various expenditures eventually proving too burdensome – as he describes in amusing and lurid detail in a chapter on "how big spenders got rich in the post-CD boom" (Knopper 2009).

An industry predicated on selling expensive, physical copies of music was not going to have an easy time adjusting to a world of easy copying and online distribution. Technology companies like Apple, Amazon and Google changed the dynamics of legal music distribution, "pirate" peer-to-peer file-sharing was enabled by technologies like BitTorrent, LimeWire and others, and the consumers changed their habits and expectations. All of this made the old music industry model impossible to maintain:

> In 2006 EMI, the world's fourth-biggest recorded-music company, invited some teenagers into its headquarters in London to talk to its top managers about their listening habits. At the end of the session the EMI bosses thanked them for their comments and told them to help themselves to a big pile of CDs sitting on a table. But none of the teens took any of the CDs, even though they were free. "That was the moment we realised the game was completely up," says a person who was there. (Economist 2008)

The result was consolidation – companies in financial trouble are bought by wealthier ones for their back catalogues as much as their current artists and repertoire. In 2007, Simon lost his job as A&R manager when his label was closed down and sold. The "Big 5" record labels that Steve Jobs had to negotiate with became the "Big 4" in 2004, and in 2011 their numbers shrank to the "Big 3" when EMI, in financial difficulties at that point, was bought by Universal.

Access is what the culture commentator Bill Wyman argues sits at the heart of the contemporary music and film industries' problems in competing with free, illegal distribution of expensively produced, copyrighted content. The problem is less about price than about *accessibility* and *convenience* for the user. This is where the content industries have fallen behind: "The easiest and most convenient way to see the movies or TV shows you want is to get them illegally" (Wyman 2011b). This convenience then combines with scale in a disastrous fashion when home broadband connections are becoming capable of faster data speeds, as Wyman describes in an article on the arrest and downfall of a prominent "cyberlocker" website which had enabled the sharing of large archives of copyrighted material:

> Not so long ago, the industry was upset about kids moving 3 megabyte MP3s around on Napster. Today, it's common to see 35 gigabyte compilations of, say, seven seasons of the TV show *House*, all conveniently bundled together. (Note that that's *ten thousand times* bigger.) Meanwhile, on the enforcement front, officials will continue to catch a few luckless file-sharers and other low-hanging fruit, none of which will have an effect on the rate of growth of the problem, much less reduce it. (Wyman 2012)

In a study of corporate responses to peer-to-peer file-sharing, Des Freedman argues that the established music industry pulls in two opposite directions in its reactions. On the one hand, it seeks to undermine the impact of file-sharing through litigation, describing it as "theft". On the other hand, the industry is "trying to take advantage of the Internet in reducing distribution costs and offering the possibility of a more direct relationship between labels and consumers" (Freedman 2003: 173). That, however, might necessitate a reinvention of the music industry's business model from what it was at the end of the twentieth century.

Case study: making music in a digital market

As Matt Mason argues in *The Pirate's Dilemma*, the fact of the ease of digital reproduction and distribution on such a massive scale is forcing a rethink of the ways in which content-producing businesses make themselves sustainable over the long term (Mason 2008). How can creativity and the production of creative goods be rewarded in new ways?

One option would be to switch off the internet, cancel everyone's broadband subscriptions and go back to distributing films, music, games and other copyrighted material in physical formats. Not likely? If so, then content producers have to look for realistic alternatives that reward the artists and makers of creative products and allow for the fact that copying and distribution is now digital, cheap (not free) and fast. Let's take musicians as an example of how artists are finding their feet in a market where they can no longer realistically expect to make their living solely from selling copies (either physical or digital) of their musical recordings. Their passion is music, but their livelihoods are made by reaching audiences who will purchase copies of their songs and albums, see them perform live, buy the t-shirts, and so on. How does that happen?

Simon says that there are a number of routes that a song or an album can go once it has been created:

> "First, you can take the recording to a record company. If you're working in a pop-genre it's not really the kind of thing an independent label or an artist can work out on their own. People say it can require a million pounds to promote a single into the pop market – and really, only the majors have got that kind of money. However, if you're *not* working in the pop-idiom, then there are ways for you to start promoting your music right away. That means putting the music into the world via radio and social media. Again, you may be doing that on a very localized level – local radio, for example – or it might be specific genre-radio, for instance if you're playing dubstep you might want Rinse FM to play it. If you had a dubstep tune, you would have to get the right underground DJs playing it, and you don't have to give them a white-label vinyl anymore, it can be sent out via MP3. Those DJs can be reached either through networks you've built up or through paying a small amount of money to a promotion company that has those contacts. So, you send the tune out via MP3 to those DJs who would potentially play it in clubs and on the right underground stations – some of which are still pirate, and some of which are licensed, like Rinse FM (which was pirate but is now a legitimate radio station). At the same time you would build your artist by adding visuals to go with the music, for example a logo. Obviously you'd probably make a cheap video you could put on YouTube. A lot of music is now distributed and enjoyed by listeners straight from YouTube, but one of the biggest websites in the UK is SBTV which mainly plays urban music – SBTV has thousands and thousands of teenage hits in this specific genre of music." (Simon, 2011)

The big problem, then, is that there are thousands of tracks going through this process. How is your track different? Simon is only partly joking when he says that, first, it has to be different by simply being *good* – better than the others competing with it. Apart from that, it's also a matter of the artists building their reputations from playing live. Most records do not become popular right away, as if by magic, coming out of nowhere. It takes time to build up a reputation for making good music. "You still need to build a career. You've made a piece of music, you've taken it to market, now it depends on what your expectations are. Maybe what you want to do is sell

5000 downloads, build a reputation, get more DJ-ing gigs as a dubstep artist" (Simon, 2011). In other words, what counts as success differs between genres of music and the cultural contexts of the musicians and their audiences.

Joe, a freelance guitarist who has toured and recorded with a number of musicians, puts a different spin on this question of what counts as success in reaching an audience for one's music. For him, live performances, merchandise sales and licensing provide a more reliable income for earning a living from his musicianship. About his experience playing and touring with Brazilian bands, he remarks:

> "The Brazilians, they see records as just another way to promote themselves. They'll put their music out online, free of charge, and basically get it to as many people as they possibly can. Then they start booking gigs and playing like crazy. I met a Brazilian band in Barcelona last year [2009] – they were on tour of Portugal, Spain and France, all off the back of songs they'd been giving away online." (Joe, 2010)

As Joe points out, for this particular band, "success" means making a living from their music through playing live and touring abroad.

Having a "profile" in this sense means that *attention* and *recognition* are extremely valuable. It takes a lot of effort for a musician to turn him- or herself into a recognizable *brand*. For DJs (short for disc-jockeys), who compete intensely for recognition and gigs, this is particularly important. Simon points out that among DJs, the stakes have been raised with the availability of cheap digital recording technology:

> "Before, DJs would be DJs and producers would be producers. Nowadays most DJs are also producers. It's almost like they get DJ work by doing their own bits of music. Of course people always did before, but now if you're a DJ and you're not

Attention economy: Information consumes the attention of its recipients, as Herbert Simon pointed out (Simon 1971). Therefore, in an information-rich environment, *attention* becomes a scarce commodity. The attention economy is therefore an economy in which information plays an important, even essential, role in the everyday lives of consumers. Such an economy hasn't done away with raw materials, manufacturing or services in the conventional sense; rather, information- or knowledge-industries play an important role alongside the older, traditional industries. Under these circumstances, an attention economy, in which the attention of consumers is valuable – as users, readers, viewers, listeners, subscribers, and so on – can operate. This is why "likes" on Facebook are valuable for advertisers. As Michael Goldhaber argued in the early years of the World Wide Web: "What would be the incentive in organizing our lives around spewing out more information if there is already far too much? [...] There is something else that moves through the Net, flowing in the opposite direction from information, namely attention. So seeking attention could be the very incentive we are looking for" (Goldhaber 1997). A decade and a half later, Google, Amazon, Facebook, Apple and Microsoft would probably all agree. Recommended reading: Clay Shirky, *Cognitive Surplus: Creativity and Generosity in a Connected Age* (2011); Charles Leadbeater, *We-Think* (2008).

also producing your own music it's quite rare. It used to be specific DJs who were brilliant at DJ-ing and other people would produce the music. Now it's almost like you have to be producing your own tunes to get the profile to get the DJ-ing gigs that are probably going to earn you the money." (Simon, 2011)

What's changed, according to Simon, is that:

"The piece of music isn't the end result – taking the recording to market is not the way to make money. Instead, it's part of the chain of things that *might* mean that you make money from DJ-ing or allow you to exploit it in other ways. For instance, a lot of urban artists have given away free mix tapes, but then have made money from selling t-shirts. It's like the music becomes – in commercial supermarket terms – the loss-leader." (Simon, 2011)

Recorded music, as a commodity, has come a long way since the big-money days of the CDs, from cash cow to loss-leader in the span of a decade.

What Simon is suggesting is that there is a business for musicians in finding their niche and establishing a strong relationship with a dedicated group of fans. He is not alone in this. The independent musician Jonathan Coulton is a rock star who appeals primarily to geeks. A former computer programmer, he turned his hand to writing funny, catchy songs about love among the cubicles. With no record label, he still makes around half a million dollars a year from touring, selling his songs and merchandise online, and licensing his music (Planet Money 2011). Coulton is an example of what Kevin Kelly refers to as the "1,000 True Fans", arguing that "the long tail" (Anderson 2006) is good for retail aggregators like Amazon, Netflix or iTunes, and for the billions of consumers who get a better deal as a result. However, it's a mixed blessing for creators. "Individual artists, producers, inventors and makers are overlooked in the equation. The long tail does not raise the sales of creators much, but it does add massive competition and endless downward pressure on prices," says Kelly. One solution to this problem is to find 1,000 True Fans:

A creator, such as an artist, musician, photographer, craftsperson, performer, animator, designer, videomaker, or author – in other words, anyone producing works of art – needs to acquire only 1,000 True Fans to make a living. [...] A True Fan is defined as someone who will purchase anything and everything you produce. They will drive 200 miles to see you sing. They will buy the super deluxe re-issued hi-res box set of your stuff even though they have the low-res version. They have a Google Alert set for your name. They bookmark the eBay page where your out-of-print editions show up. They come to your openings. They have you sign their copies. They buy the t-shirt, and the mug, and the hat. They can't wait till you issue your next work. They are true fans. (Kelly 2008)

Distribution and marketing of creative products, in other words, are in some ways changing from a mass-market model to an interactive relationship in which smaller niches of fans take a more active role (and are more willing to pay for the privilege) than a generic mass-audience. From a different perspective, we will see this revisited later in relation to marketing and advertising campaigns, and how the digital media environment encourages ongoing communications and interactivity (see Chapter 10).

SUMMARY

> For most filmmakers, the joys and pains of making and finishing their film is what defines filmmaking. In reality, the life of the film has only just begun. No one cares what hardships went into making your *chef d'oeuvre* if no one ever sees it. The true life of a film begins after it's in the can and it's sent off into the world to see if it can walk on its own. (Jenn Chen, film distributor, in Badal 2007: 53)

One key point of this chapter has been that circulation is itself a form of creative labour. Large numbers of people working in the creative industries have jobs and roles that involve putting creative products into circulation. This chapter has not sought to offer a comprehensive map of all the possibilities for how films, television, music, books or games can be circulated. Instead, we have attempted to shed light on the fundamental processes of circulation – the work that continues long after the initial development and production of a film is complete, or the writing and recording of a song.

RECOMMENDED READING

Badal, Sharon. 2007. *Swimming Upstream: A Lifesaving Guide to Short Film Distribution*. Oxford: Focal Press. Practical advice for the independent maker of short films, from festivals to TV and cinema distribution.

Fill, Chris. 2009. *Marketing Communications: Interactivity, Communities and Content* (5th edition). Harlow: FT/Prentice Hall. A wide-ranging introduction to marketing communications.

Greenberg, Joshua M. 2008. *From BetaMax to Blockbuster: Video Stores and the Invention of Movies on Video*. Cambridge, MA: MIT Press. An illuminating, entertaining history of how video rental, as a distribution technology and a business, changed consumers' relationship to films.

Hackley, Chris. 2009. *Marketing: A Critical Introduction*. London: Sage. An overview of marketing concepts and practices, combining a critical perspective with a sense of what goes on inside marketing and advertising agencies.

Moore, Karl and Niketh Pareek. 2010. *Marketing: The Basics* (2nd edition). London: Routledge. Concise introduction to marketing for readers fresh to the discipline.

PART 3

The Creative Economy

We now turn our attention to financing models and how they relate to particular types of institution, product and sector. In Chapter 9 we focus on large media organizations which originate and distribute content, taking case studies from broadcasting and publishing. As we saw in Chapter 3, large broadcasters and other content-makers tended to be vertically integrated until the 1980s, when, in many countries, vertical disintegration "streamlined" these organizations so that commissioning and distribution remained vertically integrated, while some or all of production was outsourced. In this chapter, therefore, we focus on the relationship between the producers of content and the commissioners whose job it is to "feed the hungry machine" as one interviewee put it. This content is produced by independent production companies or individual freelancers, as well as by in-house staff. We will investigate the commissioning process, through which this work is allocated — a standard practice across all the "content industries".

Moving on from these large media organizations, in Chapter 10 we take in a broader view of content and services. We look at what creative agencies do, how they relate to clients, and how the client-led business relationship differs from the commissioning structures discussed in Chapter 9. We also consider other models of finance, including public funding, the complexities of film financing, and the emerging kinds of self-funding and crowdfunding enabled by digital technologies and online social media — which recall older forms of patronage, sponsorship, and the self-financed ventures of independent artists and producers. Finally, in Chapter 11 we conclude the book by considering the role of *change*: the changing relationship between culture and commerce; the relationship between work and personal circumstances in the creative industries; and how business models and structures change over time.

9

Institutional Commissioning and Financing Structures

The main question of this chapter is how media organizations, from broadcasters to publishers, procure new programmes, images and stories. Due to the changing technological environment of the media markets, which have made new powerful players in media distribution and content production (e.g., Google, Apple), established media organizations have been forced to adapt their business models and working practices. Taking case studies from television and magazine publishing, we look at the way their business models have evolved, in particular regarding the significance of brand identity. In light of that, we consider the implications these changes have had for commissioning content.

BUSINESS MODELS IN THE TELEVISION SECTOR

The contemporary television sector features a range of business models, for both **public service broadcasting** and **commercial broadcasting**. Television services usually operate on either a **free-to-air**, pay-per-view or subscription basis. Free-to-air television services generate revenue through advertising, public funding (e.g., government subsidy or TV licence fee), donations, sponsorship or a combination of such sources. Early broadcasting ventures, such as the BBC, were set up according to the free-to-air model, aimed at a national audience, but in the late twentieth and early twenty-first centuries, new communication technologies, such as cable, satellite and digital, have developed in tandem with new models of revenue generation (such as subscription and pay-per-view) and an increasingly international reach. Organizations may operate according to different models in different territories. BBC television channels, for example, are available free-to-air in the UK, where the BBC is funded by UK TV licenceholders, but elsewhere in the world these channels may be accessed via subscriptions to cable and satellite.

Public service broadcasting (PSB) and commercial broadcasting: Public service broadcasting has as its priority to be a resource for the public, through news, entertainment, current affairs and educational programming. Commercial broadcasting, by contrast, has the aim of making a profit to the broadcaster, through the sales of advertising and sponsorships. In most European countries, public service broadcasters get some form of state funding, which in the UK takes the form of a licence-fee which goes to the BBC, which is therefore barred from carrying advertising on domestic channels. The BBC, however, is not the only public service broadcaster in the UK – the main broadcasters all have a public service remit as a condition of their broadcasting licences (ITV, Channel 4, Five, and BSkyB). The funding models are mixed (e.g., European public broadcasters feature advertising) (Downey 2007). Public service broadcasters and commercial ones differ in their ethos: the public service ethos of informing, educating and entertaining (see Born 2004) is fundamentally different from running a for-profit business. Education has been seen by many as both a core function of PSB, and under threat from cost-cutting imperatives (Grummell 2009; House of Lords 2009). More generally, as governments have sought to rein in the budgets of public service broadcasters in the past few decades, for example the slimming-down of the BBC in the 1990s (Born 2004), some have argued that the public service broadcasting model is being reinvented in practice across Europe (Bardoel and d'Haenens 2008). In the digital environment, Public Service Publishing (PSP) has been proposed as a more appropriate concept, encompassing online, interactive media and services as well as traditional broadcasting, see for example the objectives of Digital Britain (DCMS 2009). Recommended reading: Georgina Born, *Uncertain Vision* (2004); Peter Lunt and Sonia Livingstone, *Media Regulation* (2012).

A television company may produce and distribute all of its own content. Examples of such an approach range from large-scale, vertically integrated state broadcasters to small-scale, local and specialist television services. However, in an international, multi-platform media landscape, content and platform are no longer bound together and this has led to many television companies making a clearer distinction between their production, distribution and broadcast activities. There is more than one production and distribution model they might adopt. At the other end of the spectrum from full vertical integration, they might, for example, operate a publisher model, that is, they might broadcast content made by independent producers and other broadcasters but not produce content in-house.

Some publisher TV companies will both commission original programming from independent producers and acquire the rights to broadcast existing content (i.e., programmes that are already made). Channel 4 in the UK is an example of this approach. The programming of other companies, including many cable channels, or new online platforms, such as Hulu, on the other hand, is comprised mainly or entirely of acquisitions of existing content. This content may be acquired from other broadcasters or from independent producers.

Many other companies operate a mixed model, producing content in-house as well as commissioning original content from independent producers and acquiring the rights to broadcast existing content. Television stations, which are affiliated to a **television network**, will carry a proportion of programming provided by the network, a proportion of programming produced locally and a proportion of acquired existing content (referred to in the USA as **syndicated** content).

Within a particular organization, the production, distribution and broadcast divisions may operate highly autonomously. The production division of one television company may be commissioned to make programmes for broadcast on another television network, for example. Television companies will also seek to distribute their in-house content beyond broadcast on their own channels. The distribution arm of their business will sell the distribution rights to particular programmes to different territories worldwide.

The international reach of television services extends beyond international sales and acquisition of content. As we learnt above, national broadcasting services may be available to international audiences and many broadcasting ventures are set up as international services from the start. The satellite broadcaster Sky is one such example. A different, but salient example is Al-Jazeera, an Arabic language broadcasting network, set up with funding from the state of Qatar. Although financed by a national government, Al-Jazeera's target audience was the Arabic-speaking world in general and it quickly became an influential and controversial voice, with an international audience and reputation. In 2006 it launched an English-language channel to further extend its international reach, along with a news website.

Broadcasters' international approach to the production and acquisition of content is also manifest in co-productions, particularly with documentary and drama series, and also in the international sale of scripted and non-scripted formats, which we will investigate in further detail below.

The plethora of television channels, platforms and business models in operation, along with the international reach of television services, means a large number of potential commissioning opportunities for anyone seeking to write, direct or produce television programmes. This multitude of opportunities is, however, rather bewildering in its variations and complexities. In order to understand these more fully, we will return to our television production case studies from Chapter 7, as a starting point for working through some aspects of the commissioning process. We will put particular emphasis on pitching and the commissioning of content from independent producers and freelance writers, since this is the position that many creative producers will find themselves in and is perhaps the most daunting situation to navigate.

COMMISSIONING IN TELEVISION

In Chapter 7, we heard from Lisa and Anne, the in-house producer and executive producer of a drama series, and from Antony, the independent producer/director of a single documentary. After some difficulties, Antony secured a commission for a TV documentary strand. In order to do this, Antony pitched his idea to the commissioner for the strand. In the case of the in-house production, Anne, the BBC executive producer, needed to get the approval of the Drama Controller in order to get her project **green lit**.

The commissioning process for BBC Drama is not, however, an exclusively in-house process. The BBC needs to commission drama scripts from freelance screenwriters, since, in common with other broadcasters, it does not employ in-house screenwriters. The BBC also commissions at least 25% of its content from independent producers, just as Channel 4 commissioned Antony's documentary programme. Indeed, in 2012 the BBC commissioned nearly 50% of its programming from independent producers (Kanter 2012)

Independent writers and producers, seeking to get their television idea into production will need to get their project green lit through the same commissioning hierarchy as an in-house production. However, they may access it at different points, depending on various factors, as we will go on to discuss.

HOW DO WRITERS AND PRODUCERS GET TV COMMISSIONS?

All television companies that commission original content, whether they are terrestrial, cable, satellite or online, will have commissioning executives whose job it is to handle this process. The precise structure within which these commissioning executives operate, however, will vary from company to company, depending on its size and operational strategies and priorities. Media organizations also undergo fairly regular restructuring, usually as the result of a change of management. So these structures rarely stay exactly the same. In 2012, our case study, BBC drama, was part of BBC Vision, the content division. There were in fact many senior staff within BBC Vision, whose job involved overseeing drama content. These included the channel controllers responsible for the overall direction for all the programming of their particular channel. In addition, there were several different senior managers, all with particular responsibility for drama: the director of drama productions; the controller of drama commissioning; the controller of series and serials; the senior executive producer for drama production; the head of BBC films, which funds single dramas for theatrical release, and the chief creative officer, who oversees in-house production of drama and other genres, such as comedy.

These channel and genre senior executives clearly had overlapping briefs, requiring collaboration on content commissioning and scheduling. As the BBC commissioning guidelines explain, 'To get a programme commissioned it has to work for both the Channel and the Genre' (BBC 2012a). However, the first port of call for an independent producer or writer is not, in fact, any of these senior managers. Independent producers are instead directed lower down in the commissioning hierarchy to dedicated commissioning editors, whose job it is to commission independent content. At the time of writing, there are two commissioning editors for independent drama. There are also separate commissioning editors for regional programming (i.e., content produced outside London, both in-house and independent), for which the BBC has to meet commissioning and production quotas. These commissioning editors will develop a slate of projects, for which they will ultimately seek approval further up the commissioning hierarchy, with the drama controller, who will liaise with the channel controllers.

Because the BBC is a publicly funded institution, it publishes extensive information about its structures and operations (including the salaries and expenses of all its executives). Not all television companies may observe this level of transparency, but they should usually make available information about their commissioning structures and priorities, as the BBC does with its commissioning guidelines (BBC 2012a).

In practice, however, writers and producers will often tend to follow a more informal route to getting a television commission, at least in the early stages. They will attempt to discuss their idea in person, before they submit it formally. If they already have a contact within the television company, they will start with their contact. This contact may not necessarily be the commissioning editor. Writers, in particular, may have developed a relationship with an in-house script executive (also called script editors), producer or executive producer, in which case they will take the project to them. Although script executives, producers and executive producers are working on projects handed to them by commissioning executives higher up the chain, they also have the flexibility to develop projects they have found or initiated themselves as part of their slate. They then seek definitive approval higher up the chain to get the project green lit. Freelance producers and production companies will also develop relationships with executive producers as well as commissioning editors. There are, therefore, multiple entry points through which independents may pitch ideas to and develop projects with the television company, although ultimate approval is centralized at the top.

Case study: drama commissioning at the BBC

The top-down approach to content commissioning, which characterizes most broadcasters, has been criticized for various perceived faults, including being overly centralized, risk-averse and too bureaucratic. The controller-led structure described above replaced a producer-led structure, which existed before deregulation, when the BBC was mainly producing content in-house (Born 2004). An independent producer interviewed in 2006 complained that commissioning editors "are interested in having power and making decisions and seeing the global picture. It's not really about creativity" (Hesmondhalgh and Baker 2011: 110). In 2009, drama writers and producers also complained about what they saw as a "systemic failure" in commissioning, which they blamed on a management structure "which emphasizes brands over writing" (Rushton 2009b). However, BBC Controller of Drama Commissioning Ben Stephenson has publicly defended the practice of "seeing the global picture" as vital to successful commissioning. In an interview with the trade magazine *Broadcast*, he says:

> Clearly it can't be a free-for-all and it would be disingenuous to say it could. The job is not just about choosing the best programmes – it is about taking an overview of what should sit together. (Rushton 2009a)

In 2009, Stephenson was responsible for a budget of around £24 million, according to Rushton. It is the drama controller's job to determine the overall direction of BBC drama, which includes both genre and channel considerations. He will consider projects brought to him by the drama commissioning editors (both in-house and independent productions) in relation to his overall strategy. Of course, priorities change over time, as is evident from two interviews Stephenson gave to *Broadcast* in 2009 and 2010: in April 2009 Stephenson is reported as saying that crime drama is one of his priorities for 2010 (Rushton 2010). However, in January 2010 he is reported as saying that he now wants to steer away from crime shows (Rushton 2010). His new "shopping list" is not genre-specific but focuses on particular priorities for particular channels. He asks for:

"More …

- BBC1: 9pm shows that redefine the mainstream, including ones that no commercial broadcaster would make
- BBC2: "Addictive, intelligent" serials of up to six parts to air at 9pm
- Filmic singles that can attract world-class talent
- BBC3: The next *Being Human* – shows that make the most of a writer's "singular imagination" for a younger audience
- BBC4: A broader range of art and history, including adaptations of "lost classics".

Less …

- BBC1 series for 7pm on Saturday. Slots are already full with *Merlin* and *Doctor Who*
- BBC1 series for 8pm on a Sunday. "We'd rather invest our money at 9pm". (Rushton 2010)

Although this "shopping list" does not spell out the channel identities, they come through fairly clearly. BBC1 is defined as a mainstream channel, but distinguished by innovative programming of a scale and ambition that fulfils its public service remit. BBC2 is seen as a bit more experimental and sophisticated. BBC3 targets a young demographic. BBC4 has an arts and culture focus.

If we jump now to 2012, these identities remain consistent. The BBC1 overall commissioning tagline promoted on its website was "big experiences we all want to be part of" (BBC 2012b). Its drama commissioning brief was still for "returning series and serials that offer range and distinctiveness for broad audiences". There was also a particular call for "story-telling that takes us into the lives of people from different backgrounds in the UK" (BBC 2012b). BBC2's overall tagline, on the other hand, was "A spirit of bold creativity at its heart". Commissioners continued to seek "scripts that demonstrate the intelligence, sophistication and creative ingenuity that our viewers have come to expect," in particular "fine writing that is sharply contemporary in its depictions of life in Britain and around the world" (BBC 2012c).

BBC3, apparently "never afraid to try new stuff" (BBC 2012d), was defined as a channel which nurtured new talent and acted as a "laboratory for BBC One and BBC Two". Much of its focus was on comedy and entertainment, however it also called for drama ideas, where it sought "fresh high-concept ideas as well as stories that reflect the lives and aspirations of our target audience" (BBC 2012d).

Since it is funded by a licence fee paid by all owners of television sets, the BBC needs to demonstrate that it is meeting the needs of a wide range of audiences across its various channels. Its overall brand identity is the opposite of niche (compare this to the example of HBO later in this chapter). The key brand values the BBC aims to promote, as an organization and across all its channels, are excellence, inclusivity and diversity. Stephenson states that: "The ability for the best writers and directors to do their best work goes to the heart of what BBC1 – and the BBC – is about" (Rushton 2010) and says that "It would be hard to feel we were at the top of our game if we didn't offer range and variety to appeal to all licence-fee payers" (Rushton 2009a).

Brand identity

Brand identity has become increasingly important in a multi-channel television landscape. An individual executive producer or commissioning editor may love an idea brought to them by a writer or a producer, but he or she will have to abide by the particular channel, genre and strand priorities set by channel, genre and strand controllers. Television companies seek to promote a particular brand identity, both for the company and the individual channels they operate, and they will be looking to see whether any idea pitched to them is a good fit for their brand. You can get a sense of the particular identity of a channel by watching the content it programmes and by keeping abreast both of the information it publishes about itself and of what is reported in the industry trade press. However, brand identities are not static. They evolve and can change quite dramatically. US cable channel HBO, for example, began in the 1970s as primarily a sports and movies channel, but in the 1980s started using original programming as a way of differentiating its channel identity from other cable services. By the 1990s it had become a prestige brand, with a reputation for high quality drama (such as *The Sopranos* (1999–2007), *Six Feet Under* (2001–2005) and *Sex in the City* (1998–2004)). Free of the restrictions that free-to-air TV networks had to abide by (on swearing, representations of sex, violence, etc.), HBO aimed its adult-oriented content primarily at an affluent, educated audience who could afford to pay for it. Suggesting that the content it offered was available nowhere else, HBO's brand tagline at this time was "It's not TV. It's HBO". Thus the high-end quality of its programming provided a justification for its high subscription fees (C. Johnson 2012: 30).

If writers and producers are aware of how a company and/or channel identity is evolving or what gaps they might be looking to fill, they can take advantage of the opportunities it opens up. One recent example is satellite broadcaster Sky's substantial expansion of its original programming, in which it committed to raising its programming budget by 50%, with the extra spend going on comedy, arts and drama. Sky's move was motivated by a similar aim to that of HBO: to achieve a more distinct identity and a brand with appeal to an upmarket audience. Having reached near saturation point through its established strengths of sport and movies, it needed a new strategy to keep on expanding its customer base.

Stuart Murphy, director of commissioning for Sky Entertainment (including drama, comedy and arts), defined Sky's strategy as being initially about "fewer, bigger, better," which then evolved into "bigger, better, better loved" (Campbell 2012b: 25).

Sky's quality offensive began in 2011 with comedy. It commissioned several new comedies and succeeded in attracting talent previously attached to the content of terrestrial broadcasters. Sky's move sparked an upsurge of comedy commissioning by other broadcasters in an effort not to lose their **market share** to Sky (Parker 2011: 1). This was definitely the moment for writers and producers to pitch comedy ideas since TV channels were actively seeking such content and were expanding their provision.

FINDING A ROUTE IN

As we saw in the section on networking in Chapter 5, it is clear that if you are a writer or a producer seeking a television commission, you need to know who the people are in the commissioning chain at every broadcaster. You need to find out about them and what they are looking for – by reading information published by the broadcaster and in the trade press and by attending industry events. Once you have done your homework about who's who in commissioning, you then need to decide who best to pitch your ideas to. As well as knowing the particular people in the commissioning chain, this also means knowing which television company and channel is most likely to be interested in the style and genre of your programme idea and what their current priorities are.

You also need to find ways to get your work and your face known to commissioning executives. If an independent does not have an existing contact within the commissioning structure, they will seek to make such contacts, through networking at industry events, such as festivals. Face-to-face communication is considered a vital part of achieving a successful commission. This is not to say that drama has never been commissioned by somebody simply sending in a script "cold". But it is considered a less likely route to success.

Furthermore, as we heard from Lisa, the TV producer interviewed in Chapter 7, those involved in commissioning do not just wait for projects to come to them; they actively seek out projects. They approach agents, attend theatre productions, read books and explore a range of other routes in the hunt for writers. They will also approach writers and producers they already know with programme ideas.

New talent

For new talent, there may well be particular routes in. At the BBC all new writers and unsolicited scripts are directed towards the BBC Writers' Room. Also, the Writers' Room runs competitions and competitive training schemes for new writers as well as listing competitions and training provided by other broadcasters and organizations. Television companies also run schemes for new directors and producers.

Continuing and returning dramas

Continuing dramas and long-running television **returning dramas** will have a large stable of writers that they draw on. This may take the form of a team of writers working together, or of individual writers writing particular episodes, or indeed a combination of both. Writers (or their agents) seeking a commission from one of these series would approach the series editor/producer directly (the **showrunner** in the USA).

Independents need each other

Writers, directors and producers also need to be alert to each others' activities, since it may well be through an independent producer that a writer or director gains a television commission, or indeed vice versa. Likewise freelance producers take on productions for production companies. Producers also need to develop relationships with writers and directors and their agents. The process is similar to the relationship with the broadcaster. A writer will either pitch their idea and/or send a treatment or script to the company, or the company will seek them out through their agent, or directly, particularly if they have an existing relationship. A director will send their **showreel** to a production company or the company will seek them out through an agent. A writer may also find a freelance producer who is interested in their idea and seeks out a commission via an independent production company or straight to the broadcaster.

The international dimension

Since independent production is an international operation, independent producers are increasingly seeking international commissions, sales and co-production arrangements. The biggest recent trend has been in international sales of formats (both scripted and

"Super-indies" and the international television market: The increasing international focus of television markets has driven consolidation in European independent production to create so-called "super-indies" — large independent television production companies which have merged with or acquired others across different territories (including Europe, Australia, the USA and India). These consolidators include companies such as Endemol (Netherlands), All3Media (UK) and Fremantle Media (based in London, but owned by German media conglomerate Bertelsmann). Such companies were briefly seen as a potential threat to the UK's independent production sector. The fear was they would agglomerate into a handful of companies, as the Hollywood studios had done, and wield disproportionate influence in the market — even preventing smaller new entrants altogether (Kirkegaard 2004). There were several reasons for this, but here it suffices to name three: First, the rise of the *format* as a valuable asset in the international TV market, the logic of which seems to drive towards consolidation rather than diversity of production (Kirkegaard 2004; Chalaby 2011). Second, certain production companies came to have great influence over the main UK broadcasters, for example Endemol, whose *Big Brother* became Channel 4's most successful show, which the broadcaster in turn relied on for reliably healthy advertising sales. Third, and perhaps most importantly, due to changes in legislation in 2003 that enabled independent producers to retain ownership of programmes they made for broadcasters, these companies could now build valuable intellectual property *assets*. In turn, these assets allowed them to attract investors, scale up their operations, take on larger projects and compete internationally (Chalaby 2010).

In a 2006 report on the UK independent production sector, however, the media regulator Ofcom found that, while certain production

unscripted). Israel has recently been very successful in selling drama formats abroad, *In Treatment* (2008–2011) and *Homeland* (2012) being two high-profile examples of Israeli dramas remade in America. Danish drama *The Killing* (*Forbrydelsen*) (2007–2009) was also recently remade in the USA (2011–2012), while both Swedish and British adaptations of the Swedish crime novel series *Wallander* have been popular in Britain. The international market in factual formats is the most active of all. In 2012, David Clarke, of Cineflix Productions, listed factual formats from Singapore, Turkey and New Zealand as all part of his company's current slate (Clarke 2012: 15). The rights to British reality show *Love Thy Neighbour* were recently sold by a British production company to a Spanish production company, despite having done badly in the UK (Rosser 2011: 13).

Whether they are based in Australia, the United States, Europe or anywhere else in the world, producers and broadcasters are increasingly thinking in terms of formats with international potential. This goes alongside international sales of completed programmes, which is another source of income that producers and distributors need to exploit. The international television market is expanding, with new digital channels appearing all the time. These new channels cannot necessarily afford to commission and produce original programming themselves. So they need to buy in existing content.

As well as forging permanent affiliations, broadcasters and production companies also enter into co-productions, on a project-by-project basis, with other broadcasters and production companies. As we saw in Chapter 7, US public broadcaster WGBH co-funded BBC drama *The Mystery of Edwin Drood* (2012) and is a regular co-production partner on their period dramas. Often, however, it is the independent producer, rather than the broadcaster, who secures the co-production funding. High-end TV dramas are expensive to finance and are rarely financed solely by one broadcaster. The process of finding finance for such drama can often be more like the approach taken to feature films, in which a range of funding sources are put together in a package, as we will see in the next chapter.

companies could be termed "super-indies" because of their size, they were not sucking all the air out of the UK market (Ofcom 2006: 21). Certainly, it seems unlikely that it is possible to reverse the trend towards international consolidation in a global marketplace. However, in a recent survey of independent production, trade magazine, *Broadcast*, found that a number of 'true indies', that is, production companies not owned by a larger group, were also generating significant turnover through international trade (Broadcast 2012).

New platforms for content

The commissioning landscape has been further opened up for content producers and distributors by new video on-demand platforms. Distributors had already found a new outlet for existing content with video-on-demand providers such as Hulu and Netflix. More recently, Netflix has moved into commissioning original content, as has online video portal YouTube, entering into more direct competition with broadcasters. These are new opportunities that independent producers and writers can exploit. The routes are various and more or less direct, but one thing is clear: writers and producers need to be alert to the different content platforms and markets that exist, and must be active networkers in order to get a commission.

COMMISSIONING AND THE BUSINESS OF MAGAZINE PUBLISHING

Here we will look specifically at the commissioning process for magazines in order to give a sense of what the process is like from the point of view of the maker of the original content, the writer (and sometimes the editor), and how it fits into the business model of magazine publishing.

As organizations, large magazine publishers combine "industrial" structures of production with temporary, deadline-driven short-term projects (Ekinsmyth 2002). On the one hand, there is the "in-house" apparatus of permanent staff charged with keeping the magazine appearing on schedule, from writers and photographers to editors, copyeditors, designers, to sales and marketing. This involves repeated processes of planning, production and publication, with the cycle planned months ahead on the editorial calendar. A monthly magazine is assembled out of empty slots that get filled in with recurring features, often by staff writers (e.g., reviews, advice, opinion, "what's on," etc.), one-off features (i.e., longer stories or interviews), pictures and advertising. Much of the space in the editorial calendar is filled in with the work of freelance writers and photographers.

It's important to note (particularly for freelancers researching which editor to pitch a story to) that job titles and duties vary among magazines and publishing groups. For example, the proportion of full-time members of staff who work "in-house" differs between publications. Not all members of the editorial team will be permanent members of staff, so deputy/commissioning editors are sometimes "staffers" and sometimes freelancers (like Denise, interviewed below).

In the magazine industry, groups such as Condé Nast, National Magazine Company (or NatMags, for short), Bauer Media, Emap and Haymarket own a number of magazines, with each title managed independently in relation to the group. At the top of the hierarchy sits the publisher (who manages the editors of individual titles) along with the advertising and marketing managers (managing teams of marketing and advertising executives). Often these groups will specialize in certain forms of publishing, for example B2B (business-to-business) publications, trade publications aimed at professionals and specialists, or consumer titles, themselves differentiated by topics such as fashion, lifestyle, entertainment, motoring, technology, and so on.

A magazine editor is responsible for producing each issue on time and on budget. The publisher decides the length of each issue, the ratio of editorial to advertising (e.g., 60% editorial, 40% advertising), and the budget – decided on the basis of advertising sales and revenue from earlier issues. The brief and the budget will tell the editor how much copy (i.e., written text) will be required for each issue, and on the basis of that she or he will plan the content – what the readers will eventually see in the issue. The editorial team, led by the editor, usually consists of an editorial assistant, art director and deputy (or commissioning) editors who are responsible for specific sections of the magazine (McKay 2000). They will commission work from writers, photographers and researchers, either working from home or at the magazine's offices on a daily rate. Commissioning is tightly constrained by each issue's budget. Deputy editors will negotiate payments with freelancers and have responsibility for buying in the right amount of material while keeping within the budget allocated to their part of each issue.

A magazine has a certain production cycle, all leading up to the final print-deadline for each issue, with material being written, edited, corrected and laid out at certain times. This is why deadlines are so important – even sacred – for journalists and editors. Copy is collected, edited, subedited (corrected for style, punctuation, grammar), and typeset (put into the layout the reader will see on the printed page). This has to happen before the print-deadline, which is when the issue has to be ready and sent out for reprographics, printing and distribution.

What we have outlined here is a generic model of magazine publishing, an approximation of a "standard" way of doing business that is not applicable to all publishers, and most importantly, might not be around very much longer in the present form dictated by the technical and economic necessities of printing and distribution. However, this combination of in-house staff, working in a semi-industrial hierarchy from publisher through editor to writers, photographers, subeditors and designers, can serve as a model for content-production across multiple media platforms – from blogs and websites, to print, video and audio. To illustrate this further we will now consider, through the experience of a young freelance writer, how the traditional commissioning process of traditional magazine publishing persists, even when print is no longer at the centre of the operation.

Case study: the jobbing writer – how does a freelancer get published, online and in print?

Denise, a freelance journalist and magazine editor based in London, says that the process of getting published starts with both having an *idea* for a story or a feature article and knowing which *publication* would best be suited to this idea. "Then you need to find out who the commissioning editor is – or the editor of [the section] where you think [the story] belongs. That will vary depending on the publication."

Some publications may have editors responsible for different sections of the printed magazine, and some will have a specialist editor for online content. It's important to do the research first because while some publications maintain a distinction between their online- and print-content, some do not: "For *Time Out*, for example, you wouldn't contact the online editor to write a review article – you would speak to the commissioning editor for that section. So, whether it's food, films, music, shopping, you must speak to the commissioning editor of that section." Denise emphasizes that it pays to do the homework: "The most important thing is to work out who to ask, and from there you can ring the editor or call an assistant editor – you ring them, identify the person, get their email address. Once you've got the email address you write up a really strong pitch" (Denise, 2012).

When pitching a story, it's important to understand what the audience might be and who the publication aims to reach in the first place: "There are so many different publications now – online or offline. You have to be really knowledgeable about styles and style guides of publications and whether your writing actually fits that and whether it will reach their demographic." On top of that, Denise says that "the most important thing, really, is to make sure you don't make any mistakes." Factual errors, such as wrong names, dates and places, will get a pitch binned immediately. "Always fact-check, down to the last detail, otherwise you'll waste their time and you'll waste your time. If your name ever cropped up again they probably wouldn't want to work with you" (Denise, 2012).

Denise has worked on the editorial side as well, as the deputy editor of the style section of a weekly magazine. She found herself surprised to find where the pitches were coming from:

> "I found that the majority of people who are trying to pitch work to you weren't actually freelancers. Your competition [as a freelancer] is PR people, and they already have facts and they already have access to a lot of information. If you're interviewing someone as well, they'll already have that access. So you have to be really aware of what you can bring to the table – your *hook* in your pitch has to be absolutely exceptional." (Denise, 2012)

In journalism, a story hook is the interesting or unexpected fact or twist that will catch and hold the reader's attention. As with any kind of pitch, the same thing applies to commissioning editors (or indeed, to anyone whose job it is to spot and develop stories or other content for development and publication).

But the story hook is not the only part of a pitch that matters for capturing an editor's attention. The credibility of the writer matters as well. Denise points out that editors are reluctant to devote resources and space to writers whose work they haven't already read and assessed. Building a portfolio of writing is therefore essential in order to get noticed. Denise advises freelance writers not to pitch to a daily newspaper unless they have a news story that's guaranteed to be picked up. "The best thing is probably to start small and build yourself up towards something bigger," she suggests:

> "If you're interested in music or fashion, or whatever, you start with a blog. Then you start contributing to other blogs, and then you contribute to online magazines – they're called online magazines when they have exceptionally high numbers of uniques [i.e., a high *unique visitor count*] – they'll be higher than your average blog. Then you build up slowly like that so you start gaining a portfolio of a body of work. [You should] put all your work online so if you're ever in an interview or in a situation where they'll want to see your work you can show them with just one link. Editors don't really want to take on someone who's never written anything before for anyone. They want to see examples of work, and variation if possible." (Denise, 2012)

For magazines, which publish in print either weekly or monthly, *timing* is tremendously important – that is, being aware of the publication schedule and looking ahead into the future for what kind of stories might be needed months down the line. "If something's happening in July you need to start moving on it long before July" (Denise, 2012).

As a freelancer, Denise has to be aware of the editorial calendar of a magazine before she pitches a feature to the editor. The editorial calendar is signed off by the editor some time in advance, so that a weekly magazine may work two weeks ahead for shorter items and two months in advance with features. Denise points to a weekly magazine like *Time Out* as an example:

"[They work] two weeks ahead, so what goes into a magazine that comes out this week would have been written two weeks ago, because it takes a while to go through subbing [subediting]. You can have two months' worth of *Time Out* issues locked completely for features, where there's not really any room to manoeuvre as a freelancer."

By comparison, a monthly publication will work two to six months into the future, depending on the topics it covers. However, magazines do not live by features alone. They will have topic-areas where things happen quickly, such as fashion and music, and these areas offer opportunities for freelancers to get short pieces published on relatively short notice.

Denise advises writers who are trying to build a portfolio of published work to follow the action: "As a freelancer it's probably best to work in an area where there's lots of things going on," like the music scene. As an example, she mentions the coverage of Bloc Festival, an electronic music event held over two days at London Pleasure Gardens in July 2012. Bloc Festival was cancelled following serious technical problems on the opening night. A few days later the production company responsible went into administration (Hancox 2012; Michaels 2012). The first news that something was going wrong at the start of the festival, with complaints about malfunctioning ticket scanners and overcrowding at the venue, spread through tweets from the audience. The story was picked up by specialist blogs and online magazines, with the first posts appearing mere hours after the first tweets went out. Music blogs and online magazines need to publish quickly to pick up the online traffic through social media:

"You have people like *The Quietus*, *FACT Magazine*, all these music magazines competing to make sure their article gets out first. If their article is the first article, that's what people will see and it will get tweeted the most – the one that goes up on Facebook and gets liked and commented on more than the other ones." (Denise, 2012)

What follows on from the Twitter updates and the initial, hastily written reports are feature articles about the event and its repercussions. For Denise, the interesting stories are about why this happened, what went wrong, and what it might mean for the future of the festival that the production company went into administration. This is how stories get picked up in the digital environment, she points out: "That's kind of the nature of journalism now – a lot of stuff is instantaneous. You start to see something on Twitter, starts to happen – you hear about it from friends, you check up on something, the story just unravels itself."

However, picking up on news or current stories is also about talking to people:

"There's never any harm in ringing people up, asking about stuff. There's nothing wrong with just going and finding out – no one's going to shoot you for it. It's almost like being a secret agent or something. You can just go ask loads of questions about whatever's going on – you have to be interested, you have to have enthusiasm. And if you meet someone who's willing to talk to you, you never know how that's going to turn out. It's where you really start out in terms of stories, before you pitch it. You really need to have a strong pitch, and the backbone of that is going to be who you've spoken to, what's been said and whether that's going to work well for the publication that you're going to put it towards." (Denise, 2012)

When researching a feature about East London, Denise mentions that she interviewed the manager at Rough Trade, an independent record store off Brick Lane. "He let me in on loads of information, some of which was embargoed – he told me but I couldn't write about it. However, because I had this information I could go and pitch it to someone. Rough Trade were expanding, opening a New York Rough Trade, and he told me their plans with that, like they've got a couple of bands coming up playing in the store, really big bands." Famously, Radiohead played a concert at Rough Trade when *In Rainbows* came out, which generated a lot of publicity. Denise mentions that pictures of Thom Yorke, the singer in the band, handing out newspapers in the street before the "secret" gig, generated "a storm of media" – and she was alert to the possibility of something similar happening again. "Bits of information like that" are tremendously useful for journalists looking for material that might be relevant two or three months down the line, says Denise. "It's important to know when you're on to something, and to use your time wisely when you're aware of the timescales."

In planning where their work might fit in, Denise insists that freelancers must look beyond the printed page. Magazines have websites and blogs which are not subject to the same editorial calendar as the printed version. For example, *Time Out* has a popular blog: "You could more easily write freelance for the blogging section, even if it doesn't make it into the actual magazine." Similarly, she points to *Vice* magazine, which operates a popular blog site and a number of other online media properties: "They very rarely have a freelancer write something that will go in the print-magazine. Most of that stuff will go online, and they [the writer] will build a portfolio through *Vice* online before it goes anywhere near the magazine." For *Vice* and other magazines, their website will, therefore, serve as a test-bed for new writers and new ideas that will later filter into the printed publication.

However, Denise warns that magazines are often reluctant to take on new freelancers, whether it is for online or print, since they often already have lists of writers they have worked with. Here, Denise echoes similar sentiments, familiar from the film and TV production sector (Holgate and McKay 2009: 159), when she says: "They're going to use people that they know over people that they don't know." The value of work experience and internships at magazines and newspapers, says Denise, is that they are an opportunity to become known to the commissioning editors and deputy editors who make decisions. To get on to the list of trusted freelancers "you have to know them, or you have to intern".

> "When you're starting off it's fairly useful to intern at different publications, because you get inside the offices and meet people that way and talk to them. And you make yourself known around. Then you have a list of people who you can pitch to later if you have something – that's the nature of building contacts. I worked at *Mixmag* while I was still at university, however I'm really up to date with people because I have them all on LinkedIn or I've got them in my Twitter: I know when jobs have changed, when people have left, when there are new editors. This is important because you don't want to be emailing someone who doesn't work [at the publication] anymore. Also, if someone does leave, it's quite interesting to work out where they're going to. Say someone leaves *Mixmag* to go work for *NME*, and they've gone from being a reviews editor to being *the* editor, then suddenly you have a stronger contact in a different publication who already knows you." (Denise, 2012)

SUMMARY

In this chapter we have concentrated on examples from TV production and magazine publishing in order to illustrate how media organizations handle commissioning, how the commissioning process works from a business point of view, and how this is experienced in practice.

RECOMMENDED READING

Campbell, L. (2012) 'The *Broadcast* Interview, Stuart Murphy, Bringing Sky Down to Earth', *Broadcast*, June 29. A useful insight into Sky's brand strategy.

Harcup, Tony. 2009. *Journalism: Principles and Practice*. London: Sage. A wide-ranging introduction to journalism techniques and practice.

Herbert, Joanna. 2011. *Writers' & Artists' Yearbook 2012*. New York: Bloomsbury USA. A list of commissioning editors and key contacts at media organizations and publishers.

Johnson, C. (2012) *Branding Television*. Abingdon: Routledge. An in-depth study of branding strategies in UK and US television.

McKay, Jenny. 2000. *The Magazines Handbook*. London: Routledge. Highly recommended introduction to the magazine industry, the business of magazines, the role of the journalist and key jobs in the industry.

Musburger, Robert B. and Gorham Kindem. 2009. *Introduction to Media Production: The Path to Digital Media Production*. Oxford: Focal Press/Elsevier. A guide to media production for newcomers and seasoned professionals.

Peterson, Franklynn, and Judi Kesselman-Turkel. 2006. *The Magazine Writer's Handbook* (2nd edition). Madison, WI: University of Wisconsin Press. A comprehensive practical introduction to the US magazine business and freelancing for writers.

Quinn, Catherine. 2010. *No Contacts? No Problem! How to Pitch and Sell a Freelance Feature*. London: A&C Black. A step-by-step guide for researching stories, preparing pitches, and how to deliver them to commissioning editors.

10

Clients, Funders and Going It Alone

While the previous chapter dealt with mass-media business models, here we will look at other ways of initiating and resourcing content and services. First, we consider the client–agency relationship, looking at creative agencies, specifically how they relate to clients, and how the client-led business model differs from the commissioning structures discussed in Chapter 9. It relies on a more artisanal relationship, involving the rendering of services, bespoke production and working to brief. We will then go on to consider both the role of public funding and various entrepreneurial models of finance, noting some continuities between the funding structures we discuss here and older models of patronage and entrepreneurship, as discussed in Chapter 2.

WORKING TO BRIEF: THE CLIENT RELATIONSHIP

In the digital media environment, all businesses are in the media business: a construction company may need a social media manager, a bank needs a website, a university might want a mobile app developed, and an insurance company might put on an event, live-streamed online. This is not to mention conventional advertising, marketing, events and public relations, all of which are part of the creative industries. The difference between creating content through commissioning, for distribution by a media organization, and working to brief for a client who requires creative services (e.g., an advertising campaign) is that the latter example does not involve the core product of the client's business. While the BBC's core output is TV, radio and other media content, and Vice, Monocle and other publishers commission and distribute content, the same does not apply to an advertising campaign that a bank buys from an agency. In the former example, the interests of the audience are of primary importance; in the second, the needs of the client come first.

In some ways, the working relationships between designers (e.g., graphics, interactive media, interior and garden) and clients resembles that described in the preceding chapter between producers and commissioners. However, there is an important difference between the two when it comes to working to a **brief**. The designer may still be pitching ideas, but to a much more precise client brief, and the creative process will be shaped by that brief, with associated **milestones** and **deliverables** (West 1993). Many of the practitioners that we have interviewed for this book, particularly those in creative services, mention how important the brief is for each project they work on.

Advertising and marketing: creative and media agencies

Much of this work takes place in and through agencies of various kinds. They encompass, as we remember from Chapter 6, creative *goods* as well as *services*. We have been focusing in the previous chapter on what Caves (2000) would call creative originals and creative content producers, but here we look more closely at providers of creative services and experiences. As with all such typologies, they must be taken with a grain of salt – the actual business environment moves and changes, sometimes outpacing descriptions that aim to simplify and understand it. In the creative industries, the changes can be very rapid, not least because of the ways in which technological developments have altered the business fundamentals, particularly the relationship between media and consumers (Flew 2012: 111–132). The making and distribution of content is couched within systems that take symbolic goods (or "content") as their input, and turn them into multiple kinds of experiences. As Bilton and Deuze remark in their introduction to *Managing Media Work*:

> Over the past 20 years economic, technological, social, and cultural changes have conspired to devalue cultural content and place a stronger emphasis on the services and systems that convert raw symbolic goods into meaningful and valuable experiences for consumers. Consequently creativity is closely linked to the management of cultural production and cultural distribution (Bilton and Deuze 2011: 34)

Advertising and marketing (and public relations) provide creative production and services to their clients, from ideas through production to distribution. These three categories, taken together, could all fit Chris Hackley's description of an advertising agency as "an organization which manages and sells knowledge: knowledge about advertising, about consumers and about creative craft" (Hackley 2000: 239). As we will see below, in interviews with marketing and advertising professionals, these three elements – what they sell as professionals – are tightly interwoven in practice.

This is a sizeable industry, employing a large number of full-time, freelance and portfolio workers. The marketing, advertising and PR sector are remarkably integrated, not least because of the role played by communications groups. A single communications group will routinely own a number of smaller brands, for example media agencies for buying media space, creative agencies to come up with the content of marketing campaigns, PR agencies, and specialist agencies that focus on specific types of media or activity. Communications groups often build these portfolios of subsidiaries strategically, buying small agencies to acquire their talent, specialist know-how and experience. For example, the large communications groups, especially WPP and Publicis Groupe, "have been building up their digital arsenals as marketers shift spending from traditional media to the Internet, mobile applications and other digital formats" (Pfanner 2012b). These acquisitions enable the large groups to pitch for work in areas where their existing agencies do not have substantial in-house expertise.

Pitching

Whether an agency belongs within a communications group, an agency network, or is run as an independent, they will all compete for clients' business in a similar way – by pitching for work in response to a brief set by the client (although some larger clients will only deal with a select group of agencies invited to pitch).

David, an executive producer at an interactive agency, describes his experience of the pitching process, and his role within his own agency:

> "I am the front or forward-facing persona of the company. I will go to the agencies or the brands and I pick up the briefs and understand what it is they're trying to achieve. What's the one thing that we can bring to the table that can win this project for us. Then I come back inside the office and engage the right people, make sure we've got the right teams, the right people in the teams, how much time it's going to take, how much it's going to cost, what's the idea, what's the treatment, and then compile that back and then submit that, and hopefully win it." (David, 2012)

The competition in the marketing communications sector is fierce. Each week, trade magazines such as *Campaign*, *Marketing Week* and *Advertising Age* cover the latest news of which large clients are looking for a new agency for their next campaign or brand overhaul, with agencies pitching competitively for these new briefs.

The blurred distinction between creative and media agencies

The traditional role of a media agency is to plan, buy and monitor a client's media schedule. They operate "wholesale", buying media time and space in great volume (TV, radio, print, outdoor, online). They then sell it on to their clients at more favourable rates than individual clients (or individual creative agencies) would be able to negotiate on their own. For example, a media agency would buy multiple advertising slots on a popular programme from a TV broadcaster, and then sell those slots to different clients depending on how the specific programme would fit the products being advertised, the target audience, and other media planning considerations.

Creative agencies, on the other hand, specialize in coming up with ideas and content for advertising campaigns, usually in response to a brief or a strategy proposed by the client. However, this category is very loosely defined and incorporates a broad range of creative services, which, in practice, are not so clearly segregated from the work done at media agencies. Historically, one reason for that might be that advertising agencies began, in essence, as media planning and buying agencies:

> Advertising agencies evolved in a piecemeal fashion from being media space brokers, reflecting the changing needs of proprietors, as well as those of evolving media and consumer industries. Many early agencies had no division of labour at all: the account person (called senior clerk) (McFall 2004: 140) would win and maintain the account, design the advertising, do the research, and also the media planning and buying. (Hackley and Kover 2007: 74)

Over time the distinction between creative agencies and media agencies emerged as a full-fledged specialism. However, this distinction was repeatedly put in doubt by our interviewees. Derek, an **account planner** at a London-based advertising agency, says that the agency he works for tends to represent itself according to what it can deliver for individual clients: "Digital agency, integrated agency, advertising agency, marketing agency – depending on how they frame things" (Derek, 2012).

Responding to a similar question of how his agency presents itself to clients, David mentions that this is something his team considers extensively. In the competition for new work, agencies seek to define themselves and distinguish their own work, style and expertise from that of others. Therefore, self-definition is often very important because they have to be able to explain what they do and how they do it in ways that will sound compelling to potential clients and professional partners.

In reply to the interviewer's question whether he considers his company to be a production house rather than a creative agency, his answer is an emphatic "no". "We make things, but we also think about it. You could say creative production – we're a creative interactive agency. The definition is very hard to pin down, and it's kind of what we're struggling with ourselves" (David, 2012). As David puts it, the distinctions have become blurred, partly because agencies don't distinguish anymore between what used to be called "verticals" – TV, radio, print, separate forms of media:

> "There used to be kind of your TV agencies and the digital agencies, and the digital agencies used to design and build and make all the stuff. They'd do the MySpace stuff and the animated gifs and the banner ads, and the Facebook ads and the microsites, and then they started doing outdoor stuff and connect it and the digital guys started doing more and more. And the TV agencies said 'Shit, we need some of that' and they started doing more and more, and really the creative advertising agencies now, a lot of the digital, traditional digital agencies, don't have the skillset in-house to execute a lot of the ideas they come up with. [...] I mean kids don't watch that much TV – they don't watch it so the whole divvying up of budgets, the whole 'where does content live?,' how you connect with people, what does this stuff do, YouTube – everything is just in

flux again, and I feel like it's going to be in flux for quite a while. Lots of people are vying to work in those different spaces. There's lots of things happening in lots of different places." (David, 2012)

The history of digital agencies illustrates this blurring of categories and specializations that has encouraged a proliferation of different agencies. Digital agencies emerged when the web became part of the consumer media market in the 1990s. Before 2002, when broadband started to gain significant market share in the USA and Europe, their business focus tended to be narrow: website-related services, banner advertising and simple media that could work over low-bandwith internet connections. With the mass-adoption of fixed-line broadband, mobile data connectivity, smartphones and the use of social media to share video and other high-bandwidth content, they have become mainstream. All creative, marketing and public relations agencies are now, to some extent, digital agencies. Kylie, a community manager for a professional training organization, explains:

> "Full-time employment of digital specialists was not generally necessary in large businesses, like banks, retailers, and so on. Therefore, agencies were established to serve this growing need. [...] There was a challenge to traditional business models, in that digital operations grew to be essential for a range of companies that previously didn't have to pay attention to such things, and despite the declining revenue caused by the shift to digital in areas like publishing, news, music, et cetera." (Kylie, 2009)

Agencies specializing in content management systems, web-building and publishing platforms became the biggest players in the digital sector, she suggests, because "the internet has turned almost everyone into publishers" (Kylie, 2009).

It's worth emphasizing that, as Kylie points out, all businesses are now in the media business in some way, especially if they deal with consumers. Before websites, Twitter feeds, Facebook pages and the various other forms of online presence that are now routine, businesses that were not in the media business did not normally *own* media – with the exception of those who put out catalogues or put up display advertising in their own retail space. They would, for the most part, buy advertising space in small and easily measured chunks, from broadcasters and publishers. Furthermore, they did not have to think about how their businesses could *earn* mentions in various media beyond interviews and favourable coverage – a far cry from the relationships that brands now try to navigate with consumers through social media.

This distinction between *paid*, *owned* and *earned* media is useful for thinking about marketing in a digital media environment (Burcher 2012) because the relatively simple "push-media" channels of broadcasting have been supplemented and transformed by always-on "pull-media", such as interactive websites, social networking services (Masterson and Pickton 2010: 290). While brands can now establish their presence in this space, with their own Twitter accounts, Facebook pages and the like, the more complicated development is that their consumers have access to many of the same tools – for example, user-generated reviews and comments that can be published instantly on services like Twitter, Yelp, TripAdvisor and Rotten Tomatoes even before the customer leaves the restaurant, hotel, or film screening.

One result of this, from the point of view of marketing and advertising, is that agencies that previously defined themselves either as "creative" or "media" now find themselves competing with one another for the same briefs, as David describes it:

> "I would say that a media agency handled media specifically. They'd look at where the creative [content] runs, the right use of media for that creative. But again, the complexity of now – media agencies talk to Facebook, and Facebook feeding creative ideas, so it's a problem that I had at [my former creative agency], that [it and a large media agency] are vying for the same client as to who wins the creative idea." (David, 2012)

Jess, who oversees a team of researchers at a London-based media agency, explains that there is a difference between media agencies and creative agencies. People still watch TV, they still listen to radio, they still read newspapers. The long-established forms of broadcast media may be changing in response to new online platforms and the popularity of mobile media that take advantage of the capabilities of smartphones, but they are not going away anytime soon. However, she concurs that the distinction between creative and media agencies is getting blurred in the digital environment:

> "The creative agency are the people who make the ads, and the media agency are the people who plan where the ads go. Historically [they have been] very separate, well since the nineties – so my lifetime. [...] Now, because of digital and how digital started and who got there first, the rules are blurring because, for example, creative agencies might not understand user groups in the way a media agency understands how a platform works and how users might interact with it. We might have a better idea how the creative [content] should play and what content should go on that than necessarily a creative agency, who might come up with a brilliant original idea, but then again might think the other way around. [...] When we were all in our little boxes, working together was quite easy because we understood the rules of engagement. [Now] there's more of a power struggle with clients about what comes first, who is the lead agency, what is the purpose – what is our box. And from our side, we feel the creative agencies are very threatened by that because historically they were the lead and ideas were what came first." (Jess, 2010)

However, Jess makes it clear that just like creative agencies, and other service-providing agencies, media agencies pitch and work to a specific brief on each project: a marketing campaign, by the time it reaches the eyes and ears of consumers, through TV, radio and other media, is the result of a complex negotiation between the client, creative agency and the media agency.

Communications, campaigns, interactions: what agencies sell their clients

Replying to the question "What it is that a media agency sells?", Jess starts by talking about how a campaign comes into being at her media agency:

> "In terms of a campaign, it totally depends on the client. Quite often these days what happens is the client comes to us and says, 'I need to sell this much stuff, and to do that I think we should do this.' So whether that's 'I want to advertise to 18–22 year olds,' or 'I need to sell this many cars,' and quite often we're now briefed with the creative agency so media and creative at the same time are briefed to come back with a plan or ideas and how they get those to that basis could be very different. So media agencies probably take the target consumer and investigate their lives and how where they go, what they like doing, what they like with the brands they like, their attitudes to things, that's all fed into a sort of melting pot of ideas and media to come out with a plan which can be a year before you see anything on television. Buying media is a huge part of that – once they have a plan – but to do a Christmas campaign you're probably booking in March." (Jess, 2010)

When asked the same question, Jeremy, a director of research, points out that "in services is quite often hard to say that 'we produce *this* specific thing, or the supply chain is *this*'" (Jeremy, 2010). Using data from specialist research companies like Nielsen, Forrester and Mintel, Jeremy's team turns consumer research into actionable insights for their clients' marketing strategies and campaigns:

> "I suppose what we do is [that we] take information, whether it's information about GDP per head in a country, or information about how many people have access to broadband in a country, or iPhone sales figures, or anything like that, and we use that to help the client communicate with their audiences in the most effective way. So, for example, you would look at something like the penetration rate of smartphones in Japan before you were looking at whether you should do a smartphone app for your brand and their consumers in Japan. Or you would look at the demographics of people in one country who watch a certain sort of TV channel and then you would decide whether that would be the right route to advertise to the target market for those people in that country. That's effectively how media works. [...] So, it's kind of understanding who the consumer is, and also what the clients are trying to do or what the clients should be trying to do, and really try to match the two things together." (Jeremy, 2010)

In marketing and advertising, the range of services has extended from the bread-and-butter *campaign*, which has a beginning and an end, to open-ended strategies and activities that serve the interests of a brand in a longer-term dialogue, relationship or communication with its customers.

Increasingly, the focus is shifting away from self-contained campaigns. Jeremy, in his role as a strategic thinker and researcher at a **communications group**, remarks on the changing nature of campaigns in the digital media environment:

"These days it's less about campaigns and more about sort of ongoing communication. [With social media] it's less about this is a specific campaign we're doing, it's more about [a] conversation with the audience and these are the sorts of things – this is the way we want the brand to be perceived. And everything we do really has to reflect this. And so in a way customer service is the new marketing, or customer service is part of the new marketing, because it used to be the case that you'd have a solid campaign, start on this date, finish it on this date, catch your breath again, you know, three months later do something else. But now it's much more about people are interacting every day, people are wanting to interact every day, and if they send you – if they send the brand an email or write on the brand's Facebook page or whatever, you know, they expect something back within hours, or minutes." (Jeremy, 2010)

Media agencies traditionally monitor and measure the effectiveness of their campaigns, in part to account for the return on investment (ROI) to the client – in essence, to demonstrate to the client's representatives what they are getting for their money (Fill 2011). By emphasizing interaction, Jeremy argues that this conventional monitoring role has to extend to all media that an agency uses on its clients' behalf. At the same time, these interactions become more complex, often combining media platforms and physical spaces in novel ways. For example, certain agencies specialize in creating shareable moments – interesting experiences that people might encounter in public, post pictures of via Facebook, Instagram, Twitter or the like, or interact with in some way (participating in a game, for example) that can generate social media interactions with which the brand will be associated. Sometimes, this will take the form of sophisticated installations in public spaces intended to amuse, surprise and engage those who encounter them. For this type of work, larger agencies often turn to smaller, specialist **boutique agencies**.

Shareable experiences: An event, space or interaction designed to give the user something to share on a social networking service. When used as a marketing tactic, these will be affiliated with a brand or a product, often in a subtle fashion. Often these are simple interactive experiences which are nevertheless technically sophisticated underneath. Examples, of which there are many, include interactive installations by The Fun Theory (Rolighetsteorin), a Swedish agency (search for "The World's Deepest Bin", "Piano Stairs" and "Bottle Bank Arcade" on YouTube to see their work documented in action). Some will attempt to create physical representations of online experiences, for example the "Ariel Fashion Shoot", a physical installation located in Stockholm Central Station, a "live gaming experience" controlled through a Facebook interface (documented in a video on the ArielNordics YouTube channel).

Delivering on a brief

A brief can range from simple to complex, from low-budget to big-budget, involving anything from one person to multiple teams. As executive producer, it is then David's responsibility to lead the project from the pitching stage, once his agency has won the pitch, into production and delivery:

> "If we do win it, I oversee the project, while it goes through production and delivery. It's kind of creative oversight, strategically what projects are we taking on. [...] It's whatever you can imagine it. Things from sorting out internal problems, signing off cabling overhauls, managing some of the staff – God, it's a lot. It's quite nice… it's kind of… I was a producer for a while, so I'm now executive producer which means I don't have to do much producing. It's more organizing. It's a very subtle thing because they have great producers here that do all the legwork. [As executive producer] I oversee the output, like you see on feature films at the end." (David, 2012)

As David illustrates, the process of turning a brief into deliverables has different stages. These differ depending on what is being delivered, whether it's a service like a marketing campaign or a product like a prototype.

Jess, describing the four types of role that people fill within the media agency she works for, identifies them in terms of how they relate to the pitch, the brief and its delivery. First, the client-facing or client-side person "who makes the boat run on time, [...] interacts with the client, makes sure the money comes in, chases the markets and stuff – generally makes sure it all works" (Jess, 2010). Second, "the business planning team" who "answer the questions that need answering. Whether that's 'how was my advertising working in the past?' or 'who is my preferred consumer?' or 'what do I need to do to differentiate myself from the marketplace?' That's handled by the business planning team who are the people who answer the questions." Third, "the middle part is the invention people [who move the process on] to concept ideas, where we think about where these ideas are best placed – whether that's tactical ideas like doing whole huge events [or] more of a campaign idea." Finally, the implementation team "buy the media, they make sure everything's in the right place and they get the best price" (Jess, 2010). It's interesting to note that within Jess's agency the division of labour is broadly similar to that of advertising agencies (West 1993; Hackley 2003; Hackley and Kover 2007): the client-facing role (**account manager**) is distinguished from that of the researcher or strategist (**account planner**), "ideas-people" (the creatives) and implementation (production) in the process from brief to deliverable.

PUBLIC FUNDING

In many countries, government funding is available to support cultural activities, including creative practice, in a range of sectors. This includes subsidies and grants for the performing and visual arts as well as for film and digital media. Usually intermediary organizations are set up with government funding to manage allocation of and application for funds, such as the National Endowment for the Arts in the United States, the Australia Council for the Arts, or the UK Arts Councils. Typically, such organizations provide funding both for specific projects and for organizational development.

Different governments have different priorities and policies with regard to the arts. The bottom line of course is how much funding they make available. The recent global economic downturn has meant cuts in public funding for the arts. Beyond this, governments may decide to prioritize particular sectors or approaches. A traditional approach to public funding has been to see the arts as justified as "a positive public investment in the enhancement of human lives ... held to raise the general level of people's abilities to become better people, living a more autonomous and fulfilled life" (O'Connor 2009a: 392). We might broadly characterize this approach as one of patronage. As with the case study of Renaissance painting that we looked at in Chapter 2, patronage of the arts is rarely, however, a purely altruistic pursuit, but has always been associated with the accrual of status and influence. In the case of national funding of the arts, governments also seek, through such cultural enhancement, to advance the international profile and status of the nation.

This rationale for public funding has not disappeared; indeed, it is central to the official strategies of all three of the American, Australian and British public arts funding bodies cited above. However, in the broader discourse of public policy, in the second half of the twentieth century, it was superseded in many countries by a new focus on the interplay of cultural and economic factors in creative production. One of the key policy concerns that came out of this was to address issues of **market failure** (Garnham 2005; O'Connor 2009a; Oakley 2009a). Then, as we discussed in Chapter 1, towards the end of the twentieth century, an emphasis on cultural production as a key source of wealth creation and a driver of the new "knowledge economy" coined the term "creative industries" that we have been using throughout this book.

In many parts of the world, including the USA, Europe and Australasia, government discourse on the funding of creative production has therefore increasingly been in terms of an economic return on investment, rather than a cultural investment in the public good. As we discussed in Chapter 4, this development resulted in a public policy focus on growth in creative production and meant that arts organizations were increasingly required to put forward an economic and business case for their activities. However, as we also discussed in Chapter 4, at the same time, regeneration policy also provided a strong remit for community engagement and social inclusion.

Example: celebratory arts company

Emergency Exit Arts is a celebratory arts company, established in 1980. It puts on events, often on a large scale, outdoors and in public spaces, including street theatre, processions and firework displays, employing a range of visual and performance arts. Emergency Exit Arts receives annual public funding from Arts Council, England (ACE), through which it finances some of its activities. In order to qualify for this funding, which was allocated through competitive application, the company had to produce a business plan, demonstrating how it will contribute to meeting the five ten-year goals of ACE, which are:

> Goal 1: Talent and artistic excellence are thriving and celebrated. England is regarded as a pre-eminent centre for artistic excellence.
>
> Goal 2: More people experience and are inspired by the arts.
>
> Goal 3: The arts are sustainable, resilient and innovative.
>
> Goal 4: The arts leadership and workforce are diverse and highly skilled.
>
> Goal 5: Every child and young person has the opportunity to experience the richness of the arts. (Arts Council England 2012)

These goals combine a continued insistence on the arts as necessary to the public good (Goals 1, 2 and 5) with an argument for public funding as a lever for private investment and a commitment to ensuring "that artists and arts organisations continue to feed the creative industries with talent, skills and ideas" (ACE 2012). ACE elaborates these latter objectives in its strategy document as examples of the "sustainability" and "resilience" it champions in Goal 3.

How does Emergency Exit Arts meet these goals? We might assume that its established track record in production of large-scale public events provides evidence that it meets the first two goals of excellence and audience reach. With regard to the Goal 3 aim of sustainability, it certainly operates a mixed model of funding. It undertakes commissions from a variety of private and public clients nationally and internationally. It has designed weddings, provided events both for arts festivals and corporate hospitality and put on firework displays for local authorities. It also undertakes a large number of educational projects, working with a range of education providers, including local schools, thus contributing to Goal 5. As far as Goal 4 is concerned, the company's long experience probably again counts in its favour, as does its longstanding practice of working with artists from diverse disciplines and cultural backgrounds.

Despite operating a mixed model of finance, a large amount of the company's activities is nevertheless financed through public funding. Its firework displays and work in schools are examples of public funding accessed through local government entertainment and education budgets. The company has also received funding from ACE, along with other government-funded sponsors, to lead a programme of community engagement through the arts, as part of the lead up to the UK hosting of the Olympic Games in 2012. These activities are indicative of the dominant slant of the company's activities towards community and public events. Through this focus, they have for many years, under various funding regimes, accessed public funding for regeneration, aimed at social inclusion and community engagement.

Funding for community and educational activities is indeed a crucial source of funding for many arts companies, who need to keep constantly abreast of changing policy and priorities, not necessarily only arts policy, but also in other areas of government policy which may indirectly provide funding for the arts. For example, in addition to the Olympic funding cited above, Emergency Exit Arts has also taken advantage of public health initiatives, in which government funding has been made available, to raise health awareness through cultural activities. In a funding environment, in which cultural activities are increasingly valued instrumentally, either "as an input into other economic activities" (Oakley 2009a: 407) or as mechanisms for social inclusion, rather than in themselves, arts companies have to be increasingly inventive, indeed what we might call entrepreneurial, not only to secure private finance, but also in order to successfully pitch for public funding. They need to be able to both spot the opportunities that are available and take advantage of them by directing and presenting their activities to funding bodies accordingly.

ENTREPRENEURIAL APPROACHES

In describing the activities of arts companies in securing public funding as entrepreneurial above, we drew on the association of entrepreneurship with creativity, problem-solving and having an eye for spotting gaps in the market. In this section, however, what we term an entrepreneurial approach is more specifically an approach whereby a creative producer takes a product to market, assuming some or all of the burden of financial risk. In this model, the creative product is treated as a commodity. However, as we will see, just as public arts funding aims at making the arts more entrepreneurial, equally creative producers who invest money (their own and/or those of investors) in a project may be driven as much, if not more, by passion and necessity, as by the profit motive. Moreover, so-called commercial creative production may also draw on public funds. It is, as ever in creative production, often very hard to separate the art from the commerce.

Case study: film financing – putting together a package

In what is often know as the Golden Age of Hollywood, in the 1930s and 1940s, American film studios (and indeed other studios around the world) were vertically integrated organizations with large numbers of full-time cast and crew on their pay roll. They produced a large volume of films in-house every year, distributing them to exhibitors, which they also very often owned. Since the 1950s, this has no longer been the case. Instead of producing feature films in-house, US studios develop, finance and distribute films, but the actual hands-on aspects of production are carried out by independent production companies which pitch projects to the studios, in a similar way to that discussed in the last chapter in relation to television. The films are distributed via theatrical exhibition, but also through DVD, television and other non-theatrical sales.

Films financed and distributed by the six Hollywood **majors**, are often referred to as "studio films". Their films dominate the international film market. However, other film studios exist, beyond these six, if by 'film studio' we mean a company which produces (i.e., commissions and finances) and distributes films on a large scale. These include the North American **mini-majors** as well as companies based in filmmaking centres elsewhere in the world, including India, Russia and China.

The major film studios often fully finance projects, but they may also spread the risk by co-financing instead. **Independent** filmmakers also put together financing packages which do not involve large film studios at all. Co-finance packages can involve a range of investors and types and levels of investment. One of the quirks of such packages, as we will go on to see, is that organizations that we might think of as coming in at the end of the production cycle, such as distributors, actually come in right at the beginning. Another is that organizations that have nothing to do with the film industry may invest in a film, either as a tax reduction strategy or as a capital venture. Let's look at a few examples.

Pre-sales

One of the major ways in which contemporary feature films are financed is through pre-sales. This is when the rights to the film are sold before the film is made, either to a sales company – which will sell the rights on internationally to distributors in different territories – or directly to a distribution company, or indeed via both routes. A UK film producer, for example, might approach both a UK distribution company and an international sales agency. Distributors will give the producer a **minimum guarantee**, which he or she can use to part finance the production of the film. For big projects, sales companies may also sometimes offer a minimum guarantee. In other cases they may charge no sales fees up front, taking only a percentage of sales. Distribution companies seek to recoup the advance they have given, and of course also a profit, through distribution of the film.

One recent example is *The Woman in Black* (Watkins 2012), which was co-financed by US/UK-based company Exclusive Media and distributor, Alliance Films, who are based in the UK, Canada and Spain. The film's producer, Hammer Films, is part of the Exclusive Media group, which is able to provide financial backing for film development and production through its sales and distribution division. Rather than coming in at the end of the process, then, sales and distribution were in at the very start of the process, as Robert (Senior Vice President Acquisitions and Productions WW, Alliance Films) explains: "It's very rare that we screen a film completed and we buy it. We buy on script with a few elements attached… whether it's the director and a key actor and we always know who the producer is" (Robert, 2012).

In the case of *The Woman in Black*, in fact, Alliance acted not simply as distributor, but as a co-producer on the film, since it was investing 50% of the budget. Alliance also acts as sole financer and executive producer for the films of US producer Jason Blum, producer of *Paranormal Activity*. As producers they own the films they finance and benefit from a larger share of the film's profits, having assumed a sizeable, but carefully calculated, financial risk. Robert says that his company will fully finance or co-finance around four films a year. They only do so having run detailed financial models to determine what they consider to be a manageable level of risk.

However, a large number of Alliance Films' investments will be smaller percentages of a film's budget, typically between 7.5% and 14%, for which it gains distribution rights to the territories in which it operates: Canada, the UK and Spain. Each of the company's subsidiaries, Momentum Pictures in the UK and Aurum Producciones in Spain, has autonomy and may buy rights to distribute a film only in their particular territory, or the company may buy rights across the three territories. The film *The King's Speech*, for example, was picked up by Canada and the USA, but not by Spain.

Whether coming in as producer or distributor, however, the majority of the company's distribution deals will be done on script, with only a few acquisitions of finished films. The same is true of international sales companies, to whom talent agencies will first send scripts, as Robert explains:

> "They'll put it out to tender to a few sales companies and then the sales companies will provide international sales estimates to see how quickly the film can get financed... The sales company will pay a minimum guarantee to take on that film and get it financed and they'll take a fee for all the sales." (Robert, 2012)

Sales companies sell films to distributors, although distributors also deal directly with producers and talent agencies. Thus sales and distribution have become, via pre-sales, a key engine of film development and production in the film industry.

As we saw with the television case study in the last chapter, many companies in the film sector include development, financing, production through to distribution and sales within their operations, but they keep these operations separate and will have different involvements in different projects, sometimes coming in at every stage, sometimes just one or two. Often these companies have expanded from a focus on one particular aspect to become involved in other areas of the process. The distribution company Exclusive Films, for example, was first set up in the 1930s by the founder of Hammer Productions to distribute its films. By the end of the 1930s, however, the production company had ceased trading, while the distribution company continued, distributing other companies' films. Reversing the initial relationship, Exclusive Films later re-launched Hammer Film productions in the 1940s as the company's film production arm, a relationship still enduring through the more recently formed Exclusive Media group. Many media organizations, including the Hollywood majors, have gone through similar reorganizations, reinventions and reincarnations, often as a result of company mergers, sales and acquisitions. These produce, in effect, vertical integration, but in a somewhat looser mould than that which was in operation in the original Hollywood studio system.

Television companies also finance feature films. BBC Films and Film4 Productions (the film production arm of Channel 4), for example, are important sources of finance for UK films. They will put equity into the film, acting as (executive) producers or co-producers.

Public funding for film

In many countries, government funding is available to support film development, production, **completion** and distribution. In some instances the full amount may be provided. In others they will advance a percentage of the budget. The funding strategies of these schemes vary from country to country. Often they may have a remit to support new and emerging talent. One example is the UK's low-budget scheme for London filmmakers, Microwave, administered by the regional film council Film London, which recently funded the film *Ill Manors* (Drew 2012), the debut feature by singer Ben Drew, aka Plan B.

As discussed above, in relation to public funding in general, government support of film production also has other varied and differing objectives. It is often seen as having the dual remit of both maintaining and developing a country's national cultural heritage and its international profile. The recently established Doha Film Institute in Qatar, for example, has as its goal to "kick-start an entire film culture and industry" (McNab 2011). It does not focus exclusively on homegrown talent, but has a strategy of investing in high-profile international films, such as *Black Gold* (Annaud 2011), as well as a slate of films from the Middle East and North Africa. The Danish Film Institute, on the other hand, focuses on Danish films and has helped Danish directors develop a strong international profile, even though few Danish films are actually profitable. Danish films tend in fact to be reliant on government support (McNab 2011). Other film funds, such as the now defunct UK Film Council, put much more emphasis on recoupment of funds, treating investment in film production as a commercial investment rather than as a form of government subsidy.

Government film funding may also address more specific briefs. Bilingual countries, such as Canada or Belgium, earmark funding for films to be made in each of the country's official languages, while in Britain film funding, raised by the government through the National Lottery, targets regional filmmaking (alongside a national film fund) to try to reduce the hegemony of London.

Tax schemes

Government support may also be granted through mechanisms such as tax shelters and rebates on money spent on film production, which are available in many countries.

Such schemes are used by governments as a way of both attracting international film productions and supporting local production.

Private equity investment

Sometimes part or total film finance may come from private investors. Depending on the film project, the nature of these investors varies from venture capital companies and **"high-net-worth" individuals** seeking an investment, to personal funds committed by cast and/or crew (see case study below), to **crowdfunding** (see below). The decision to go this route may be motivated by lack of access to other finance. The kind of pre-sales guarantee discussed above is rarely available to first-time filmmakers. They may only be able to gain access to funding from sales and distribution companies once the film is completed. Equally, private equity investment may be a route taken by established filmmakers and investors. American businessman Steven Rales has financed three films by US director, Wes Anderson, through his production company Indian Paintbrush, including *Fantastic Mr. Fox* and *Moonrise Kingdom*, as well as *Jeff, Who Lives at Home*, by the Duplass Brothers. In China the film industry has also seen great interest from Chinese investors in recent years (Kay 2011). Equity investors in a film will take a share of the film's profits, and also its losses.

Loans

The difference between a loan and an equity investment is that the loan needs to be paid back (usually with interest) to the lender regardless of the success of the film. However, if the film is very successful, the lender will not receive a higher return, whereas the equity investor will receive a percentage of the profits. As with equity finance, both low- and high-budget films may be financed through debt finance. A first-time producer may borrow from friends and family, for example. An established producer may go to a media bank or other organization which offers debt finance to films.

Putting the puzzle together

The film *This Must Be the Place* (Sorrentino 2011) provides a good example of the way that producers take advantage of a range of sources to finance their films. The film, directed by established Italian director Paolo Sorrentino, starred US actor Sean Penn as a retired rock star. It was shot in English, on location in Ireland and the United States. The combined track record of director and actor gave the film its particular USP and, when financing the film, the Italian production company, Indigo Film, secured a minimum guarantee from Italian distributor Medusa Distribution. They then explored international financing options, as the film's producer, Carlotta Carlori, explains:

> The film's original script was set in the UK but, after carrying out some location scouting, we realized the film didn't have enough British elements to qualify for local funding… So Paolo did some research and realized Ireland was a plausible context for a retired rock star. We contacted Element Pictures who secured funding from the Irish Film Board and helped access the local tax credit, Section 481. (Carlori, in Wiseman 2012: 23)

The director also chose particular US states to film in, based on the best tax incentives on offer. In addition, the finance package included Italian tax credits; a minimum guarantee from sales company Pathé, which pre-sold the film internationally; funding from European support agencies MEDIA and Eurimages; as well as finance from an Italian bank. The film also involved a French co-producer, who brought on French broadcaster France 2 (Wiseman 2012).

As this example makes clear, financing a feature film is a complex operation, which usually involves putting together a package from multiple sources. The key problem is usually in gaining the first commitment of funds. Financers are often unwilling to be the first to commit to something that hasn't already received a stamp of approval. Another problem that first-time filmmakers may have, if they have financed their film through public funding or private investment rather than pre-sales, is in securing distribution. Distributors and international sales companies are often unwilling to take on films by unproven directors, unless they can identify a particular USP or obvious target audience. Given the large number of backers requiring recoupment, it can also be hard for a film's original producer to ultimately make any money.

SELF-FUNDING

Many creative entrepreneurs mainly or fully self-finance projects and then take them to market, particularly at the beginning of their career. Affordable technologies play a key factor in this model of financing since they substantially lower the cost of both production and distribution.

Case study: self-funded feature film

Writer-director Jamie Thraves self-funded his low-budget feature *Treacle Jr.* (Thraves 2011) after already having directed two feature films – a low-budget film which was funded by Film4, and a higher budget European and Canadian co-production. Neither of these films had done great box office, although the first was a critical success. However, his second did not even receive a cinema release and was considered a misfire. As a result, Jamie had "got to the point where I felt that, rightly or wrongly, if I wrote another script, no matter how good it was, it wouldn't get funded in the UK" (Johnston 2011). So he decided to fund the next film himself. In fact, Jamie's version of self-funding was a very personal form of debt-financing, as discussed above, in that he re-mortgaged his house to fund his film. He was motivated more by the need for personal and creative achievement and fulfilment than by the prospect of financial gain, saying that his "ambition is to keep going until I make something that everyone thinks is an absolute classic" (Gilbey 2011) and that "it's re-energised my career, so it's paid off in that respect. But I've never been so broke. I'm up to my neck in debt" (Johnston 2011). However, as we have seen in earlier chapters, creative entrepreneurs are not necessarily motivated by money. We can consider his approach to be entrepreneurial, in the sense that he took on financial risk, staking his own capital on producing the film and taking it to market in an effort to recoup its costs and, ideally, make a profit. The film was finally picked up by a UK distributor and gained a theatrical release.

User-generated content/web publishing

Another self-funded audiovisual venture, the online comedy *The Misadventures of Awkward Black Girl* (Rae 2011) was aimed neither at theatrical nor at television distribution, but was released instead on YouTube, where it received more than 6 million views. When they ran out of money, the producers changed their funding model to crowdfunding (see below), raising more than $56,000 (Adewunmi 2012). Producers often take the YouTube route out of necessity (in this case due to the apparent reluctance of television channels to commission shows with majority black casts, except in the 'urban realism' genre (Adewunmi 2012). However, there is also a case to be made for online distribution channels as a choice, rather than a last resort. As film director Yousaf pointed out in Chapter 5, not all sections of society recognize themselves as being represented in mainstream film and television, which may be seen as symbols of a status quo and which they feel excludes them. Combine this with the digital habits of contemporary youth and, as Adewunmi says, "Where, therefore, are the newest generation turning in order to see a broader representation of themselves? The internet, of course" (Adewunmi 2012).

Various types of content have indeed emerged that are best suited for online platforms such as YouTube. Characteristically, such content is short-form, takes full advantage of the lack of restrictions on online content compared to film or television (in particular on bad language) and often has a DIY aesthetic. Comedy and special interest shows are particularly prominent. The business model for such shows, once they reach a certain size of audience, is a profit share of advertising with the host platform. Amateur and semi-professional internet "stars" have led the way in this area. Some of them have then achieved a high enough profile to attract mainstream interest and make the transition to television.

Even more significantly, web distribution is itself becoming more professionalized, having recently seen the launch of a series of channels on YouTube, run by television production companies. This is an example of a frequent phenomenon in which the alternative feeds into the mainstream and is often subsumed by it. It remains to be seen whether online platforms will become fully professionalized and policed by gate-keepers, or whether they will remain a site hospitable to fringe and alternative activity.

CROWDFUNDING

A "patron" or even investor does not have to be a single person or business entity. Online, a form of funding creative projects, prototypes and even art works has taken shape. Crowdfunding is a form of financial crowdsourcing, pitching an idea to the masses through a website that serves as a marketplace. Through sites such as Kickstarter.com, small businesses or individuals will pitch ideas and ask for small up-front investment in the project, in return for getting the eventual product at a lower price – in some cases making it exclusively available to the participants.

The musician Amanda Palmer and the artist Molly Crabapple, for example, have both used Kickstarter to finance tours, recordings and artworks. Palmer split with her record label in 2010 and has been independent since then, dealing directly with her fans through online media. In the process she has found herself doing a lot more than making music:

> Sure, backers of Palmer's project could choose to get a $1 digital download, a $25 CD or a $50 vinyl, all with exclusive Kickstarter content. Those are typical rewards for music-based fundraising drives—but on the other end of the spectrum was a $10,000 private dinner with the singer… during which she would paint a portrait of you. (Two backers went for that one.) (Franco 2012)

Palmer's business model is simple: by seeking donations up-front, in exchange for downloads, CDs and other goods (or services) when the project is ready, she does not have to make the up-front investment (paying musicians, hiring a studio, etc.) herself, nor does she need a record label to do it for her, as Palmer puts it in one of her Kickstarter project updates. Recalling Steve Albini's famous essay "The Problem with Music" (Albini 1997), which originally appeared in 1993, Palmer is explicit about the costs and why she doesn't want a record label involved:

> It COSTS REAL MONEY to manufacture and distribute a record, to have a staff and a publicist, to promote an artist and tour a band. That will never truly change but now, because we can reach our fans directly without the machine, artists are empowered to call the shots and keep whatever's leftover… not the labels. (Palmer 2012)

This applies to any artist who previously would have relied on a publisher and distributor. Musicians are only one example of this relationship. In software, both small games developers and developers of smartphone apps have successfully used Kickstarter, IndieGoGo, RocketHub and similar sites for launching games or apps that previously would have gone through a publisher, or necessitated risky self-funding.

The online crowd can be a source of labour as well as finance. The term "crowd-sourcing" was coined by Jeff Howe, a writer for *Wired* magazine, agglomerating "crowd" and "outsourcing" to describe "the new pool of cheap labor" which consists of "everyday people using their spare [time] to create content, solve problems, even do corporate R & D" (Howe 2006). Using examples like iStockphoto.com, Howe describes a new type of online business that makes their money from coordinating and taking a cut of what James Surowiecki called "the wisdom of crowds" (Surowiecki 2005).

One use of crowdsourcing technology is to divide large tasks into small "micro-tasks" that can be delegated to a crowd of people. Mturk.com, Amazon's Mechanical Turk is perhaps the most famous example of this: an online marketplace for getting tasks completed by humans over the web. Named after a famous hoax in the eighteenth century, a wooden man with a turban on its head that played chess like a master but was said to run on clockwork, the Mechanical Turk turned out to have a man hidden inside. Amazon's Mechanical Turk makes no secret of the humans, calling the system "artificial artificial intelligence" when it was launched in 2006 (Economist 2006; Mieszkowski 2006). The "Human Intelligence Tasks" (HITs) put out to workers tend to be small and simple, yet difficult for computers, such as evaluating search results, selecting categories for products, or transcribing audio. Requesters, who put the tasks out into the marketplace and set the price, are usually businesses, but individuals and academic institutions have used it as well, including social scientists recruiting participants for research (Berinsky, Huber, and Lenz 2012).

Crowdsourcing has also been applied to creative work. Talenthouse.com, for example, features contests (or "creative invites") for art and design projects, fashion, film/video, music and photography. Other specialist sites for marketing and advertising include Zooppa.com and CrowdSpring.com. On Zooppa, briefs are posted as contests that creatives can enter, submitting designs, videos, scripts or whatever the client calls for, with the winner getting paid for what the client decides to use. The downside for the creatives is that the chance for winning each contest can be small, but the upside is that if they win, the money is often less important than the resulting cultural and social capital – the distribution their work gets, the association with a famous brand, and the possibility of getting picked up by a large agency. Talenthouse, for example, has in the past partnered with BBH and other large creative agencies, with an internship thrown into the mix for the contest winner (Elliott 2009). Sensing a trend, communications groups have acquired specialist crowdsourcing agencies, for example the Havas group buying a small agency named Victors & Spoils "to come up with ad concepts in collaborative fashion, rather than using traditional models like teaming up a copywriter and an art director at an advertising agency" (Elliott 2012).

Case study: crowdfunding independent journalism

In March 2012, a project titled *Matter* raised $140,000 in one month through the crowdfunding site Kickstarter. Initially aiming for $50,000 to produce a proof-of-concept version, the response outstripped anyone's expectations. The founders envisioned a lean publication distributed via e-readers and mobile apps, specializing in long-form science and technology journalism, charging readers $0.99 per story (McAthy 2012). Linking these stories through a unified brand, produced by a distributed editorial team, *Matter* fits neither the description of a magazine nor a website in the traditional sense.

Long-form investigative journalism is expensive, time-consuming and labour-intensive, not to mention requiring legal backup to protect against libel suits. The Kickstarter funding in March 2012 enabled the *Matter* team to start producing three stories for publication in the autumn. Unlike a conventional magazine, *Matter* aims to publish each story as a separate publication, focusing on the long-form feature to the exclusion of everything else a traditional magazine might do. In this, *Matter* follows a "less is more" principle, preferring to get the dedicated attention of a relatively small group of regular readers, rather than attempt to reach the largest possible number of consumers: "There may be an apparently infinite supply of material; there is certainly not an infinite supply of attention. Being bigger and carrying more stories may not always be the best way to get that attention," writes co-founder and editor Bobbie Johnson (2012a). *Matter*'s business model is, in other words, premised on the suspicion that "the age of the broad publication [is] pretty much over — or at least those publications which try to do all things for all people are much harder to start now" (Johnson 2012b). Already having secured 2,500 individual contributions through Kickstarter, *Matter* will partly rely for its marketing strategy on readers to tweet and promote their stories on social media, as well as the return custom of an expanding pool of readers coming back month after month to purchase articles.

SUMMARY

Financing is a complex process which takes many forms, some quite specific to the particular sector. New financing models are developing in tandem with new technologies and new media platforms and forms, one of the results of which is that self-funding is a much more feasible option for print and broadcast media than it might have been in the past.

RECOMMENDED READING

Fill, Chris. 2009. *Marketing Communications: Interactivity, Communities and Content* (5th edition). Harlow: FT/Prentice Hall. A wide-ranging introduction to marketing communications, including the functions of different agencies within the marketing communications process.

Hackley, Chris. 2003. "Account Planning: Current Agency Perspectives on an Advertising Enigma." *Journal of Advertising Research* 43 (2): 235–245. Based on interviews with planners and other advertising professionals. Good review of the literature and full of interesting quotes on job roles in advertising.

Hackley, Chris and Arthur J. Kover. 2007. "The Trouble with Creatives: Negotiating Creative Identity in Advertising Agencies." *International Journal of Advertising* 26 (1): 63–78. Explores the stereotype of the "creative" as the unruly rebel among the "suits" of the advertising agency, and how different the reality of advertising work is from this mostly fictitious image.

Jones, Chris, Genevieve Jolliffe, and Andrew Zinnes. 2010. *The Guerilla Film Makers Pocketbook: The Ultimate Guide to Digital Film Making*. London: Continuum. An accessible update to the well-known *Guerilla Film Maker's Handbook*. We particularly like the case studies of individual digital films in Chapter 6.

West, Douglas. 1993. "Restricted Creativity: Advertising Agency Work Practices in the US, Canada and the UK." *The Journal of Creative Behavior* 27 (3): 200–213. A comparison of working practices in advertising in three national contexts.

11

The Changing Economic Landscape

Change is constant in the creative industries, because they generate new things without guarantees that they will be embraced by audiences, consumers, customers or clients. Films bomb, music goes unheard, advertising campaigns sink without a trace. This makes working in the creative industries both compelling and challenging. On the one hand, they offer opportunities to work in exciting environments with intelligent, stylish and talented people; on the other hand, they constantly challenge workers to keep up with new developments and new skills. There is always the risk of one's experience and training becoming technically outdated or aesthetically outmoded. In this closing chapter we look at the three overarching themes of the book in terms of how they relate to *change*. How does the relationship between culture and commerce change? How do personal circumstances and work routines change? And how do structures and models in the creative industries change over time?

Recall that we started this book by pointing out that the category "creative industries" is not found in nature: it is made to serve a particular purpose, for government, businesses and institutions. The concept of the creative industries is born out of changes in government priorities and policy, themselves pushed along by technological and cultural changes. As we saw in Chapter 1, the creative industries concept was an attempt to bring together what was previously termed cultural policy and industrial policy, bringing the arts into contact with large-scale industries such as mass-media entertainment and the information technology sector (Garnham 2005; Hartley 2005).

The "creative industries" might lose their relevance and meaning under new, changed circumstances. In the 1990s, the mingling of the creative arts with industry represented a profound change in funding for the arts. Instead of being seen as an expenditure, arts funding began to be seen as an investment in an area that directly and indirectly fed into commerce (McRobbie 2002), and supported innovation, jobs and investment beyond the confines of "the art world". Viewed in this way, the very idea of creative industries represents a collapse of the distinction between art and commerce, so dearly held by the artistic **avant-garde** (Bürger 1984). As a result, if the creative industries, including the fine arts, start to be seen as a general source of innovation and creativity, feeding into other sectors, such as services and manufacturing, then it's possible that they cannot be so easily distinguished from the rest of the economy on the basis of "creativity" or expressive value anymore. We may, in other words, find ourselves in a moment "after the creative industries" (Banks and O'Connor 2009). Therefore, we cannot take the terminology of this book for granted. The concept of the creative industries may itself fall victim to the rapidly changing socio-economic activities and relationships that it was intended to describe in the late 1990s. Circumstances, technologies, and the experiences of the people on the ground may eventually put new terms and new concepts in its place.

The iPhone Will Fail: Published just after the release of the first iPhone, a short opinion-article predicted: "Apple iPhone Will Fail, in a Late Defensive Move." The iPhone, proclaimed Matthew Lynn, was a doomed product from the start, because Apple was entering a crowded market for mobile phones, already dominated by giants like Nokia, Motorola and Sony Ericsson; the network operators would resist this new kind of mobile phone; and finally "the iPhone is a defensive product. It is mainly designed to protect the iPod, which is coming under attack from mobile manufacturers adding music players to their handsets. Yet defensive products don't usually work — consumers are interested in new things, not reheated versions of old things" (Lynn 2007). This article does the rounds on Twitter every time a new version of the iPhone comes out, as a joke. However funny it is, Lynn's article is far more valuable as a lesson in how novelty is sometimes perceived. The article itself was perfectly reasonable *at the time*. The arguments about the competition and the network providers were relevant, but years later it's easy to see that by focusing on things as they were, the author couldn't see the potential for success in the innovations that the iPhone introduced: a touchscreen that actually worked, the iOS operating system and interface, and the ability to run apps. None of this was self-evident in 2007.

CREATIVITY AND COMMERCE: NOVELTY, RISK AND CHANGE

Cultural change, aesthetic change, technological change, economic change – the list goes on. These changes are not easily separated; they come along all at once, wrapped up in one another: As we finish this manuscript for a book intended for printed publication, the publishing industry is going through enormous changes driven, in part, by the rise of e-publishing, the easy availability of convenient e-readers, and the commercial success of mass-market electronic books. This is a technological change that affects the economics of book publishing (and therefore employment opportunities), the aesthetics of book design (why bother designing for printing on paper if the majority of readers will see a novel on the screen of a smartphone, tablet computer, Kindle, Kobo, Nook, or other e-reading device?), and in the long run we will see some cultural changes in the way we relate to books, magazines, long-form journalism and other written forms of communication that have been shaped by print over the course of centuries (see Chapter 2).

Making something new, commercially, is an inherently risky business. On the one hand, audiences are easily bored, they want to see, hear and experience something interesting or different; except when they don't. Knowing in advance what will work, sell, attract an audience, become popular – the best market research in the world cannot say anything with certainty. It is this inherent risk that puts pressure on businesses in the creative industries, if they are successful, to attempt to preserve that success and increase the return on investment by hedging against future risks through diversification, increased size, new partnerships and extended networks. Even when public funding is involved, for example in subsidized arts, there is risk – the use of public money is subject to popular disapproval, restrictions on what can be done with it, and the shrinking of the government's purse in lean times.

The risks that businesses take on tend to get passed on to all those with a stake in them, not least the employees, freelancers and portfolio workers. In this book we have frequently referred to Georgina Born's *Uncertain Vision* (2004), which documents the cultural, organizational and economic shift from in-house production to commissioning at the BBC during the 1990s. One way of reading Born's book is as a study of change, and how people dealt with it in their professional lives. What began as a political change cascaded down through the BBC and other publicly-funded broadcasters in the UK, vastly increasing the market opportunities for independent production companies. In the space of little more than a decade, they have become a powerful force in UK media production, with international "**super-indies**" exporting both finished programmes for broadcast in the international markets, and branded formats for licensing and adaptation for various national languages and national contexts. At the moment, these players look firmly established and invincible, just as the integrated production model did in the 1980s – and we don't know what might be around the corner for them.

CHANGING WORK ROUTINES AND WORK CULTURES

We do know, however, that many of our interviewees owe their careers to their ability to deal with change, and to adapt their talents, skills and experience to new circumstances. This often means that while it's useful to leave school, college or university with specific knowledge, skills and training, the most valuable skills our informants point to have to do with the underlying "soft skills" of research, communication (written and verbal presentation), and a certain confidence in trying new tools, new ideas and new ways of working. For example, a recent film studies graduate, working as a runner at a large production house in Soho, remarked that she would have liked to have come away from university with a bit of training in InDesign, PhotoShop, Adobe Bridge and Final Cut 7, but she had picked up what she needed on the job. To her own surprise, years of studying film theory turned out to be immediately useful for researching treatments for advertising, along with a "breadth of reference" – her ability to recognize films cited by the directors and creatives who write the briefs.

From the (very different) point of view of an employer, Jess, who manages a research team at a large media agency, sees training in social sciences and journalism as a great asset, because she needs researchers who are interested in people and are able to look beyond themselves and their own prejudices and frames of reference when gathering background information for marketing campaigns:

> "I tend to hire people who have done sociology, psychology, and anthropology [because they] have an interest in people. And that's fundamentally what we do. And if you don't have that interest, all the numbers in the world and creating pretty charts isn't going to work, you're going to have to create an insight from that. [...] That's why I tend to hire people who have a different background, so I just hired a journalist, for example, who's changing direction [...] because they know how to question, they know how to think about something and have an opinion but they're not scared of changing that opinion." (Jess, 2010)

Jess speaks from a position of a manager. The availability of trained journalists for work in marketing, in this case, is a by-product of the changing fortunes of other businesses in the creative industries. Newspapers had been shedding staff at the time of the interview, while Jess's media agency was in need of researchers. Recent research indicates that, at present "advertising, architecture and writing and publishing are the ones offering more job stability and higher economic rewards, while craft, performing arts, film and television and fine arts graduates are facing uncertainty and poorer work conditions" (Comunian, Faggian, and Jewell 2011: 305). This uneven distribution of jobs indicates that creative workers, from graduates and newcomers to more seasoned professionals, will sometimes have to switch sectors. For them, the ability to adapt their skills to new contexts is essential.

Changing personal circumstances

Creative workers do not remain in their twenties forever. Maturing, having relationships, children and responsibilities – a career in the creative industries involves dealing with changes on the home front as well as in the workplace. Freelance or portfolio work, particularly if the job is flexible about when the work is done, can be a way for parents to accommodate work alongside family responsibilities. Debra Osnowitz, in her study of freelance professionals in the USA, cites the example of Sherry, an editor, translator and project manager:

> [Sherry] thought she might solicit work that she could intersperse with household tasks. She might confine herself to small projects while her children were young, she speculated, without compromising her credibility as a professional. As long as she met commitments, she believed, she would remain professionally viable, and as her children grew older, she could again seek projects she found more demanding. (Osnowitz 2010: 159)

However, a career in some areas of the creative industries can be hard to sustain through different life-stages. On average, across the sector, a freelancer worked 77% of a full working year in 2009 (down from 83% in 2005). On average, 69% of freelancers have a contract:

> The average contract length at one month was enjoyed by 38% of the freelance workforce, followed by more than one month but less than three (26%). Only 16% enjoy a contract of over six months. […] Overall, 55% of contracts contained provision for holiday credits, 23% for sick leave and 6% for maternity/paternity leave. (Skillset 2011: 29)

These numbers indicate that there is a great deal of research to be done in topics beyond the scope of this book (because we focus on introducing the creative industries to those starting out), particularly about questions of sustainability. How do creative media workers convert their training and experience from their years of freelancing into other kinds of work when their life circumstances change, for example when having children? Shalane, the assistant film editor, mentioned this:

> "Quite a lot of people I know have children. Most of them… no I take that back. I was going to say that most of them have partners with more sensible jobs, but that's not true at all. It is a big pressure when you have a family and a mortgage because if you're not working for X amount of months, you know, if it's just you can sort of take care of it but if you've got kids, there is that sort of pressure to just take whatever comes up, so that you're working. I'm not really sure how they've balanced it, to be honest, it seems quite a scary thing to do, especially if you're being self-employed, so as a woman, if you have a baby I'd take a year off, six months off. Which can be a career-killer – just gone for a year." (Shalane, 2011)

As it turns out, there is a significant cohort of people who "move on" to something that's more sustainable than project-based freelancing, particularly for parents. When asked about people she knows who have left film/TV production and post-production, Shalane is both reluctant to think about alternative career paths for herself and aware that some of her friends have left to work in other sectors, and that there are other options open to her with the kind of skills and experience she has:

> "People who I know, 'cause I'm a bit younger – well I'm not younger but I started later so I'm younger in the industry – people I know who have left, just completely left and have gone – I know a guy who works in a bank now – a lot of people go towards advertising, which is sort of a natural trajectory for it because you're still in media. But like I said a lot of them left because they either didn't have a ton of interest in the industry to begin with, or they just couldn't hack it for as long as was necessary." (Shalane, 2011)

Not being able to "hack it" for younger people is often related to the challenge of living, working and eating in London on a tight budget while gaining a foothold in the industry.

> "Internships are often unpaid, running is minimum wage – national minimum wage is £11.70, that's barely enough to live on in London. If you don't have somebody helping you out, and it's really a low wage to be asking somebody to be on for an extended period of time, and you either stick it out and get what you want or you leave the industry, or – this has happened as well to a lot of my friends – they'll take whatever the first promotion is. It's hard to see when you're 20 years old and you make £12,000 a year in London, you're just going to take whatever comes along." (Shalane, 2011)

"Sticking it out" as a runner, Shalane says, can feel like there is no reward for the hard work, so the temptation to go elsewhere is always present:

> "Yeah, and a lot of them have changed their minds and they've decided that they maybe don't want to be editors 'cause they don't know how to go down that road, or whatever, and you just really have to sort of stick it out there, and it's increasingly difficult to do the longer you have to work for a small wage or it just seems like there's nothing at the end of the – when you're running it seems like 'what's going on here? I can make more money working in a bar.'" (Shalane, 2011)

Of course, those who decide *not* to persist in the creative media industries, whether they're young people trying to get into the game or older workers looking for a career change, don't just fall off the edge of the map. They tend to have cultural capital that is valuable in other lines of work – their education, skills and experience translate into work elsewhere in the creative industries. For example, with a background in media, some of Shalane's acquaintances have successfully migrated into marketing communications:

> "[They have gone into the] bookings and project management side of things [because] something with a softer skillset is easier to learn, so they'll go to other places where they can do some similar work as far as managing teams of people and managing times. [They look] after accounts, money and things like that." (Shalane, 2011)

For Shalane, who is seriously invested in her identity as a creative professional, the thought of a change of direction at this point in her career is understandably not particularly attractive. When asked what she might do if she decided to leave the post-production sector, Shalane comes up short. It's a difficult question, asking someone to imagine alternative uses for the experience, skills and contacts they've built over the past five years.

> "Nothing! There's nothing I could do. [...] Teaching, of course, but that would still be in the vein of – so I know, for example, people who do as a supplement to editing and things like that teach at [a] film school. [...] I don't know. I don't know what I would do if I left the industry.... Yes... sorry." (Shalane, 2012)

Nevertheless, many people do decide to pursue alternatives. Media occupations and professions have long seemed particularly prone to "a substantial outflow in mid-career" (Tunstall 2001: 5). According to more recent figures "there is a steady exit of people in their 30s and 40s" from the UK creative media industries such as film, television and radio (Skillset 2011: 48). Some of the reasons why older workers, free-lancers in particular, choose other occupations have to do with the relative inflexibility of deadline-driven project-working, so common in media production.

For older workers, there are further challenges that are not offset by experience and a long track record. First, there is the constant threat of one's skills and training becoming either outdated or falling out of fashion. Creative work is often as much about style as technical skills, and changing aesthetic standards can make as much of a difference as technical changes (Platman 2004: 589). Second, one's network of contacts can quickly become outdated. Given "the regular turnover of commission-ers" (Platman 2004: 585) there is a real risk of dropping off the radar of editors and commissioners without constant renewal and updating. Finally, an interruption in the flow of work, for example because of childrearing, other caring responsibilities or health problems, equally risks pushing the freelancer off the aforementioned radar.

CHANGING STRUCTURES AND MODELS

Institutions that were founded upon one medium, for example newspapers, have struggled to redefine themselves and reshape their business models to accommodate decreasing print circulation, with papers such as *The Guardian* shifting their busi-ness online and onto mobile media while still publishing a printed daily newspaper from an integrated newsroom that does not separate web from print. Meanwhile, *The Daily Mail*'s MailOnline website has had great success by being produced and pre-sented differently from the newspaper – becoming the world's most popular English-language website (pushing *The New York Times* to second place) in November 2011 (Wheeler 2012). While the older models of mass-market entertainment and broad-cast media are changing, they have not gone away and will not vanish anytime soon. As the example of *The Guardian* and *Daily Mail* shows, there's life yet in the old bones as they stumble from print to digital.

The music industry in the UK, to take a different example of an established media business, is still dominated by big players despite their loss of size, revenue and power in recent years (Cluley 2009). In this context, we have previously mentioned the UK's "super-indies" – film and TV production companies that have grown big from ownership of the content they've produced, the international market in TV programming, and the international sales of formats such as *X-Factor* and the *Idol* contests (see Chapter 9). However, there are good business reasons why investors put money into cross-platform content, with the intention to create tomorrow's media giants, as with the recent expansion of Vice Media Group (Bercovici 2012). These content investments rely on new approaches to reaching audiences (and particular audience segments) through social media and various forms of sharing and engagement, as we explored in Chapter 10. Obviously, they are ripe with potential for structural changes – not least at the level of content commissioning that creative workers encounter in their professional lives.

Case study: apps

App development for smartphones and tablets is one of the most vibrant, innovative areas of the creative industries. It is a cottage industry of sorts, unlike large-scale software development or games development for consoles and computers, but has generated many small businesses. Apple's App Store created a marketplace and a model for selling simple software straight from developer to the user (with Apple serving as intermediary and taking a cut for billing, cataloguing and vetting the apps on offer). App developers can be individuals with a good idea, a simple product and a straightforward business model, ranging from individuals to small studios and teams. We might say that the Apple App Store and Google Play represent a form of crowdsourcing – hundreds of thousands of apps are available, with only a fraction of them gaining an audience share and generating revenues. This works like the crowd-sourced creative work we mentioned in Chapter 10, with the consumers standing in for judges in the contest of the apps. The apps that do make an impression and gain visibility through trending on the "most downloaded" lists are the ones that succeed, then. For example, Marco Arment created Instapaper, an app for saving web pages for reading later on a mobile device, and has turned it into a little business through the App Store. When interviewed in early 2012, he was still the only employee of Instapaper (Planet Money 2012).

Apps are small, relatively cheap to develop, and some of them become bestsellers. *Angry Birds*, a simple game in which the player shoots birds from a slingshot at fortresses built by pigs (they stole the eggs, hence all the anger) came to dominate the screens of smartphone users in 2011. The Apple App Store opened for business on 10 July 2008. Three years later, *The Economist* reported that this small "bite-sized software" (Economist 2011) had become the reason why Apple and Google dominate the smartphone market, while rival technology brands such as Nokia and RIM languished in the doldrums. "The bounty of software available for Android and iOS, as varied as racing games and apps for managing recordings on cable boxes, is a chief reason the mobile phone market has settled into a two-horse race" (Wingfield and Chen 2012). Meanwhile, Rovio Entertainment, the maker of *Angry Birds*, was seen as the leading hope of the European technology start-up sector (Pfanner 2012a) when a mere four years ago most people wouldn't have known what an app was.

Apps are an instructive example of how much and how quickly established business structures can change. In this case, it's not just the mobile phone, software and games sector that's changed – consumers have come to regard their smartphones as the hub of their digital lives. That's where they get their email, their Facebook messages, Twitter updates, news, where they play games, and consume content that previously would have come to them via television, radio, newspaper or a desktop computer. In other words, this is an important development for the content industries – publishing, music, film, television, and so on. As we have seen with the examples of *Vice* and *Monocle*, content is increasingly seen as platform-agnostic, accessible on whatever device the consumer has at hand, and those devices do not differentiate between print, video or audio – it's data, content, entertainment, news, and so on.

JOBS THAT DON'T EXIST YET

The creative industries regularly generate job descriptions that previously did not exist – terms like "app developer" or "community manager" crop up suddenly and become ubiquitous. Attending industry events such as Social Media Week or Internet Week (both of which are international, taking place in many cities across the world), one is constantly reminded of how rapidly terms, contexts and expectations change. At a Social Media Week session (London, February 2012) titled "Social Media Skills Gap?", recruiters, talent managers, and social media professionals debated the skills that they look for in graduates they hire. A panelist who introduced herself as working for "a word-of-mouth agency" (itself a rather novel specialization) said that what she looked for in graduates were basic professional skills like organization, delegation, prioritization and crisis management – not to mention that they need to understand that to be a Facebook user is not the same as being able to use Facebook to fill an advertising or marketing brief. This raised a question from a student in the audience who remarked that this kind of information wasn't exactly on her university curriculum: "How do I find out what [employers] might want from me?" The answer she got was to start early, begin researching roles and professional pathways two years before she might expect to start applying for jobs, but at the same time, she was helpfully advised by another panelist that these roles and pathways change all the time.

There is no simple trick to reconciling these two imperatives, but it helps to be aware of them. In this book we have tried to help our readers do that by paying attention to the fundamentals that cut across the creative industries – the types of work, social encounters and relevant skills that the different creative sectors have in common. Working at a word-of-mouth agency sounds novel and interesting, but the core skills the panelist mentioned have nothing to do with gossip, chitchat, or rumour; she wants someone who can fulfil a brief (and handle a crisis, let's not forget). The same can be said of the other skills, activities, habits and structures that we describe as being shared across the creative industries. More importantly, they will apply to jobs that don't exist yet, in businesses yet to be established. The aim of this book has therefore been to get our readers started in understanding how these fundamentals might apply to their own situation – doing the research while remembering that it will inevitably all change.

RECOMMENDED READING

Arden, Paul. 2003. *It's Not How Good You Are, It's How Good You Want To Be*. London: Phaidon. A short, witty book on creative thinking and seeing things differently, drawing on Arden's long experience in the advertising industry.

Fendley, Alison. 1996. *Saatchi & Saatchi: The Inside Story*. London: Arcade. The story of the golden age of London advertising agencies in the 1980s, as seen through the story of what was briefly the world's largest advertising agency.

Goldman, William. 2000. *Which Lie Did I Tell?: More Adventures in the Screen Trade*. London: Bloomsbury. Highly entertaining essays about Goldman's own changing fortunes in the Hollywood film industry.

Knopper, Steve. 2009. *Appetite for Self-Destruction: The Spectacular Crash of the Record Industry in the Digital Age*. New York: Simon & Schuster. A history of the music recording industry and its ambivalent (and seemingly disastrous) relationship with technological development.

Muir, Gregor. 2009. *Lucky Kunst: The Rise and Fall of Young British Art*. London: Aurum. A memoir of the Young British Artists before they were famous, and of Hoxton and Shoreditch while they were still grotty.

Reynolds, Simon. 2011. *Retromania: Pop Culture's Addiction to Its Own Past*. London: Faber. Essays about the contemporary compulsion to mine the films, music and television of the past. Along the way, Reynolds offers a funny, provocative look at the role of change and novelty in the products of the creative industries.

Glossary

30 days credit: In business a certain window of time is usually allowed between receipt and payment of an invoice. 30 days is a standard window and is often stated as the terms of credit on invoices when they are issued. However some **debtor** companies (such as large media companies employing freelancers) may stipulate terms of up to 90 days before they pay their **creditors**.

Account manager: In advertising, the main client contact and liaison between the client and the agency (account planner and creative team), with responsibilities for the brief, the budget and on-time delivery – the "client leadership" person, as one of our interviewees at a London media agency put it (Jess, 2010). Account managers often work closely with account planners (Hackley 2003). Charles Saatchi famously required his "account men" to be "tall, elegant with nice voices and good manners" because "they got on better with clients than ones who were short, fat, and ugly and swore" (Fendley 1996: 33).

Account planner: In advertising and marketing, a planner writes the formal creative brief and works with the account manager (who handles client contact and the budget) and a team of creatives to put it into action. The planner represents the point of view of the consumer within the agency: gathering "raw material" on brand positioning, market analysis and consumer insights, and pulling this material, references and ideas together into a proposition that can be presented back to the client (Grabher 2002a; McLeod, O'Donohoe, and Townley 2009). Planners, therefore, combine research, marketing strategies, and innovative ideas for reaching consumers (see e.g., Burcher 2012). An excellent study of different attitudes to the account planner role and the literature around it can be found in Hackley (2003).

ADR: Automated Dialogue Replacement, i.e the recording of dialogue as part of post-production: either because of sound quality issues or script changes.

Agents and **Agencies:** See page 53.

Assembly: The assembly edit is the first edit put together by the editor, who organizes the scenes in story order and makes a first selection of shots and takes to cover each scene.

Attention economy: See page 171.

Avant-garde: A French term for the advance guard of a military formation, those who move ahead, scoping out the terrain for the main army following behind. In art, this applies to an approach to aesthetics that privileges the new, the radical, the shocking, that which breaks with tradition and shows the way towards something new in art, literature, film, music, etc.

BBC World Service: The British Broadcasting Corporation's international broadcasting service for news and information, in a variety of national languages. It has successfully presented itself as an independent, impartial news source, not the voice of the British government. Until 2010 it was funded by the Foreign Office, and regarded as a separate operation from the licence-fee funded core services of the BBC. Recommended reading: James Wood, *History of International Broadcasting*, Volume 2 (2000).

BBC Worldwide: The commercial arm of the British Broadcasting Corporation. Its aim is to "maximise profits on behalf of the BBC by creating, acquiring, developing and exploiting media content and media brands around the world". BBC Worldwide acquires the commercial rights to the BBC's content, for example *Dr Who*, *Planet Earth*, *Top Gear* and other well-known series, for distribution across various platforms (digital, DVD, etc.) and merchandising (e.g., Stig figurines). BBC Worldwide also owns a number of other media brands, including the *Lonely Planet* travel guides.

Bohemia: See page 78.

Boilerplate: Standardized segments of text, often used as clauses in contracts, proposals or other documents featuring stock elements.

Books or **the books:** All businesses need to keep records of income and expenditure. Today such records are often kept electronically, but in the past they would have been recorded in a book and the practice is still referred to as book-keeping.

Boutique agencies: Boutiques provide specialist or niche services for clients such as copyrighting, developing creative content and other artistic services (Fill 2009: 290). Often they compete with larger agencies by offering an alternative source of ideas, new ways of thinking about a problem, or certain styles or approaches.

Brand, Branding: See page 132.

Brief: A specification or description of what a client needs from a bespoke product or service. If a brief is about services (e.g., marketing plan, research), then that service is tailor-made and exclusive to the client. In the case of a product delivered in response to a brief, both the physical deliverable and the associated intellectual property (e.g., a brand logo) usually belongs solely to the client. Usually, a briefing process starts with an initial contact and discussions, followed by a client brief. The brief serves as the basis for a contract (stipulating project **milestones** and key **deliverables**), followed by approval and signing off. At that point the brief can be put into action, with staff time and resources devoted to it, according to the budget.

Business model/structure: The method by which a business generates value and makes money. A business model is based on making a tangible product, providing a service, or a combination of both – with value creation being the main objective. Every business, no matter how informally it is conceived and run, will have some strategy to generate revenues and profits. Sometimes this can take the form of the "story" that the business tells about itself, or the value proposition it presents to its customers. See Chapter 4 for a more detailed discussion of this concept in the context of the creative industries. Recommended reading: Colin Barrow, *Starting a Business for Dummies* (2007); John W. Mullins, *Getting to Plan B* (2009); *Harvard Business Review on Business Model Innovation* (2010).

Call sheet: A call sheet is distributed by the production office to each member of the crew at the end of each day. It contains vital information on the schedule for the following day, such as scenes being shot, location, key cast, equipment, props, etc., and directions to get to the location, if it is a location shoot. Since the schedule may change as the shoot progresses, it is important for the crew to receive a daily update.

Campaign: See page 161.

Capital and **Capitalism:** See page 32.

Cash flow: Money flows in and out of a business or project as income is received and costs are incurred. It is important to pay careful attention to cash flow, to ensure that cash is available when needed. If the balance between incoming and outgoing cash is not carefully managed, a business can have problems with liquidity (i.e., cash to spend) even if overall it is profitable. (**30 days credit** can be very useful here, but, equally, businesses need to remember that their **debtors** will also be taking advantage of credit windows).

Casualization: The trend towards the employment of casual workers on a temporary basis (ranging from day-to-day to fixed-term contracts) instead of employing workers on a full-time basis or as employees over a longer term.

Classical and **Classicism:** In art and aesthetics, classical can refer either to Greek and Roman culture, literature and art, or in a general sense to works of art that have stood the test of time and have been read, played, viewed and enjoyed long after their time of origin. Classicism, by contrast, is an aesthetic movement which harks back to the Greek and Latin models of craftsmanship, and classical rules of harmony and proportion. Classicism is often contrasted with Romanticism, which set itself against a rational, rule-focused approach to art, appealing to the senses, emotions and wild nature instead.

Closed shop: An arrangement between a trade union and employers under which the employers agree to hire only union members, and all employees must be members of the union in order to stay employed. Since 1992, all forms of closed shop employment have been illegal in the UK, on the grounds that such arrangements violate individuals' right to free association.

Co-production: Film and television drama productions are expensive, involving a lot of crew, cast and other resources. Therefore they are very often financed by a number of organizations together. This is a co-production. Co-productions are often international, with each financing organization able to exploit the distribution rights in their territory to recoup costs and make a profit.

Collective bargaining: When employees negotiate with an employer through an organized body, such as a trade union, representing the interests of its members.

Commercial broadcasting: See page 178.

Commissioner/controller: See page 142.

Commissioning guidelines: Most large media organizations will have published guidelines for commissioning. For example, the BBC commissioning guidelines are available at www.bbc.co.uk/commissioning. These guidelines give information about who to contact, what kind of content particular channels and genres are currently looking for and how to submit proposals through the BBC's electronic submission system.

Commodity: In economics, a commodity is a generic thing like oil, wheat, coffee and the like. Commodities are often raw materials used to make other products. It can also refer generally to anything of use that can be bought and sold – for example, time (the labour-time of the worker or the billable hours of the professional).

Communications groups: The largest fish in the marketing pond, these "Behemoths" (as David refers to them) are umbrella organizations or holding companies for subsidiaries that operate independently from one another. Large communications groups, such as Publicis, Carat, Zenith Optimedia and WPP, own many agencies that all have similar specialisms, often in competition with one another, because by having multiple options within the same "family" of companies they can attract clients who compete with one another in the same market without conflicts of interest arising. The same communications group might, for example, do business with two competing car manufacturers through two separate agencies.

Completion: Given the difficulties in raising full film finance, independent filmmakers sometimes take the risk of shooting a project and producing a first cut, or perhaps a trailer of selected scenes, and then seeking completion finance to fund post-production.

Conglomerate: A large company composed of many subsidiaries, sometimes in very different businesses, often identified as a "group" of companies. Often a conglomerate forms when a company seeks to expand through acquisition rather than growth, buying up smaller businesses and gathering them into its portfolio. In the creative industries, media conglomerates like Viacom or Time-Warner will own many different companies across film, radio, music and other forms of media. In advertising, the WPP and Publicis groups own many different media agencies and creative agencies in order to accommodate clients who are in competition with each other (e.g., car makers or drinks companies) under the same umbrella without conflicts of interest.

Content: See page 12.

Continuing drama: A drama that continues and never ends, i.e., a 'soap'.

Convergence: See page 6.

Copyright: See page 1.

Corporation: In contemporary usage a corporation is a large company or a public organization. Historically, the term comes from the Latin *corpus* (body), in the sense of a collective body given the status of a *legal person* (as distinct from a *natural person*, or individual).

Creative clusters: See page 85.

Creativity and **creatives (artistic and cultural):** See page 4.

Creditor: A person or entity who/which is owed money by another person or entity.

Crowdfunding: The practice of funding the production of a project through payments made directly by the future audience, rather than finance from an intermediary organization, such as a broadcaster, a publisher, etc. The model is becoming more and more common, particularly for digital media such as games, but is also applied in areas such as book publishing. Recommended reading/resources: Kickstarter.com; Jeffrey Howe, *Crowdsourcing: Why the Power of the Crowd is Driving the Future of Business* (2008). See Chapter 10 for further discussion and examples.

Culture: See page 7.

Cultural Capital: See page 116.

Cut: A commonly used alternative term for edit.

DCMS: Department for Culture, Media and Sport (in the UK).

Debtor: A person or entity who/which owes money to another person or entity.

Deregulation: See **Regulation and deregulation**.

Deliverables: The outcomes listed in the brief. In advertising and marketing this will be a list of specific media objects (e.g., how many TV adverts, radio adverts, display adverts, etc.) or specification of events or activities to be completed as part of a campaign or a project.

Designs: See page 3.

Development: See page 59.

Direct and **Indirect costs:** A direct cost is one that can be directly attributed to a particular product or other cost object (i.e., anything, such as a project, office, activity etc. which needs to be specifically costed). Examples would include the materials for manufacturing a particular shoe, or cast and crew fees on a television production, and so on. An indirect cost is one that is clearly related to a cost object, but is less easy to trace and calculate. This might include, for example, such items as rent and utilities or accounting and legal services. Often they are costs that relate to many cost objects and, for any one cost object, they may be calculated on a percentage basis.

Director: In audiovisual production, the director works with the producer to supervise and execute the creative realization of the project. He or she works particularly closely with the actors, the production designer, the director of photography and other heads of department in pre-production, production and post-production. The director of a company, on the other hand, is the person who runs the company.

Disruption: See page 163.

Division of labour: See page 35.

Dot-com and **Dot-com bubble:** See page 65.

Ecology: See page 52.

Economy of scale: When the level of production goes up, for example with bigger factories or more efficient machines, costs go down. This results in savings, proportionate to the increase in production.

Editor: In journalism and broadcasting, the editor is the person who commissions external projects and/or approves in-house projects (such as articles and programmes) and oversees their development and execution. As well as the editor in chief, a magazine or newspaper will have editors of particular sections, such as features or news. Likewise in radio and television there will be editors of different areas, such as news and entertainment, as well as series editors for programme strands. In film, TV and radio the same word also denotes the person who edits together the raw footage into the finished programme, a highly important creative and technical role.

Employee: In this book we make a distinction between a freelancer, who is self-employed and an employee, who is employed by a business, which gives them a different status with regard to tax and national insurance payments and state benefits linked to unemployment.

Enlightenment: The Enlightenment was an intellectual movement that emphasized reason, science and individual autonomy. Set against Church dogma, traditions and the fixed class divisions of European aristocracy, the Enlightenment was a philosophical and political movement, profoundly influential to this day. Recommended reading: Peter Gay, *The Enlightenment: An Interpretation: The Science of Freedom* (1996, orig. 1969); Lloyd Spencer, *Introducing the Enlightenment: A Graphic Guide* (2010).

Enterprise or arts and culture schemes: Many countries provide funding schemes to support both business (enterprise) and the arts. Creative businesses and organizations can potentially tap into both. They might, for example, seek finance for business and running costs from enterprise schemes and project funding from arts and culture schemes. Some arts and culture funding will also cover overheads costs. See also **Public funding**.

Entrepreneur: See page 52.

Execs: The colloquial term for all the people involved in the production at an executive level, i.e., the executive producer upwards.

Executive producer: Oversees all aspects of the production, editorial and financial and is usually responsible for hiring the writer, director and producer. He or she is involved in all key decisions on the production, but does not get involved in the day-to-day running of the show, which is the producer's job.

Fine cut: The developed and revised edit, achieved as the result of fine-tuned decisions about story, performance and other elements, which have proceeded from the viewing of the original assembly.

Fixed costs: Costs which do not vary per unit, according to the volume of the product or the service produced. Fixed costs include overheads, such as office rent, utilities, etc. Caves (2000) elucidates the way that fixed costs are proportionally high in the theatre, compared to other sectors in the creative industries, which benefit from the low marginal costs of mass-production. It costs a huge amount of money to produce a feature film, for example, but, once the costs of producing this 'master' have been covered, the costs per unit of making the hundreds, thousands or millions of exhibition prints, DVDs or digital copies for download, are very small. To put on a theatre production, on the other hand, the costs of putting on the 100th or 1,000th performance of a play (theatre rent, cast and crew fees, etc.) do not vary, but remain as high as for the first performance. They are therefore fixed costs.

Footage: A term used to designate unedited audiovisual material. It dates from the days of film stock, which was measured in feet, but continues to be used in relation to digital material, even though the latter is not of course literally measurable in feet, or indeed metres.

Fordism and **Post-Fordism:** See page 40.

Format: See page 143.

Free-to-air: Broadcast services which are available to anyone with the appropriate equipment to receive them, i.e., they are not subject to subscription or pay-per-view costs, or restricted through some other means, such as encryption. The term is also used in relation to cable and internet services.

Freelancer: See page 45.

Gentrification: When something is transformed to suit middle-class tastes and sensibilities. In aristocratic society the gentry were the next class down from the nobility (the word comes from the same root as *gentle*), a term that later applied to the industrial and post-industrial middle classes. In urban areas, gentrification often follows on from the migration of artists and other creatives with little money but a lot of social and cultural capital. They make a neighbourhood "cool", shops, coffee houses and restaurants follow in their path, and soon the moneyed classes arrive to drive up the real estate prices, displacing the previous locals and the artists to start the process somewhere else (Zukin and Braslow 2011).

Gift economy: The exchange of goods and services without the expectation of an immediate *quid pro quo* or payment. In anthropology this term was initially applied to traditional societies in which gift exchange supported communal values and strengthened social ties. More contemporary uses of the term can be seen around open-source software, copyleft, file-sharing, open-access publishing and Creative Commons licensing (Berry 2008; Kelty 2008).

Green light: If we imagine that a production is waiting at the traffic lights to see if it can go ahead, then it is when it gets the green light that it hits the accelerator and takes off into production. A widely used term, 'green light' is often employed as a verb, e.g., 'the film has finally been greenlit', etc.

Gross income: Total income, before tax, national insurance or any other deductions. **Net income** is income after deductions are made.

Gross value added (GVA): The value of all newly generated goods and services, minus goods and services that are consumed when producing it (intermediate consumption). In the case of individuals and businesses, this is simply called value added, and is subject to the Value Added Tax (VAT) that we all pay on goods and services.

Hero: The central role of the hero within the story has given rise to the practice of referring to other central features of the production as heroes, such as a hero location or a hero prop.

High growth firms: "A high-growth enterprise is an enterprise with average annualised growth greater than 20% per annum, over a three-year period" (OECD 2007: 82).

High-net-worth individual: Business jargon for "rich person with money to invest".

Hot-desking: When people use a workspace with no individually designated desk or office, simply using whichever one is available. It usually consists of a basic configuration of seating, desk and communications equipment, sometimes just a shared space with wireless internet access and seating for laptop use.

HR (Human Resources): Administration (hiring and firing), management and training of personnel is, in larger businesses or organizations, the role of the Human

Resources (HR) department. Implicit in the title is the sense that the staff are regarded as an asset for the organization, a key "resource" for its operation.

Imprint: One publisher will own many smaller publishing companies, or *imprints*, which will specialize in different kinds of books for different audiences. Sometimes these will be run as stand-alone independent companies, and in other cases the imprint will be a matter of branding rather than company structure.

In-house: See page 144.

Independent or **indie** for short: Who or what is an independent in the creative industries is a relative judgement. Independents are those who come after and/or differentiate themselves from the established institutions that already exist. Leadbeater and Oakley (1999) used the term to describe the new wave of creative and entrepreneurial freelancers and SMEs that they saw emerging in Britain at the end of the twentieth century. In film you're an indie if you're not a major studio. In television the split is between in-house and independent production. Independent publishers and record labels are differentiated from large conglomerates. However, so-called independent companies may turn out in fact to be subsidiaries of much larger ones (see **super-indies** on page 186). They may have started out as independents, but are they still? Often media conglomerates accord a high degree of autonomy to independents that they buy up, aware that their value lies in their unique creativity. Such companies then often continue to be referred to as independents. A certain attitude and style tends to come from not being part of established and large-scale financial and institutional frameworks. If this style and attitude persist, then an individual or a company might continue to be considered an independent, even if technically part of an established institution. In film and music in particular, being an 'indie' is about an ethos and artistic style.

Indirect costs: See **Direct and indirect costs**.

Industrial Revolution: See page 24.

Informal recruitment: See page 105.

Intellectual property: See page 1.

Keeping an Eye Out: See page 15.

Knowledge workers: See page 18.

Licences and **Licensing:** A licence is a contract between a *licensor*, who owns the intellectual property in question, and a *licensee*. The former gives the latter the right to do something, for example reproduce, manufacture, market and sell. Licences come in many forms, and they can apply to artworks, designs, technologies and patents. A licence can be granted for a flat fee, a royalty, or a combination of the two. They are usually limited by time (days, months, years), purpose and use. Recommended reading: Richard Caves, *Creative Industries: Contracts between Art and Commerce* (2000); Lawrence Smith-Higgins and Miles Rees, *Intellectual Property* (2007).

Limited company: see "Business structures" box on page 83.

Line manager: The next one up in an organizational hierarchy; a manager with direct responsibility for an employee.

Line producer: The line producer works for the producer on the hands-on running of the production. He or she has a particularly responsibility for the budget and making sure that the production stays within it.

Lock and **Picture lock:** This is the point at which the picture edit (i.e., the edit of the image and sync sound from the shoot) is completed and agreed and no more changes can be made.

Loss leader: A product or service sold below cost (or even offered for free) in order to attract customers who will later spend more on other things. Hardware, such as video games consoles might be sold cheaply in order to gain customers who will then spend money on video games and other content. Music tracks might be given away in order to build a fan base, whose members will then pay to attend live events.

Majors and **Mini-majors:** The Hollywood majors, or major film studios are: 20th Century Fox, Warner Bros, Paramount, Columbia, Universal and Disney. The term 'mini-majors' is often given to other film studios, such as Lionsgate, which approach the majors in size.

Market and **Marketplace:** See page 30.

Market failure: A term used in capitalist economics to describe a situation in which a free market in goods and services (the default ideal of capitalism) is not working efficiently. It might, for example, have produced a monopoly, i.e., one company effectively controls the market and excludes new entrants, thus stifling competition, an essential principle of the free market. Market failure is often seen as a motive/prerequisite for government intervention.

Market share: Proportion of total sales in a national market or within a class of commodities. For example, market share can be calculated in terms of the sales of a particular product (e.g., Brand X mobile phones) as a proportion of all mobile phones sold in the UK, or in Europe. It can also be measured by class, for example, mobile phones as a proportion of telephones sold in a particular market.

Market valuation: The value of a company based on the price of its shares at that moment. Share prices fluctuate depending on whether investors think the company is a promising investment or not, and therefore market valuations tend to be volatile, especially for companies that are publicly traded on the stock market. When companies are privately held, by comparison, valuations are often more speculative (since the shares aren't being valued from day-to-day by the stock market) and subject to complex negotiations between the buyers and sellers. Recommended reading: Peter Antonioni, *Economics for Dummies* (2010).

Marketing: The UK Chartered Institute of Marketing (CIM) defines marketing as "the management process responsible for identifying, anticipating and satisfying customer requirements profitably". The American Marketing Association (AMA) has a slightly different definition: "Marketing is an organizational function and a set of processes for creating, communicating, and delivering value to customers and for managing customer relationships in ways that benefit the organization and its stakeholders". Both the AMA and the CIM have useful reference sections on their websites with explanations of technical marketing terms. They can be found at www.marketingpower.com and www.cim.co.uk. Recommended reading: Edward Russell, *The Fundamentals of Marketing* (2010); Karl Moore and Niketh Pareek, *Marketing: The Basics* (2010). For more discussion of marketing, see Chapters 8 and 9.

Microbusiness: Defined by the European Commission as a business with 0–9 employees.

Middle Ages (and **Medieval**): Approximately one thousand years of European history bookended by the fall of the Roman Empire in 475 AD, and the Renaissance (*c.* 1450 AD). The Church dominated all of Europe, through divinely ordained kings that ruled over relatively small feudal states, characterized by a strict division between the peasantry, aristocracy and the clergy.

Milestones: Literally, a stone marking the distance along a road. In advertising and other project-centred industries, a milestone is an event or achievement that marks a significant stage in the development of a project, usually the delivery or completion of an important element of the project.

Mini-majors: see **Majors.**

Minimum: The logic of mass-production and reproduction is that, once you have committed the resources to producing one item, it costs only marginally more money to produce each subsequent one (Caves 2003; Hesmondhalgh 2007). Yet each item can be sold for the same amount of money. Therefore, as long as you can sell them all, the more items you can produce from the same design, or the more copies you can make from a master, the higher your profits. Likewise, when taking on a job for a client, manufacturers will tend to stipulate a minimum run, which they judge will allow them to recoup their costs and make an acceptable profit.

Minimum guarantee: A guaranteed minimum payment offered by a sales or distribution company, irrespective of the ultimate sales figures and income of the film. Additional payments may be agreed, dependent on the success of the film.

Neoliberalism: See page 50.

NESTA: National Endowment for Science, Technology and the Arts (in the UK).

Networking: Seeking out and making use of meetings and connections with people in the same field as oneself. This is useful for sharing information, providing mutual help, support, finding work, and learning about new developments. In the creative industries, having a network is a great asset, particularly for freelancers and portfolio workers. Professional bodies, local groups of practitioners, conferences, events (openings, premières, and the like), workshops and seminars organized by and for professionals – all of these can be valuable networking opportunities. See also "Online networking" box on page 111.

Ofcom: Office of Communications, the regulatory body for communications and media (in the UK).

Outsourcing: The opposite of in-house. When tasks or roles are outsourced, a business hires another company or freelancers to do it for a fee, instead of employing someone to do it, thereby reducing their staff overheads (the costs of employing people). Companies usually outsource the highly technical, routine or standardized elements of their business, while retaining their "core" functions in-house. For example, a publisher in London might outsource all proofreading to India, while retaining editorial staff in-house.

Overheads: The ongoing costs of running a business, as distinct from the costs of producing/supplying a particular product or service. It is a term often used interchangeably with 'indirect costs', since it largely designates the same items. However 'indirect costs' is a more precise accounting term.

Partnership: see "Business structures" box on page 81.

Patents: See page 3.

Patron and **Patronage:** See page 25.

Picture grading: The process of adjusting and manipulating picture qualities, such as colour, saturation and tone, to achieve consistency and particular stylistic effects.

Pitch/pitching: See page 61.

Platform: See page 5.

Platform-agnostic: In digital media, shared standards (e.g., HTML or "hyper-text markup language") enable software to work across platforms such as operating systems and web-browsers. This gives the advantage of not having to design for specific systems, hardware or supporting software, but the downside is that functionality will often be limited, because platform-agnosticism is bought at the price of not relying on the particular features of the platforms themselves. Therefore, platform-agnostic software is often something simple like a web-page.

Policy: See page 8.

Portfolio working and **Portfolio career:** See page 63.

Post-Fordism: See **Fordism.**

Pre-production: See page 59.

Precarity: See page 17.

Producer: A producer in audiovisual production is the person who initiates the project and takes it through to completion. This may include raising finance and coming up with the idea and will certainly include creative and organizational supervision of the project, working closely with both creative personnel, such as writers, directors, designers and editors, and organizational and technical personnel, such as production managers, accountants and sound engineers, as well as pitching to and liaising with editors, commissioners and financers. In this book we also use the term more generally, when we refer to 'creative producers'. We use this latter term to refer to people who work in some capacity in creative production, but not necessarily as audiovisual producers.

Production and **Post-production:** See page 60.

Production chain: See page 7.

Production company: A production company is a company that produces audio or audiovisual material. They may specialize in a particular area, such as commercials, radio or feature film, corporate or community work. Video game production companies are usually referred to as *developers* or *studios*.

Profit: The difference between total revenue (i.e., money coming into the business) and all costs incurred in running the business. Regulations governing tax can be quite complex but, broadly speaking, the tax that you pay will be calculated on profit, rather than total revenue (also called turnover).

Project-based work: See page 48.

Project: See page 47.

Prototype: A prototype is a sample or model of a product that is being developed. 'Sample' is the term often used in the contemporary fashion sector, while 'prototype' is commonly used in sectors such as product design and the games industry. It is usually assumed that there will need to be a series of prototypes, before the desired product attributes, such as look, functionality, etc., are achieved.

Public funding: See page 31.

Public service broadcasting and **Commercial broadcasting:** See page 178.

R&D (research and development): A term that comes from military and high-tech industries, for the secretive phase during which new materials, techniques, processes and products are devised.

Recce: Short for *reconnoitre*, from the French. Also employed in a military context, it is widely used in the audiovisual industry, in which the organization of productions is in fact often compared to that of military campaigns, given their scale and complexity. It designates the process of visiting and checking out locations, prior to the shoot, in order to determine all the opportunities and problems that they present and work out the logistics for dealing with them.

Regeneration: See page 85.

Regulation and **Deregulation:** See page 51.

Renaissance: Meaning "rebirth", this is the name of a period in European history from the middle of the fifteenth century to the mid-seventeenth century. Giorgio Vasari, the Italian artist and critic, gave the period this name in his book *The Lives of the Artists* (1550). Vasari argued that the artists of the Renaissance had initiated a movement of invention and renewal, inspired by the art of Greek and Roman antiquity. Renaissance art was also made possible by the wealthy and powerful merchant families of Florence and other Italian city-states, who provided **patronage** to artists like Michaelangelo and Leonardo da Vinci. While the period is named after its art, it was also characterized by political and religious upheaval, new technologies (e.g., shipbuilding, navigation), discovery of parts of the world previously unknown to Europeans, and the beginnings of colonial exploitation of the riches of the "New World" of the Americas and further afield (see Brotton 2006).

Residual payments or residuals: A term used in the film and broadcast industries to designate royalties paid to content originators, such as writers and actors, each time a production is re-screened or broadcast, after its original run. The term 'royalties' is a more general term, which designates payments made for the ongoing use of an asset, including **intellectual property**. All original copyright holders, including writers, musicians and actors, are potentially entitled to royalties for reprints, re-releases, reruns, etc., of works containing their original content and royalties will constitute a clause of the contract they sign with publishers, producers, etc. A successful creative product (such as an album, book or film) therefore has the potential to generate a long-term income stream for its author(s), which could be quite substantial. However, writers, performers and other copyright originators may sometimes be asked to sign royalty 'buy outs' as part of their contract, i.e., to agree a one-off fee and waiver all royalty payments.

Returning drama: A drama that returns for several seasons.

Revenue: See **Profit**.

Rights: In the context of film production, this refers to the **copyright**. As a term, 'rights' can also designate other intellectual property rights (IPR), such as **trademarks**, **patents** or **licences**.

Risk/return ratio: The proportionate relationship between how much is risked and the possible gain that might result. With a low risk/return ratio, not much is risked and not much is likely to be gained – it's a low-stakes gamble. When the ratio of risk to return is high, however, a lot of money, time and resources might be gambled on the possibility of a high return, as in the case of a blockbuster movie for which the initial outlay of tens of millions of dollars is riding on a strong showing at the box-office (Caves 2000; Flew 2012).

Rushes/dailies: The footage that has been shot that day, which is viewed by the executive producer, the producer and director, other heads of department (HODs) and sometimes the rest of the crew.

Sample: It is common practice in the fashion sector for companies to produce samples of new lines, which can be tested and evaluated before going into mass-production of the new design. Hence the sample sale, which clothing brands will put on from time to time and which, as keen shoppers will know, can be the source of great bargains. Samples are also often unique, as many sample products do not in the end make it into full-scale production.

Script editor (sometimes also called **script executive):** The person who works with the writer to develop the script. In television, script editors often move up the career ladder to become producers and executive producers.

Seed funding: The initial finance provided to startup projects or businesses to help the enterprise reach a position in which it is able either to sustain itself or raise more substantial finance.

Self-employment, self-employed: See page 81.

Shareable experiences: See page 202.

Shares: If a company is owned by more than one person, the ownership of the company is divided into shares. The number of shares owned by each shareholder designates the proportion of the company that they own. The total capital of the company divided by the number of shares is the face value of each share. However, the market value of each share may be higher than this. If investors consider the company to be on the up and likely to bring them substantial dividends in the future, they will buy shares for higher than their face value.

Showreel: Like the artist or designer's portfolio, this is a collection of work by a director, actor, cinematographer, etc., which evidences their track record and showcases their specialist skills. It may be distributed by its owner via DVD or online and usually consists of short clips highlighting both the range and quality of their work. New directors often direct short films or scenes to create a showreel. Such productions are also useful for other crew, such as cinematographers, sound recordists and actors. The latter may also use the services of companies who offer a showreel production service. Casting directors, producers, agents and other individuals and organizations involved in financing projects and hiring cast and crew will usually want to see a showreel of your work.

Showrunner: When the creator of a series takes on both lead writer and creative producer responsibilities, i.e., they are running the show, in the USA they are called a showrunner. The term is less used in the UK. However, on successful shows, the series creator and lead writer (such as Russell Davies on *Dr Who*, or Lynda La Plante on *Prime Suspect*) usually also becomes involved in overseeing the production, as well as the writing, and is credited as the executive producer. This is the screen credit also accorded to US showrunners.

Slate: The development or production slate of a company is the list of projects that they are developing or producing at any one time, which one might imagine as being chalked up on a slate. The metaphor is particularly apt in that, although projects may stay on the development slate for many years without being made, they may also be wiped off it as easily as they are chalked on to it.

SME: See page 48.

Soft skills and hard skills: See page 118.

Sole proprietor, sole trader: See "Business structure" box on page 81.

Sound spotting: The adding in of additional sound effects.

Startup: A small business in the very early stages of developing a product, launching it or gaining a foothold in the market. The term entered popular use in the dotcom era, when many entrepreneurs took advantage of the low barriers to entry to start small companies to put their business ideas into practice. Sometimes called *the startup phase*, this is seen as a transitory period in a company's life, leading either to it becoming established or failing. This is why venture capitalists (VCs) keep a close eye on startups – it's the phase at which an investor can get into a promising business at the outset, investing capital against an ownership stake in the company which will become valuable if it succeeds.

Story: It is not only in drama productions that commissioners will be looking for a good story. Documentaries are often expected to follow the same narrative structure as mainstream film drama, i.e., telling the story of a central character, striving to achieve a goal, overcoming problems along the way and (usually) achieving their goal and undergoing some kind of transformation (emotional, physical or spiritual, ideally all three). Recommended reading: Bernard's *Documentary Storytelling* (2007) .

Super-indies: See page 186.

Syndication/syndicated content: Content that is published simultaneously or consecutively through a number of outlets, for example, a syndicated newspaper column, a radio programme or television show broadcast on a number of local channels.

Technology: See page 28.

Television network: A network of television stations supplied with content from a central organization. Usually these are nationwide networks, such as the American networks ABC, NBS and NBC. The broadcast centre provides them with a certain amount of content, with the rest of their programming made up of local and **syndicated content**.

The four Ps: See page 161.

The long tail: See page 159.

Track laying: The process during which the various audio tracks, which will go to make the final soundtrack of the programme are produced, edited and combined with the picture. Besides the dialogue recorded synchronously with the picture, elements will include atmosphere tracks (e.g., background street or country noises); spot effects (such as doors slamming, gun shots), music and many other possibilities.

Trade associations: See **trade unions**.

Trade guilds: Associations of artisans have had a long history and an international presence. In Europe they were often originally lay organizations of craftsmen from different trades, affiliated to the Church, who joined together to effect good works. As well as serving the Church, they would also support their members in times of hardship, helping them and their dependents if they were sick, paying for funerals, providing charity for widows and orphans, and so on. They also focused on improving work prospects for their members, conserving trade secrets, securing trade, and so on. In the Middle Ages the trade guilds emerged as a powerful presence in the community, able to control labour, production and trade in their spheres of influence. Thus, as a member of a guild, you were supported and protected. However, membership was only obtained through lengthy apprenticeship. It could be hard to gain an apprenticeship and, if you were not a member of a guild, you would face many obstacles to practising a trade.

Trade unions (labor unions in the USA): Organizations of workers that engage in collective bargaining with employers on behalf of their members. Unions primarily negotiate pay and conditions of employment, including pensions, holiday pay and health insurance. Trade associations, by contrast, are groupings of businesses in specific industries, also known as industry trade groups or business associations, which represent the shared interests of members. Trade associations often lobby politicians for legislation favourable to their members, regulatory changes or seek to affect public policy on their behalf.

Trademarks: See page 3.

Treatment: A narrative account of the story that is being proposed for a drama or a documentary project. It can vary in length but for television drama it may often be about 10 pages long. It is widely used in development and commissioning as the basis for deciding whether or not to commission a script.

UNCTAD: United Nations Conference on Trade and Development.

UNESCO: United Nations Educations, Scientific and Cultural Organization.

USP: Unique Selling Point or Unique Selling Proposition – what differentiates a product or service from others.

Value: See page 26.

Venture capital: The term used to describe capital invested in a project where there is high degree of risk – a startup company, for example, or, in the creative industries, an expensive speculative project such as a feature film. In order to appeal to investors, the high-risk potential is usually off-set by the equally high potential of substantial gain. The startup company might, for example, be in a high growth area, such as digital technologies.

Vertical integration and **Vertical disintegration:** See page 49.

Working title: The term used to indicate that the title given to a film or television project during development and production is provisional and may change before distribution. It was, furthermore, the name chosen by the highly successful British production company founded by Tim Bevan and Sarah Radclyffe and responsible for a wide range of successful films, including *Four Weddings and a Funeral* (1994), *Billy Elliot* (2000), *Johnny English* (2003) and *Tinker, Tailor, Soldier, Spy* (2011). It is now a subsidiary of media conglomerate NBC Universal.

References

Adewunmi, Bim. 2012. "Why Black British Drama Is Going Online, Not on TV." *The Guardian*, July 12.

Albini, Steve. 1997. "The Problem with Music." In *Commodify Your Dissent*, 164–176, ed. Thomas Frank. New York: W.W. Norton & Co.

Allen, Kathleen R. 2008. *Complete MBA for Dummies* (2nd edition). Hoboken, NJ: Wiley.

Allen, Paul. 2011. *Artist Management for the Music Business*. Oxford: Focal Press.

Amin, Ash, ed. 1994. *Post-Fordism: A Reader*. Oxford: Blackwell.

Anderson, Benedict. 1991. *Imagined Communities* (Revised edition). London: Verso.

Anderson, Chris. 2006. *The Long Tail: Why the Future of Business is Selling Less of More*. New York: Hyperion Books.

———. 2009. *The Longer Long Tail: How Endless Choice is Creating Unlimited Demand*. New York: Random House Business.

Anderson, Christopher. 2000. "Disneyland." In *Television: The Critical View* (6th edition). Oxford: Oxford University Press.

Annaud, Jean-Jacques. 2011. *Black Gold*. Drama

Antonioni, Peter. 2010. *Economics for Dummies* (2nd edition). Chichester: John Wiley.

Arthur, Charles. 2009. "Are Downloads Really Killing the Music Industry? Or is it Something Else?" *The Guardian Technology Blog*, June 8. www.guardian.co.uk/news/datablog/2009/jun/09/games-dvd-music-downloads-piracy.

Arts Council England. 2012. "Our Goals and Priorities." *Arts Council England*. www.artscouncil.org.uk/funding/apply-for-funding/national-portfolio-funding-programme/how-we-made-our-decision/our-goals-and-priorities/.

Badal, Sharon. 2007. *Swimming Upstream: A Lifesaving Guide to Short Film Distribution*. Oxford: Focal Press.

Baines, Paul. 2008. *Marketing* (2nd edition). Oxford: Oxford University Press.

Banks, Mark. 2006. "Moral Economy and Cultural Work." *Sociology* 40 (3) (June 1): 455–472.

———. 2007. *The Politics of Cultural Work*. Basingstoke: Palgrave Macmillan.

———. 2009. "Fit and Working Again? The Instrumental Leisure of the 'Creative Class'." *Environment and Planning A* 41 (3): 668–681.

Banks, Mark and Justin O'Connor. 2009. "After the Creative Industries." *International Journal of Cultural Policy* 15 (4): 365–373.

Banks, Miranda J. 2010. "The Picket Line Online: Creative Labor, Digital Activism and the 2007–2008 Writers Guild of America Strike." *Popular Communication: The International Journal of Media and Culture* 8 (1): 20–33.

Bannock, Graham, Ron Eric Baxter, and Evan Davis. 2003. *Dictionary of Economics* (4th edition). New York: Bloomberg Press.

Bendjelloul, Malik. 2012. *Searching for Sugar Man*. Drama

Bardoel, Johannes and Leen d'Haenens. 2008. "Reinventing Public Service Broadcasting in Europe: Prospects, Promises and Problems." *Media, Culture & Society* 30 (3): 337–355.

Barrow, Colin. 2007. *Starting a Business for Dummies* (2nd edition). Hoboken, NJ: Wiley.

Barrowclough, Diana and Zeljka Kozul-Wright. 2006. *Creative Industries and Developing Countries: Voice, Choice and Economic Growth*. London: Routledge.

Batschmann, Oskar. 1997. *The Artist in the Modern World: A Conflict between Market and Self-Expression*. Cologne: DuMont Buchverlag.

Baxandall, M. 1988. *Painting and Experience in Fifteenth-century Italy: A Primer in the Social History of Pictorial Style* (2nd edition). Oxford: Oxford University Press.

Bazelon, Emily, John Dickerson, and David Plotz. 2011. "The Political Gabfest: The Crazy Negotiating Posture Gabfest." *Slate Magazine*. www.slate.com/id/2290092.

BBC. 2012a. "Commissioning TV – How We Commission." www.bbc.co.uk/commissioning/tv/how-we-work/how-we-commission.shtml.

———. 2012b. "Commissioning TV – BBC One." www.bbc.co.uk/commissioning/tv/what-we-want/service-strategies/bbc-one.shtml.

———. 2012c. "Commissioning TV – BBC Two." www.bbc.co.uk/commissioning/tv/what-we-want/service-strategies/bbc-two.shtml.

———. 2012d. "Commissioning TV – BBC Three." www.bbc.co.uk/commissioning/tv/what-we-want/service-strategies/bbc-three.shtml.

Becker, Howard Saul. 1982. *Art Worlds*. Berkeley, CA: University of California Press.

Bell, Matthew. 2010. "Monocle: 'It's the Media Project that I've Always Wanted to Do'." *The Independent*, August 1. www.independent.co.uk/news/media/press/monocle-its-the-media-project-that-ive-always-wanted-to-do-2040516.html.

Beniger, James R. 1986. *The Control Revolution: Technological and Economic Origins of the Information Society*. Cambridge, MA: Harvard University Press.

Bennett, Tony, Lawrence Grossberg, Meaghan Morris, and Raymond Williams. 2005. *New Keywords: A Revised Vocabulary of Culture and Society*. Chichester: Wiley-Blackwell.

Bercovici, Jeff. 2012. "Tom Freston's $1 Billion Revenge: Ex-Viacom Chief Helps Vice Become the Next MTV." *Forbes*, January 3. www.forbes.com/sites/jeffbercovici/2012/01/03/tom-frestons-1-billion-revenge-ex-viacom-chief-helps-vice-become-the-next-mtv/.

Berinsky, Adam J., Gregory A. Huber, and Gabriel S. Lenz. 2012. "Evaluating Online Labor Markets for Experimental Research: Amazon.com's Mechanical Turk." *Political Analysis*, March 2. http://pan.oxfordjournals.org/content/early/2012/03/02/pan.mpr057.

Bernard, Sheila Curran. 2007. *Documentary Storytelling: Making Stronger and More Dramatic Nonfiction Films*. Oxford: Elsevier.

Berry, David M. 2008. *Copy, Rip, Burn: The Politics of Copyleft and Open Source*. London: Pluto Press.

Berry, Ralph. 1985. *Shakespeare and the Awareness of the Audience*. London: Macmillan.

Bilton, Chris. 2007. *Management and Creativity: From Creative Industries to Creative Management*. Oxford: Blackwell.

———. 2011. "The Management of the Creative Industries." In *Managing Media Work*, ed. Chris Bilton and Mark Deuze. London: Sage.

Bilton, Chris and Mark Deuze, eds. 2011. *Managing Media Work*. London: Sage.

Blair, Helen. 2009. "Active Networking: Action, Social Structure and the Process of Networking." In *Creative Labour: Working in the Creative Industries. Critical Perspectives on Work and Employment*, ed. Alan McKinlay and Chris Smith. Basingstoke: Palgrave Macmillan, 116–134.

Blair, Helen, Nigel Culkin, and Keith Randle. 2003. "From London to Los Angeles: a Comparison of Local Labour Market Processes in the US and UK Film Industries." *International Journal of Human Resource Management* 14 (4) (June): 619–633.

Bordwell, David, Janet Staiger, and Kristin Thompson. 1985. *Classical Hollywood Cinema: Film Style & Mode of Production to 1960*. London: Routledge.

Born, Georgina. 2004. *Uncertain Vision: Birt, Dyke and the Reinvention of the BBC*. London: Secker & Warburg.

Bourdieu, Pierre. 1985. "The Market of Symbolic Goods." *Poetics* 14 (1–2): 13–44.

————. 1990. *The Logic of Practice*. Cambridge: Cambridge University Press.

Bowker, Geoffrey C., and Susan Leigh Star. 2000. *Sorting Things Out: Classification and Its Consequences*. Cambridge, MA: MIT Press.

Briggs, A. and P. Burke. 2002. *A Social History of the Media: From Gutenberg to the Internet*. Cambridge: Polity Press.

Broadcast. 2012. "Indie Survey 2012." *Broadcast*, March 23: 14.

Brotton, Jerry. 2006. *The Renaissance: A Very Short Introduction*. Oxford: Oxford University Press.

Brown, David Blayney. 2001. *Romanticism*. London: Phaidon Press

Brown, Maggie. 2007. *A Licence to be Different: The Story of Channel 4*. London: BFI (British Film Insitute).

Burcher, Nick. 2012. *Paid, Owned, Earned: Maximising Marketing Returns in a Socially Connected World*. London: Kogan Page.

Bürger, Peter. 1984. *Theory of the Avant-Garde*. Minneapolis, MN: University of Minnesota Press.

Burns, Paul. 2011. *Entrepreneurship and Small Business: Start-up, Growth and Maturity*. Basingstoke: Palgrave Macmillan.

Burton, Graeme. 2010. *Media and Society: Critical Perspectives* (2nd edition). Maidenhead: Open University Press.

Bygrave, William D. 2011. *Entrepreneurship* (2nd edition). Hoboken, NJ: Wiley.

Campbell, Lisa. 2012a. "BBC Agrees Directors UK Deal." *Broadcast*, March 29. www.broadcastnow.co.uk/news/broadcasters/bbc-agrees-directors-uk-deal/5039919.article.

————. 2012b. "The *Broadcast* Interview, Stuart Murphy, Bringing Sky Down to Earth." *Broadcast*, June 29.

Carr, David. 2010. "Inviting in a Brash Outsider." *The New York Times*, February 15, sec. Business / Media & Advertising. www.nytimes.com/2010/02/15/business/media/15carr.html.

Carr, Paul. 2008. *Bringing Nothing to the Party: True Confessions of a New Media Whore*. London: Weidenfeld & Nicolson.

Carrotworkers Collective. 2011. *Surviving Internships: A Counter Guide to Free Labour in the Arts*. London: Carrotworkers Collective. http://carrotworkers.files.wordpress.com/2009/03/cw_web.pdf.

Caves, Richard E. 2000. *Creative Industries: Contracts between Art and Commerce*. Cambridge, MA: Harvard University Press.

Caves, Richard E. 2003. "Contracts Between Art and Commerce." *Journal of Economic Perspectives* 17 (2): 73–83.

Cellan-Jones, Rory. 2001. *Dot.bomb: The Rise and Fall of Dot.com Britain*. London: Aurum.

Chalaby, Jean K. 2010. "The Rise of Britain's Super-indies: Policy-making in the Age of the Global Media Market." *International Communication Gazette* 72 (8): 675–693.

————. 2011. "The Making of an Entertainment Revolution: How the TV Format Trade Became a Global Industry." *European Journal of Communication* 26 (4) (December 1): 293–309.

Christensen, Clayton M. 1997. *The Innovator's Dilemma: When New Technologies Cause Great Firms to Fail*. Boston, MA: Harvard Business School Press.

Christopherson, Susan. 2009. "Working in the Creative Economy: Risk, Adaptation, and the Persistence of Exclusionary Networks." In *Creative Labour: Working in the Creative Industries. Critical Perspectives on Work and Employment*, ed. Alan McKinlay and Chris Smith. Basingstoke: Palgrave Macmillan, 72–90.

Christopherson, Susan and Danielle van Jaarsveld. 2005. "New Media after the Dot.com Bust." *International Journal of Cultural Policy* 11 (1): 77–94.

Clarke, David. 2012. "Global Trends, Israel and the US." *Broadcast*, March 16.

Clinton, Michael, Peter Totterdell, and Stephen Wood. 2006. "A Grounded Theory of Portfolio Working Experiencing the Smallest of Small Businesses." *International Small Business Journal* 24 (2) (April 1): 179–203.

Cluley, Robert. 2009. "Chained to the Grassroots: The Music Industries and DCMS." *Cultural Trends* 18 (3): 213.

Comunian, Roberta, Alessandra Faggian, and Sarah Jewell. 2011. "Winning and Losing in the Creative Industries: An Analysis of Creative Graduates' Career Opportunities across Creative Disciplines." *Cultural Trends* 20: 291–308.

Couldry, Nick. 2010. *Why Voice Matters: Culture and Politics after Neoliberalism.* London: Sage.

Couldry, Nick and Anna McCarthy. 2004. *MediaSpace.* London: Routledge.

Csikszentmihalyi, Mihaly. 1991. *Flow: The Psychology of Optimal Experience.* Reprint. New York: HarperPerennial.

————. 2004. "The Creative Industries after Cultural Policy: A Genealogy and Some Possible Preferred Futures." *International Journal of Cultural Studies* 7 (1) (March 1): 105–115.

Cunningham, Stuart and Peter Higgs. 2008. "Creative Industries Mapping: Where Have We Come From and Where Are We Going?" *Creative Industries Journal* 1 (1): 7–30.

Currid, Elizabeth. 2007. *The Warhol Economy: How Fashion, Art and Music Drive New York City.* Princeton, NJ: Princeton University Press.

Curtin, Michael and Thomas Streeter. 2001. "Media." In *Culture Works: Essays on the Political Economy of Culture*, ed. Richard Maxwell. Minneapolis, MN: University of Minnesota Press, 225–251.

Daniels, Gary and John McIlroy. 2008. *Trade Unions in a Neoliberal World: British Trade Unions under New Labour.* London: Taylor & Francis.

Davis, Susan G. 2001. "Shopping." In *Culture Works: Essays on the Political Economy of Culture*, ed. Richard Maxwell. Minneapolis, MN: University of Minnesota Press, 163–196.

Day, Elizabeth. 2012. "Can You Make Any Kind of Living as an Artist?" *The Guardian*, July 28. www.guardian.co.uk/culture/2012/jul/29/artists-day-job-feature.

*DCMS. 1998a. *Creative Industries Mapping Document.* London: Department for Culture, Media and Sport.

————. 1998b. "Creative Industries Mapping Document." *The National Archives.* http://webarchive.nationalarchives.gov.uk/20100407120701/www.culture.gov.uk/reference_library/publications/4740.aspx.

————. 2009. "Digital Britain: Creating the Skills for the Digital Economy." www.dcms.gov.uk/reference_library/publications/6071.aspx.

————. 2010. *Creative Industries Economic Estimates, February 2010.* London: Department for Culture, Media and Sport. www.culture.gov.uk/reference_library/publications/6622.aspx.

————. 2011. *Creative Industries Economic Estimates, December 2011.* London: Department for Culture, Media and Sport. www.culture.gov.uk/publications/8682.aspx.

Deuze, Mark. 2007a. *Media Work. Digital Media and Society.* Cambridge: Polity Press.

————. 2007b. "Convergence Culture in the Creative Industries." *International Journal of Cultural Studies* 10 (2): 243–263.

Dex, Shirley, Janet Willis, Richard Paterson, and Elaine Sheppard. 2000. "Freelance Workers and Contract Uncertainty: The Effects of Contractual Changes in the Television Industry." *Work, Employment and Society* 14 (2): 283–305.

Donald, James. 2004. "What's New? A Letter to Terry Flew." *Continuum: Journal of Media & Cultural Studies* 18 (2): 235–246.

Downey, John. 2007. "The United Kingdom." In *Western Broadcast Models: Structure, Conduct, and Performance*, ed. Leen d'Haenens and Frieda Saeys. Berlin: Walter de Gruyter, 319–340.

Drew, Ben 2012. *Ill Manors.* Drama

Dumenco, Simon. 2011. "Ad Age Magazine A-List: Tyler Brule is Editor of the Year." *Ad Age Magazine*, October 10. http://adage.com/article/media/ad-age-magazine-a-list-tyler-brule-editor-year/230271/.

Duménil, Gérard. 2011. *The Crisis of Neoliberalism*. Cambridge, MA: Harvard University Press.

Dylan, Bob. 2003. *Chronicles: Volume One*. New York: Simon & Schuster.

Economist. 2006. "Monitor: Artificial Artificial Intelligence." *The Economist*, June 8. www.economist.com/node/7001738?story_id=7001738.

———. 2008. "The Music Industry: From Major to Minor." *The Economist*, January 10. www.economist.com/node/10498664?story_id=E1_TDQJRGGQ.

———. 2009. "The Harry Potter Economy." *The Economist*, December 17. www.economist.com/node/15108711.

———. 2011. "Apps on Tap." *The Economist*, October 8. www.economist.com/node/21530920.

Edgar, Andrew and Peter Sedgwick, eds. 2008. *Cultural Theory: The Key Concepts* (2nd edition). London: Routledge.

Edge. 2012. "Get into Games 2012: EA Gothenburg, DICE and Criterion." *EDGE Magazine*, June 25. www.edge-online.com/features/get-games-2012-ea-gothenburg-dice-and-criterion.

Eisenstein, Elizabeth L. 2012. *The Printing Revolution in Early Modern Europe*. Cambridge: Cambridge University Press.

Ekinsmyth, Carol. 2002. "Project Organization, Embeddedness and Risk in Magazine Publishing." *Regional Studies* 36 (3): 229–243.

Elliott, Stuart. 2009. "Despite Downturn, Bold Moves and New Techniques." *The New York Times*, October 29, sec. Business/Media & Advertising. www.nytimes.com/2009/10/29/business/media/29adco.html.

———. 2012. "Havas Buys Majority Stake in Crowdsourcing Ad Agency." *Media Decoder Blog*. http://mediadecoder.blogs.nytimes.com/2012/04/03/havas-buys-majority-stake-in-crowd-sourcing-ad-agency/.

Evans, Graeme. 2003. "Hard-branding the Cultural City – from Prado to Prada." *International Journal of Urban and Regional Research* 27: 417–440.

———. 2005. "Creative Spaces: Strategies for Creative Cities." In *Tourism, Creativity and Development: ATLAS Reflections 2005*, ed. J. Swarbrooke, M. Smith, and L. Onderwater. Arnhem: Association for Tourism and Leisure Education, 7–10.

———. 2009. "Creative Cities, Creative Spaces and Urban Policy." *Urban Studies* 46 (5–6): 1003–1140.

Evans, Simon, ed. 2004. *Creative Clusters Conference Handbook*. Sheffield: Creative Clusters.

Febvre, Lucian and Henri-Jean Martin. 1976. *The Coming of the Book: The Impact of Printing, 1450–1800*. London: New Left Books.

Fendley, Alison. 1996. *Saatchi & Saatchi: The Inside Story*. London: Arcade.

Fifield, Paul. 2008. *Marketing Strategy Masterclass: The 100 Questions You Need to Answer to Create Your Own Winning Marketing Strategy: Including the New "SCORPIO" Model of Market Strategy*. Oxford: Butterworth-Heineman.

Fill, Chris. 2009. *Marketing Communications: Interactivity, Communities and Content* (5th edition). Harlow: FT/Prentice Hall.

———. 2011. *Essentials of Marketing Communications*. Harlow: FT/Prentice Hall.

Flew, Terry. 2012. *The Creative Industries: Culture and Policy*. London: Sage.

Florida, Richard. 2002a. *The Rise of the Creative Class: And How It's Transforming Work, Leisure, Community and Everyday Life*. New York: Basic Books.

———. 2002b. "Bohemia and Economic Geography." *Journal of Economic Geography* 2 (1) (January 1): 55–71.

———. 2010a. "Bohemian Index." *The Atlantic*, June. www.theatlantic.com/national/archive/2010/06/bohemian–index/57658/.

———. 2010b. "Creative Class Density." *The Atlantic*, September. www.theatlantic.com/business/archive/2010/09/creative-class-density/62571/.

———. 2010c. "The Density of Artistic and Cultural Creatives." *The Atlantic*, September. www. theatlantic.com/business/archive/2010/09/the-density-of-artistic-and-cultural-creatives/62575/.

Foord, Jo. 2008. "Strategies for Creative Industries: An International Review." *Creative Industries Journal* 1 (2): 91–113.

Forty, A. 1995. *Objects of Desire: Design and Society since 1750*. London: Thames & Hudson.

Franco, Marta. 2012. "Amanda Palmer on Her $1 Million Kickstarter Campaign: 'This is the Future of Music'." *Time*, July 27. http://entertainment.time.com/2012/07/27/amanda-palmer-on-her-1-million-kickstarter-campaign-this-is-the-future-of-music/.

Frederick, Jim. 2003. "The Intern Economy and the Culture Trust." In *Boob Jubilee: The Cultural Politics of the New Economy*, ed. Thomas Frank and David Mulcahey. New York: W.W. Norton & Co., 301–313.

Freedman, Des. 2003. "Managing Pirate Culture: Corporate Responses to Peer-to-peer Networking." *International Journal on Media Management* 5 (3): 173–179.

———. 2008. *The Politics of Media Policy*. Cambridge: Polity Press.

Frith, S. 1988. *Music for Pleasure: Essays on the Sociology of Pop*. Cambridge: Cambridge University Press.

Fuller, Matthew. 2005. *Media Ecologies: Materialist Energies in Media and Technoculture*. Cambridge, MA: MIT Press.

Garnham, Nicholas. 1990. *Capitalism and Communication*. London: Sage.

———. 2005. "From Cultural to Creative Industries: An Analysis of the Implications of the 'Creative Industries' Approach to Arts and Media Policy Making in the United Kingdom." *International Journal of Cultural Policy* 11 (1): 15–30.

Gay, Peter. 1996. *The Enlightenment: An Interpretation: The Science of Freedom*. London: W.W. Norton (orig. published 1969).

Gilbey, Ryan. 2011. "Life is Bittersweet." *The Guardian*, June 30.

Gill, Rosalind. 2007. *Technobohemians or the New Cybertariat? New Media Work in Amsterdam a Decade after the Web*. Network Notebooks. Amsterdam: Institute of Network Cultures. http://networkcultures.org/wpmu/portal/publications/network-notebooks/technobohemians-or-the-new-cybertariat/.

———. 2011. "Life is a Pitch." In *Managing Media Work*, ed. Mark Deuze. London: Sage, 249–262.

Gill, Rosalind and Andy Pratt. 2008. "In the Social Factory? Immaterial Labour, Precariousness and Cultural Work." *Theory, Culture, Society* 25 (7–8): 1–30.

Gladwell, Malcolm. 2000. *The Tipping Point: How Little Things Can Make a Big Difference*. London: Little, Brown.

Goldhaber, Michael H. 1997. "The Attention Economy and the Net". Text. *First Monday*. http://firstmonday.org/htbin/cgiwrap/bin/ojs/index.php/fm/article/viewArticle/519/440.

Gordy, Barry. 1994. *To Be Loved: The Music, the Magic, the Memories of Motown*. New York: Headline.

Gottlieb, Lori. 2002. *Inside the Cult of Kibu*. New York: Basic Books.

Grabher, Gernot. 2001. "Ecologies of Creativity: The Village, the Group, and the Heterarchic Organisation of the British Advertising Industry." *Environment and Planning A* 33 (2): 351–374.

———. 2002a. "The Project Ecology of Advertising: Tasks, Talents and Teams." *Regional Studies* 36 (3): 245–262.

———. 2002b. "Cool Projects, Boring Institutions: Temporary Collaboration in Social Context." *Regional Studies* 36 (3): 205–214.

Grabher, Gernot, and Oliver Ibert. 2011. "Project Ecologies: A Contextual View on Temporary Organizations." In *The Oxford Handbook of Project Management*, ed. Peter Morris, Jeffrey K Pinto, and Jonas Söderlund. Oxford: Oxford University Press, 175–200.

Green, Garth L. and Philip W. Scher. 2007. *Trinidad Carnival: The Cultural Politics of a Transnational Festival*. Bloomington, IN: Indiana University Press.

Greenberg, Joshua M. 2008. *From BetaMax to Blockbuster: Video Stores and the Invention of Movies on Video*. Cambridge, MA: MIT Press.

Greenslade, Roy. 2012. "Unpaid X Factor Interns Receive Compensation." *The Guardian*, June 7. www.guardian.co.uk/media/greenslade/2012/jun/07/the-x-factor-itv.

Gregg, Melissa. 2010. "On Friday Night Drinks: Workplace Affects in the Age of the Cubicle." In *The Affect Theory Reader*, ed. Melissa Gregg and Gregory J. Seigworth. Durham, NC: Duke University Press, 250–268.

———. 2011. *Work's Intimacy*. Oxford: Polity Press.

Grugulis, Irena and Dimitrinka Stoyanova. 2012. "Social Capital and Networks in Film and TV: Jobs for the Boys?" *Organization Studies*, August 8. http://oss.sagepub.com/content/early/2012/08/02/0170840612453525.

Grummell, Bernie. 2009. "The Educational Character of Public Service Broadcasting: From Cultural Enrichment to Knowledge Society." *European Journal of Communication* 24 (3): 267–285.

de Grunwald, Tanya. 2012. "X Factor Interns Win Thousands in Unpaid Wages." *Graduate Fog*. http://graduatefog.co.uk/2012/2091/factor-internship-interns-win-wages/.

Guile, David John. 2010. "Learning to Work in the Creative and Cultural Sector: New Spaces, Pedagogies and Expertise." *Journal of Education Policy* 25 (4) (July): 465–484.

Gurr, Andrew. 2006. "London's Blackfriars Playhouse and the Chamberlain's Men." In *Inside Shakespeare: Essays on the Blackfriars Stage*, ed. Paul Menzer. Selinsgrove, PA: Susquehanna University Press, 17–33.

Hackley, Chris. 2000. "Silent Running: Tacit, Discursive and Psychological Aspects of Management in a Top UK Advertising Agency." *British Journal of Management* 11 (3): 239–254.

———. 2003. "Account Planning: Current Agency Perspectives on an Advertising Enigma." *Journal of Advertising Research* 43 (2): 235–245.

Hackley, Chris and Arthur J. Kover. 2007. "The Trouble with Creatives: Negotiating Creative Identity in Advertising Agencies." *International Journal of Advertising* 26 (1): 63–78.

Haddow, Joshua. 2012. "Interns of the World, Unite and Take Over." *Vice*. www.vice.com/en_uk/read/interns-unite-take-over-brendan-o-neill-fuck-you.

Hammond, Richard. 2003. *Smart Retail: How to Turn Your Store into a Sales Phenomenon*. London: Pearson/Prentice Hall.

Hancox, Dan. 2012. "Bloc 2012: Making Music Out of Chaos." *The Guardian*, July 9. www.guardian.co.uk/music/2012/jul/09/bloc-weekend-2012.

Handy, Charles. 1995. *Age of Unreason*. London: Random House.

Hanks, Craig. 2010. *Technology and Values: Essential Readings*. Chichester: John Wiley and Sons.

Hansen, Høgni Kalsø, Bjørn Asheim, and Jan Vang. 2009. "The European Creative Class and Regional Development: How Relevant is Florida's Theory for Europe?" In *Creative Economies, Creative Cities: Asian–European Perspectives*, ed. Lily Kong and Justin O'Connor. Dordrecht: Springer, 99–120.

Harney, Stefano. 2010. "Creative Industries Debate. Unfinished Business: Labour, Management, and the Creative Industries." *Cultural Studies* 24 (3): 431.

Harper, Stephen C. 2003. *The McGraw-Hill Guide to Starting Your Own Business: A Step-by-Step Blueprint for the First-time Entrepreneur*. London: McGraw-Hill.

Hartley, John, ed. 2005. *Creative Industries*. Oxford: Wiley-Blackwell.

Harvard Business Review. 2010. *Harvard Business Review on Business Model Innovation*. Boston, MAs: Harvard Business.

Harvey, David. 1992. *The Condition of Postmodernity: An Enquiry into the Origins of Cultural Change*. Oxford: Blackwell.

Heath, Becky and Dom Potter. 2011. *Going for Broke: The State of Internships in the UK*. London: Internocracy.

Heebels, Barbara and Irina van Aalst. 2010. "Creative Clusters in Berlin: Entrepreneurship and the Quality of Place in Prenzlauer Berg and Kreuzberg." *Geografiska Annaler: Series B, Human Geography* 92 (4): 347–363.

Hesmondhalgh, David. 2007. *The Cultural Industries* (2nd edition). London: Sage.

———. 2008. "Cultural and Creative Industries." In *The Sage Handbook of Cultural Analysis*, ed. Tony Bennett and John Frow. London: Sage, 552–569.

Hesmondhalgh, David and Sarah Baker. 2008. "Creative Work and Emotional Labour in the Television Industry." *Theory, Culture, Society* 25 (7–8): 97.

———. 2010. "'A Very Complicated Version of Freedom': Conditions and Experiences of Creative Labour in Three Cultural Industries." *Poetics* 38 (1) (February): 4–20.

———. 2011. *Creative Labour: Media Work in Three Cultural Industries*. London: Routledge.

van Heur, Bas. 2009. "The Clustering of Creative Networks: Between Myth and Reality." *Urban Studies* 46 (8) (July 1): 1531–1552.

Hirsch, Paul M. 2000. "Cultural Industries Revisited." *Organization Science* 11 (3): 356–361.

HMRC. 2012. "Employment Status." *HM Revenue and Customs*. www.hmrc.gov.uk/employment-status/.

Hobsbawm, E. J. 1999. *Industry and Empire: The Birth of the Industrial Revolution*. New York: The New Press.

Hochschild, Arlie Russell. 2003. *The Managed Heart: Commercialization of Human Feeling*. Berkeley, CA: University of California Press.

Hodkinson, Paul. 2011. *Media, Culture and Society: An Introduction*. Los Angeles: Sage.

Holgate, Jane and Sonia McKay. 2007. *Institutional Barriers to Recruitment and Employment in the Audio Visual Industries*. London: Working Lives Research Institute.

———. 2009. "Equal Opportunities Policies: How Effective Are They in Increasing Diversity in the Audio-visual Industries' Freelance Labour Market?" *Media, Culture & Society* 31 (1) (January 1): 151–163.

Holt, Douglas B. 1997. "Distinction in America? Recovering Bourdieu's Theory of Tastes from its Critics." *Poetics* 25 (2–3): 93–120.

Holt, Jennifer and Alisa Perren. 2009. *Media Industries: History, Theory, and Method*. Oxford: Wiley Blackwell.

House of Lords. 2009. *Public Service Broadcasting: Short-term Crisis, Long-term Future?* London: The Stationery Office.

Howe, Jeff. 2006. "The Rise of Crowdsourcing." *Wired*, June. www.wired.com/wired/archive/14.06/crowds.html.

———. 2008. *Crowdsourcing: Why the Power of the Crowd is Driving the Future of Business*. New York: Crown Publishing Group.

Hyde, Lewis. 2007. *The Gift: How the Creative Spirit Transforms the World*. Edinburgh: Canongate Books (orig. published 1983).

Isaacson, Walter. 2011. *Steve Jobs: The Exclusive Biography*. London: Hachette UK.

Jansen, Wendy, Wilchard Steenbakkers, and Hans Jägers. 2007. *New Business Models for the Knowledge Economy*. Aldershot: Gower.

Jarvis, Jeff. 2012. *Gutenberg the Geek*. Amazon Kindle Single.

Jenkins, Henry. 2008. *Convergence Culture: Where Old and New Media Collide* (Revised edition). New York: New York University Press.

Johns, Jennifer. 2010. "Manchester's Film and Television Industry: Project Ecologies and Network Hierarchies." *Urban Studies* 47 (5) (May 1): 1059–1077.

Johnson, Bobbie. 2012a. "Why Less is More." *Matter*. http://blog.readmatter.com/post/23058106160/less-is-more.

————. 2012b. "It isn't a Magazine, It isn't a Website." *Matter*. http://blog.readmatter.com/day/2012/07/05/.

Johnson, Catherine. 2012. *Branding Televison*. Abingdon: Routledge.

Johnson, Steven. 2010. *Where Good Ideas Come From: The Seven Patterns of Innovation*. London: Penguin.

Johnston, Trevor. 2011. "Going for Broke." *Time Out*, July 14.

Jubert, Tom. 2011. "10 Tips on How to Become a Professional Games Writer." *Plot is Gameplay's Bitch*. http://tom-jubert.blogspot.com/2011/03/10-tips-on-how-to-become-professional.html.

Julier, Guy. 2008. *The Culture of Design* (2nd edition). London: Sage.

Kanter, Jake. 2012. "Indies Secure Largest Slice of WoCC to Date." *Broadcast*, July 12. www.broadcastnow.co.uk/news/indies/indies-secure-largest-slice-of-wocc-to-date/5044297.article.

Karlsson, Charlie and Robert G. Picard. 2011. *Media Clusters: Spatial Agglomeration and Content Capabilities*. Cheltenham: Edward Elgar.

Kavoori, Anandam P. and Aswin Punathambekar. 2008. *Global Bollywood*. New York: New York University Press.

Kay, Jeremy. 2011. "Feature Focus: Equity Finance." *Screen International* (November): 31–38.

Keane, Michael. 2007. *Created in China: The Great New Leap Forward*. Routledge Media, Culture and Social Change in Asia 11. London: Routledge.

————. 2009. "The Capital Complex: Beijing's New Creative Clusters." In *Creative Economies, Creative Cities: Asian–European Perspectives*, ed. Lily Kong and Justin O'Connor. Dordrecht: Springer, 77–97.

Kelly, Kevin. 2008. "1,000 True Fans." *The Technium*, March. www.kk.org/thetechnium/archives/2008/03/1000_true_fans.php/.

Kelty, Christopher M. 2008. *Two Bits: The Cultural Significance of Free Software*. Durham, NC: Duke University Press.

Khalsa, Balihar. 2012. "Time To Drop the Banner?" *Broadcast* (March 2): 24–25

Kimes, Mina. 2011. "From Guns n' Roses Bassist to Money Manager." *Fortune*, March 4. http://money.cnn.com/2011/03/04/pf/duff_mckagan_meridian_rock.fortune/index.htm.

Kirkegaard, Sean. 2004. "Super Indies are in Line for Tomorrow's Big Prize." *The Guardian*, August 24. www.guardian.co.uk/media/2004/aug/24/broadcasting.business.

Knopper, Steve. 2009. *Appetite for Self-Destruction: The Spectacular Crash of the Record Industry in the Digital Age*. New York: Simon & Schuster.

Kong, Lily. 2009. "Beyond Networks and Relations: Towards Rethinking Creative Cluster Theory." In *Creative Economies, Creative Cities: Asian–European Perspectives*, ed. Lily Kong and Justin O'Connor. Dordrecht: Springer, 61–76.

Kotamraju, Nalini P. 2006. "Keeping Up: Web Design Skill and the Reinvented Worker." *Information, Communication & Society* 5 (1): 1–26.

Krotoski, Aleks. 2012. "Tech Weekly Podcast: Watching the Web." *The Guardian*, April 3. www.guardian.co.uk/technology/audio/2012/apr/03/tech-weekly-podcast-gov-surveillance.

Kruhly, Madeleine. 2011. "Harry Potter, Inc: How the Boy Wizard Created a $21 Billion Business." *The Atlantic*, July. www.theatlantic.com/business/archive/2011/07/harry-potter-inc-how-the-boy-wizard-created-a-21-billion-business/241948/.

Lane, Jeremy F. 2000. *Pierre Bourdieu: A Critical Introduction*. London: Pluto Press.

Larocca, Amy. 2010. "Planet Monocle." *New York Magazine*, December 5. http://nymag.com/news/media/69921/.

Leadbeater, Charles. 2008. *We-Think*. London: Profile.

Leadbeater, Charles and Kate Oakley. 1999. *The Independents: Britain's New Cultural Entrepreneurs*. London: Demos.

Lessig, Lawrence. 2005. *Free Culture: How Big Media Uses Technology and the Law to Lock Down Culture and Control Creativity*. New York: Penguin Group USA.

Lewandowski, Natalie. 2010. "Understanding Creative Roles in Entertainment: The Music Supervisor as Case Study." *Continuum: Journal of Media & Cultural Studies* 24 (6): 865.

Lewis, Michael. 2002. *Next: The Future Just Happened*. New York: W.W. Norton & Co.

Leyshon, Andrew, Peter Webb, Shaun French, Nigel Thrift, and Louise Crewe. 2005. "On the Reproduction of the Musical Economy." *Media, Culture & Society* 27 (2): 177–209.

Lloyd, Richard Douglas. 2010. *Neo-Bohemia: Art and Commerce in the Postindustrial City* (2nd edition). London: Routledge.

Lobato, Ramon. 2010. "Creative Industries and Informal Economies." *International Journal of Cultural Studies* 13 (4): 337–354.

Lovink, Geert. 2003. *My First Recession*. Rotterdam: V2_ publishing.

Lunt, Peter and Sonia Livingstone. 2012. *Media Regulation: Governance and the Interests of Citizens and Consumers*. London: Sage.

Lynn, Matthew. 2007. "Apple iPhone Will Fail in a Late, Defensive Move." *Bloomberg*. www.bloomberg.com/apps/news?pid=newsarchive&sid=aRelVKWbMAv0.

MacFarquhar, Larissa. 2012. "When Giants Fail: What Business Has Learned from Clayton Christensen." *The New Yorker*, May 14. www.newyorker.com/reporting/2012/05/14/120514fa_fact_macfarquhar.

Malik, Shiv and Rajeev Syal. 2011. "Internships: The Scandal of Britain's Unpaid Army." *The Guardian*, November 4. www.guardian.co.uk/money/2011/nov/04/internships-scandal-britain-unpaid-army.

Markoff, John. 2011. "Steve Jobs of Apple Dies at 56." *The New York Times*, October 5, sec. Business Day. www.nytimes.com/2011/10/06/business/steve-jobs-of-apple-dies-at-56.html.

Marling, Karal Ann. 1996. *As Seen on TV: The Visual Culture of Everyday Life in the 1950s*. Cambridge, MA: Harvard University Press.

Marx, Karl, and Friedrich Engels. 2012. *The Communist Manifesto: A Modern Edition*. 2nd ed. London: Verso Books (orig. published 1848).

Mason, Matt. 2008. *The Pirate's Dilemma: How Hackers, Punk Capitalists, Graffiti Millionaires and Other Youth Movements are Remixing Our Culture and Changing Our World*. London: Allen Lane.

Masterson, Rosalind and David Pickton. 2010. *Marketing: An Introduction* (2nd edition). London: Sage.

Mattelart, Armand. 1996. *The Invention of Communication*. Minneapolis, MN: University of Minnesota Press.

Mayer, Vicki, Miranda J. Banks, and John Thornton Caldwell. 2009. *Production Studies: Cultural Studies of Media Industries*. New York: Routledge.

McAthy, Rachel. 2012. "Long-form Journalism Project *Matter* Aiming for September Launch." *Journalism.co.uk*. www.journalism.co.uk/news/digital-long-form-journalism-project-matter-aiming-for-september-launch/s2/a549767/.

McEvoy, Sean. 2000. *Shakespeare: The Basics*. London: Routledge.

McFall, Elizabeth Rose. 2004. *Advertising: A Cultural Economy*. London: Sage.

McGuigan, Jim. 2009. "Doing a Florida Thing: The Creative Class Thesis and Cultural Policy." *International Journal of Cultural Policy* 15 (3): 291–300.

McKagan, Duff. 2011. *It's So Easy (And Other Lies): The Autobiography*. New York: Orion.

McKay, Jenny. 2000. *The Magazines Handbook*. London: Routledge.

McKinlay, Alan. 2009. "Making 'the Bits between the Adverts': Management, Accounting, Collective Bargaining and Work in UK Commercial Television, 1979–2005." In *Creative Labour: Working in the Creative Industries. Critical Perspectives on Work and Employment*, ed. Alan McKinlay and Chris Smith. Basingstoke: Palgrave Macmillan, 174–192.

McKinlay, Alan and Chris Smith, eds. 2009. *Creative Labour: Working in the Creative Industries. Critical Perspectives on Work and Employment*. Basingstoke: Palgrave Macmillan.

McLeod, Charlotte, Stephanie O'Donohoe, and Barbara Townley. 2009. "The Elephant in the Room? Class and Creative Careers in British Advertising Agencies." *Human Relations* 62 (7): 1011–1039.

McNab, Geoffrey. 2011. "Can Doha Strike Gold?". *Screen International* (October): 23–25.

McRobbie, Angela. 1998. *British Fashion Design: Rag Trade or Image Industry?* London: Routledge.

———. 2002. "Clubs to Companies: Notes on the Decline of Political Culture in Speeded up Creative Worlds." *Cultural Studies* 16 (4): 718–737.

Meikle, Graham and Sherman Young. 2012. *Media Convergence: Networked Digital Media in Everyday Life.* Basingstoke: Palgrave Macmillan.

Menger, Pierre-Michel. 1999. "Artistic Labor Markets and Careers." *Annual Review of Sociology* 25: 541–574.

Michaels, Sean. 2012. "Bloc Goes into Administration Following Festival Cancellation." *The Guardian,* July 12. www.guardian.co.uk/music/2012/jul/12/bloc-liquidation-festival-cancellation.

Mieszkowski, Katharine. 2006. "'I Make $1.45 a Week and I Love It'." *Salon,* July 24. www.salon.com/2006/07/24/turks_3/.

Miller, Michael B. 1994. *The Bon Marché: Bourgeois Culture and the Department Store, 1869–1920.* Princeton, NJ: Princeton University Press.

Miller, Vincent. 2011. *Understanding Digital Culture.* London: Sage.

Monks, Leila. 2012. "The Demand for Formats Shows No Sign of Waning." *Broadcast* (April 13): 13.

Moor, Elizabeth. 2003. "Branded Spaces: The Scope of 'New Marketing'." *Journal of Consumer Culture* 3 (1): 39–60.

Moor, Liz. 2008. "Branding Consultants as Cultural Intermediaries." *The Sociological Review* 56 (3): 408–428.

Moore, Karl and Niketh Pareek. 2010. *Marketing: The Basics* (2nd edition). London: Routledge.

Morris, Peter, Jeffrey K. Pinto, and Jonas Söderlund, eds. 2011. *The Oxford Handbook of Project Management.* Oxford: Oxford University Press.

Mullins, John W. 2009. *Getting to Plan B: Breaking Through to a Better Business Model.* Boston, MA: Harvard Business School Press.

Nathan, Max. 2005. "The Wrong Stuff: Creative Class Theory, Diversity and City Performance." *Centre for Cities Discussion Paper* 1 (September). www.centreforcities.org/index.php?id=78.

Naughton, John. 2012. *From Gutenberg to Zuckerberg: What You Really Need to Know about the Internet.* London: Quercus.

Neff, Gina, Elizabeth Wissinger, and Sharon Zukin. 2005. "Entrepreneurial Labor among Cultural Producers: Cool Jobs in Hot Industries." *Social Semiotics* 15 (3): 307–334.

NESTA. 2006. *Creating Growth: How the UK Can Invest in Creative Businesses.* London: National Endowment for Science, Technology and the Arts (NESTA). www.nesta.org.uk/publications/assets/features/creating_growth.

O'Connor, Justin. 2009a. "Creative Industries: a New Direction?" *International Journal of Cultural Policy* 15 (4): 387–402.

———. 2009b. "Shanghai Moderne: Creative Economy in a Creative City?" In *Creative Economies, Creative Cities: Asian–European Perspectives,* ed. Lily Kong and Justin O'Connor. Dordrecht: Springer, 175–195.

Oakley, Kate. 2004. "Not So Cool Britannia: The Role of the Creative Industries in Economic Development." *International Journal of Cultural Studies* 7 (1) (March 1): 67–77.

———. 2006. "Include Us Out—Economic Development and Social Policy in the Creative Industries." *Cultural Trends* 15 (4): 255.

———. 2009a. "The Disappearing Arts: Creativity and Innovation after the Creative Industries." *International Journal of Cultural Policy* 15 (4): 403–413.

———. 2009b. "Getting Out of Place: The Mobile Creative Class Takes on the Local. A UK Perspective on the Creative Class." In *Creative Economies, Creative Cities: Asian–European Perspectives,* ed. Lily Kong and Justin O'Connor. Dordrecht: Springer, 121–134.

Oakley, Kate, Brooke Sperry, and Andy Pratt. 2008. *The Art of Innovation: How Fine Arts Graduates Contribute to Innovation*. London: NESTA.

OECD. 2007. *Eurostat-OECD Manual on Business Demography Statistics*. Paris: OECD. www.oecd. org/std/entrepreneurshipandbusinessstatistics/eurostat-oecdmanualonbusinessdemographystatistics. htm.

Ofcom. 2006. *Review of the Television Production Sector*. London: Ofcom. http://stakeholders.ofcom. org.uk/consultations/tpsr/statement/.

Osborne, Thomas. 2003. "Against 'Creativity': A Philistine Rant." *Economy and Society* 32 (4): 507–525.

Osnowitz, Debra. 2010. *Freelancing Expertise: Contract Professionals in the New Economy*. Ithaca, NY: Cornell University Press.

Palmer, Amanda. 2012. "Kickstarter Project Update 5: All You Ever Wanted to Know About All This Kickstarter Money & Where It's Going." *Kickstarter*. www.kickstarter.com/projects/ amandapalmer/amanda-palmer-the-new-record-art-book-and-tour/posts/232020.

Parker, Robin. 2011. "Battle Lines Drawn in Comedy." *Broadcast*, September 2.

Pearson. 2012. "Pearson Publishing". Corporate Website. *Pearson*. www.pearson.co.uk/.

Perlin, Ross. 2011. *Intern Nation: How to Earn Nothing and Learn Little in the Brave New Economy*. London: Verso.

Perrons, D. 2007. "Living and Working Patterns in the New Knowledge Economy: New Opportunities and Old Social Divisions in the Case of New Media and Care Work." In *Gendering the Knowledge Economy: Comparative Perspectives*, ed. Sylvia Walby, Heidi Gottfried, Karin Gottschall, and Mari Osawa. Basingstoke: Palgrave Macmillan, 188–206. www.palgrave. com/products/title.aspx?PID=334212.

Peters, Jeremy W. 2011. "Huffington Post is Target of Suit on Behalf of Bloggers." *New York Times Media Decoder*, April 12. http://mediadecoder.blogs.nytimes.com/2011/04/12/huffington-post-is-target-of-suit-on-behalf-of-bloggers/.

Pfanner, Eric. 2012a. "Maker of Angry Birds Shows Way for European Start-ups." *The New York Times*, May 17, sec. Technology. www.nytimes.com/2012/05/18/technology/18iht-rovio18. html.

———. 2012b. "WPP Acquires AKQA to Beef Up Digital Marketing." *The New York Times*, June 20, sec. Business Day/Global Business. www.nytimes.com/2012/06/21/business/global/wpp-acquires-akqa-to-beef-up-digital-marketing.html.

Planet Money. 2011. "The Friday Podcast: Is This Man a Snuggie? Planet Money: NPR." *Planet Money*, May 19. www.npr.org/blogs/money/2011/05/20/136496085/the-friday-podcast-is-this-man-a-snuggie.

———. 2012. "The App Economy." *NPR.org*, January 30. www.npr.org/blogs/ money/2012/01/31/146152273/the-tuesday-podcast-the-app-economy.

Platman, Kerry. 2004. "'Portfolio Careers' and the Search for Flexibility in Later Life." *Work, Employment & Society* 18 (3): 573–599.

Plunkett, John. 2012. "BBC Director General: George Entwistle Profile." *The Guardian*, July 3. www.guardian.co.uk/media/2012/jul/04/george-entwistle-director-general-profile.

Popcorn, Faith. 1992. *The Popcorn Report: Revolutionary Trend Predictions for Marketing in the 90s*. London: Arrow.

Porter, Michael E. 2005. "Local Clusters in a Global Economy." In *Creative Industries*, ed. John Hartley. London: Routledge, 259–267.

Porter, R. 1990. *English Society in the Eighteenth Century*. London: Penguin.

Portny, Stanley E. 2010. *Project Management for Dummies*. Chichester: John Wiley & Sons.

Potts, Jason and Stuart Cunningham. 2008. "Four Models of the Creative Industries." *International Journal of Cultural Policy* 14 (3): 233–247.

Potts, Jason, Stuart Cunningham, John Hartley, and Paul Ormerod. 2008a. "Social Network Markets: A New Definition of the Creative Industries." *Journal of Cultural Economics* 32 (3): 167–185.

Potts, Jason, John Hartley, and Stuart Cunningham. 2008b. "Social Network Markets: A New Definition of the Creative Industries (Pre-Publication Draft)". Brisbane, Queensland University of Technology. http://cci.edu.au/topics/economics.

Power, Dominic. 2003. "The Nordic 'Cultural Industries': A Cross-national Assessment of the Place of the Cultural Industries in Denmark, Finland, Norway and Sweden." *Geografiska Annaler: Series B, Human Geography* 85 (3): 167–180.

Pratt, Andy C. 2004. "The Cultural Economy: A Call for Spatialized 'Production of Culture' Perspectives." *International Journal of Cultural Studies* 7 (1): 117–128.

———. 2007. "Locating the Cultural Economy." In *The Cultural Economy*. Vol. 2. The Cultures and Globalization Series, ed. Helmut Anheier and Yudhishthir Raj Isar. London: Sage, 42–51.

———. 2008. "Creative Industries: the Cultural Industries and the Creative Class." *Geografiska Annaler: Series B, Human Geography* 90 (2): 107–117.

———. 2009. "Urban Regeneration: From the Arts 'Feel Good' Factor to the Cultural Economy: a Case Study of Hoxton, London." *Urban Studies* 46 (5-6): 1041–1062.

Pratt, Andy C. and Paul Jeffcutt, eds. 2009. *Creativity, Innovation and the Cultural Economy*. London: Routledge.

Prieur, Annick and Mike Savage. 2011. "Updating Cultural Capital Theory: a Discussion Based on Studies in Denmark and in Britain." *Poetics* 39 (6): 566–580.

Rae, Issa. 2011. *The Misadventures of Awkward Black Girl*. www.youtube.com/user/actingrl112.

Randle, Keith and Nigel Culkin. 2009. "Getting in and Getting on in Hollywood: Freelance Careers in an Uncertain Industry." In *Creative Labour: Working in the Creative Industries. Critical Perspectives on Work and Employment*, ed. Alan McKinlay and Chris Smith. Basingstoke: Palgrave Macmillan, 93–115.

Reidd et al. 2010. *A Creative Block? The Future of the UK Creative Industries?* London: The Work Foundation.

Richmond, Siubhan. 2012. *An Expert's Guide to Getting into TV*. e-book. London: Siubhan Richmond.

Rimmer, Matthew. 2007. *Digital Copyright and the Consumer Revolution: Hands Off My iPod*. Cheltenham: Edward Elgar.

Robb, John. 2009. *The North Will Rise Again: Manchester Music City 1976–1996*. London: Aurum.

Rodic, Yvan. 2010. *Facehunter*. London: Thames & Hudson. http://facehunter.blogspot.com/.

Rogerson, Christian. 2006. "Creative Industries and Urban Tourism: South African Perspectives." *Urban Forum* 17 (2): 149–166.

Rojek, Chris. 2001. *Celebrity*. London: Reaktion Books.

Ross, Andrew. 2003. *No-Collar: The Humane Workplace and its Hidden Costs*. New York: Basic Books.

———. 2008. "The New Geography of Work." *Theory, Culture, Society* 25 (7–8): 31–49.

Rosser, Michael. 2011. "Second Chance for *Love Thy Neighbour* in Spain." *Broadcast*, July 15: 13.

Rushton, Katherine. 2009a. "Ben Stephenson, Controller, BBC Drama Commissioning." *Broadcast*, April 1. www.broadcastnow.co.uk/news/people/ben-stephenson-controller-bbc-drama-commissioning/2015609.article.

———. 2009b. "Drama Producers Point to 'Systemic' Failures at BBC | News | Broadcast." *Broadcast*, July 23. www.broadcastnow.co.uk/news/broadcasters/bbc/drama-producers-point-to-systemic-failures-at-bbc/5003834.article.

———. 2010. "Ben Stephenson, BBC Drama." *Broadcast*, January 14. www.broadcastnow.co.uk/news/commissioning/ben-stephenson-bbc-drama/5009652.article.

Rushton, Susie. 2008. "'Monocle' Has an Eagle Eye on the Lives of the Jet Set." *The Independent*, February 18, sec. Media. www.independent.co.uk/news/media/monocle-has-an-eagle-eye-on-the-lives-of-the-jet-set-783487.html.

Russell, Edward. 2010. *The Fundamentals of Marketing*. Lausanne: AVA Publishing.

Saundry, Richard and Peter Nolan. 1998. "Regulatory Change and Performance in TV Production." *Media, Culture & Society* 20 (3) (July 1): 409–426.

Saundry, Richard, Mark Stuart, and Valerie Antcliff. 2007. "Broadcasting Discontent: Freelancers, Trade Unions and the Internet." *New Technology, Work and Employment* 22 (2) (July 1): 178–191.

Savage, Mike and Modesto Gayo. 2011. "Unravelling the Omnivore: A Field Analysis of Contemporary Musical Taste in the United Kingdom." *Poetics* 39 (5) (October): 337–357.

Schivelbusch, Wolfgang. 1986. *The Railway Journey: The Industrialization of Time and Space in the 19th Century*. Berkeley, CA: University of California Press.

Scott, Allen J. 2010. "Cultural Economy and the Creative Field of the City." *Geografiska Annaler: Series B, Human Geography* 92 (2): 115–130.

Sengupta, Sukanya, Paul K. Edwards, and Chin-Ju Tsai. 2009. "The Good, the Bad, and the Ordinary Work Identities in 'Good' and 'Bad' Jobs in the United Kingdom." *Work and Occupations* 36 (1): 26–55.

Shih, Clara. 2011. *The Facebook Era: Tapping Online Social Networks to Market, Sell and Innovate* (2nd edition). Boston, MA: Pearson.

Shirky, Clay. 2011. *Cognitive Surplus: Creativity and Generosity in a Connected Age*. London: Penguin.

Shurgot, Michael W. 1998. *Stages of Play: Shakespeare's Theatrical Energies in Elizabethan Performance*. Delaware, DE: University of Delaware Press.

Simon, Herbert A. 1971. "Designing Organizations for an Information-Rich World." In *Computers, Communications, and the Public Interest*, ed. Martin Greenberger and Johns Hopkins University. Baltimore, MD: Johns Hopkins University Press.

Skillset. 2009. *2009 Employment Census: The Results of the Seventh Census of the Creative Media Industries*. London: Skillset. www.skillset.org/research/index/.

———. 2011. *Sector Skills Assessment for the Creative Media Industries in the UK*. London: Skillset. www.skillset.org/research/index/.

Skillset and CCSkills. 2011. *Sector Skills Assessment for the Creative Industries*. Strategic Skills Assessment for the Creative Industries. London: Skillset. www.skillset.org/research/index/#ssa2011.

Smith, Chris and Alan McKinlay. 2009. "Creative Industries and Labour Process Analysis." In *Creative Labour: Working in the Creative Industries. Critical Perspectives on Work and Employment*, ed. Alan McKinlay and Chris Smith. Basingstoke: Palgrave Macmillan, 3–28.

Smith, Stuart James. 2008. *How to Make It in Music: Written by Musicians for Musicians*. London: Dennis Publishing.

Smith-Higgins, Lawrence and Miles Rees. 2007. *Intellectual Property*. London: Hodder Arnold.

Smythe, Dallas W. 2006. "On the Audience Commodity and its Work." In *Media and Cultural Studies: Keyworks*, ed. Meenakshi Gigi Durham and Douglas Kellner. Oxford: Blackwell, 230–256.

Sorrentino, Paolo. *This Must Be the Place*. 2011. Drama

Sparke, Tim. 2012. "A Meeting of Great Minds". *Broadcast* (22 June): 20

Spencer, Lloyd. 2010. *Introducing the Enlightenment: a Graphic Guide*. London: Icon Books.

Stahl, Matt. 2009. "Privilege and Distinction in Production Worlds: Copyright, Collective Bargaining, and Working Conditions in Media Making." In *Production Studies: Cultural Studies of Media Industries*, ed. Vicki Mayer, Miranda J. Banks and John T. Caldwell. London: Routledge, 54–68.

Steger, Manfred B. 2010. *Neoliberalism: A Very Short Introduction*. Oxford: Oxford University Press.

Sternberg, Robert J., ed. 1998. *Handbook of Creativity*. Cambridge: Cambridge University Press.

Stokes, David. 2002. *Small Business Management*. London: Continuum

Surowiecki, James. 2005. *The Wisdom of Crowds*. New York: Knopf Doubleday Publishing Group.

———. 2010. "Blockbuster, Netflix, and the Future of Rentals." *The New Yorker*, October 18. www.newyorker.com/talk/financial/2010/10/18/101018ta_talk_surowiecki.

Tench, Ralph and Liz Yeomans. 2009. *Exploring Public Relations*. Harlow: Pearson Education.

Thompson, Don. 2008. *The $12 Million Stuffed Shark: The Curious Economics of Contemporary Art*. London: Palgrave Macmillan.

Thornton, Sarah. 2008. *Seven Days in the Art World*. London: W.W. Norton.

Thraves, Jamie. 2011. *Treacle Jr.* Drama.

Thrift, Nigel. 2005. *Knowing Capitalism*. London: Sage.

Throsby, David and Anita Zednik. 2011. "Multiple Job-holding and Artistic Careers: Some Empirical Evidence." *Cultural Trends* 20 (1): 9.

Tunstall, Jeremy, ed. 2001. *Media Occupations and Professions: A Reader*. Oxford: Oxford University Press.

Turner, Graeme. 2004. *Understanding Celebrity*. London: Sage.

UNCTAD. 2010. *Creative Economy Report 2010*. United Nations Conference on Trade and Development.

UNESCO. 2009. *2009 UNESCO Framework for Cultural Statistics*. Paris: UNESCO.

Vanderbilt, Tom. 1997. "The Advertised Life." In *Commodify Your Dissent*, ed. Thomas Frank and Matt Weiland. New York: W.W. Norton & Co., 127–142.

Vaughan, W. 1999. *British Painting: The Golden Age*. London: Thames & Hudson.

Vice. 2012. "2012 Media Kit". Vice Media Group. http://scs.viceland.com/vice-com/VICE_UK_Media_kit_2012_Rev6.pdf.

Watkins, James. 2012. *The Woman in Black*. Alliance Films, UK/Canada.

Webb, Matt. 2010. "Week 272." *Berg London Blog*. http://berglondon.com/blog/2010/08/26/week-272/.

Weeds, Helen. 2012. "Superstars and the Long Tail: The Impact of Technology on Market Structure in Media Industries." *Information Economics and Policy* 24 (1) (March): 60–68.

Wei, Li Wu, and Hua Jian. 2009. "Shanghai's Emergence into the Global Creative Economy." In *Creative Economies, Creative Cities*, ed. Lily Kong and Justin O'Connor. Dordrecht: Springer, 167–171.

Weisberg, Robert W. 1993. *Creativity: Beyond the Myth of Genius*. New York: W.H. Freeman.

West, Douglas. 1993. "Restricted Creativity: Advertising Agency Work Practices in the US, Canada and the UK." *The Journal of Creative Behavior* 27 (3): 200–213.

Wheeler, Brian. 2012. "How the Daily Mail Stormed the US." *BBC*, January 27, sec. Magazine. www.bbc.co.uk/news/magazine-16746785.

Wilkinson, Carl. 2008. "The Vice Squad." *The Observer*, March 30. www.guardian.co.uk/media/2008/mar/30/pressandpublishing.tvandradioarts.

Williams, Raymond. 1961. *Culture and Society 1780–1950*. Harmondsworth: Penguin.

———. 1965. *The Long Revolution*. Harmondsworth: Penguin.

———. 1981. *Culture*. Glasgow: Fontana.

———. 1985. *Keywords: A Vocabulary of Culture and Society*. Oxford: Oxford University Press.

Wilson, Elizabeth. 2000. *Bohemians: The Glamorous Outcasts*. London: Taurus Parke.

Wingfield, Nick and Brian X. Chen. 2012. "Google Outsells, but Apple Keeps Loyalty of Mobile App Developers." *The New York Times*, June 10, sec. Technology. www.nytimes.com/2012/06/11/technology/apple-keeps-loyalty-of-mobile-app-developers.html.

Wiseman, Andreas. 2012. "A Special Place." *Screen International* (January 27): 23.

Wood, James. 2000. *History of International Broadcasting* (Vol. 2). London: Institution of Electrical Engineers.

Wright, Shelagh, John Newbigin, John Kieffer, John Holden, and Tom Bewick. 2009. *After the Crunch*. London: Creative and Cultural Skills. www.creative-economy.org.uk.

Wyman, Bill. 2011a. "Lester Bangs' Basement: What it Means to Have All Music Instantly Available." *Slate*, April. www.slate.com/articles/arts/music_box/2011/04/lester_bangs_basement.html.

———. 2011b. "Groundhog Decade: Hollywood is about to Repeat the Catastrophic Mistakes of the Music Industry." *Slate*, July. www.slate.com/articles/arts/culturebox/2011/07/groundhog_decade.html.

————. 2012. "So Long, and Thanks for All the Pirated Movies." *Slate*, January 20. www.slate.com/articles/business/technology/2012/01/megaupload_shutdown_what_the_site_s_departure_means_for_other_traffic_hogging_cyberlockers_.single.html.

Young, James Webb. 2003. *A Technique for Producing Ideas*. London: McGraw-Hill Professional.

Yúdice, George. 2003. *The Expediency of Culture*. Durham, NC: Duke University Press.

Zukin, Sharon. 1982. *Loft Living: Culture and Capital in Urban Change*. Baltimore: John Hopkins University Press.

Zukin, Sharon and Laura Braslow. 2011. "The Life Cycle of New York's Creative Districts: Reflections on the Unanticipated Consequences of Unplanned Cultural Zones." *City, Culture and Society* 2 (3) (September): 131–140.

Index